CHRISTIAN–MUSLIM RELATIONS IN THE AFTERMATH OF THE ARAB SPRING

À la mémoire de Bertrand

CHRISTIAN–MUSLIM RELATIONS IN THE AFTERMATH OF THE ARAB SPRING

Beyond the Polemics over 'The Innocence of Muslims'

Anna Hager

EDINBURGH
University Press

Edinburgh University Press is one of the leading university presses in the UK. We publish academic books and journals in our selected subject areas across the humanities and social sciences, combining cutting-edge scholarship with high editorial and production values to produce academic works of lasting importance. For more information visit our website: edinburghuniversitypress.com

© Anna Hager, 2024, 2025

Edinburgh University Press Ltd
13 Infirmary Street
Edinburgh EH1 1LT

First published in hardback by Edinburgh University Press 2024

Typeset in 11/15 EB Garamond by
IDSUK (DataConnection) Ltd

A CIP record for this book is available from the British Library

ISBN 978 1 3995 2844 3 (hardback)
ISBN 978 1 3995 2845 0 (paperback)
ISBN 978 1 3995 2846 7 (webready PDF)
ISBN 978 1 3995 2847 4 (epub)

The right of Anna Hager to be identified as author of this work has been asserted in accordance with the Copyright, Designs and Patents Act 1988 and the Copyright and Related Rights Regulations 2003 (SI No. 2498).

CONTENTS

Acknowledgements		vi
Transcription, Transliteration and Abbreviations		viii
Introduction: Revisiting Christian–Muslim Relations through a Minor Controversy		1
1	Beyond the Controversy: Islamist Movements and the Constraints of the Political Game	12
2	Another Understanding of Violence: From Coptic–Muslim Violence to a Far Greater Danger	32
3	The Stakes of Being Christian or Muslim: The Other Key Actors of Christian–Muslim Relations	51
4	Searching for Proximity to the Other: Redefining *Fitna* and *Dhimma*	72
5	The Core of Peaceful Relations: Rituals of Solidarity and Avoidance	98
6	Renegotiating the Promises of the Arab Spring	113
Conclusion: The Requirements for the Ideal Islamic Society		136
Notes		140
Bibliography		189
Index		219

ACKNOWLEDGEMENTS

This has been a long journey and I am very grateful to a number of persons and institutions. I am delighted to record my thanks here.

This journey started as a dissertation project at the University of Vienna, Austria, and thus I would like to thank to the university and my two PhD supervisors, Stephan Procházka and Wolfram Reiss. I was also the recipient of a PhD grant program for mobility of the OeAD – to whom I am most thankful – which allowed me to conduct research in the Middle East. During that time, I benefitted from institutional support and I would like to express my deepest gratitude to the following: in Beirut, especially, the Faculty of Religious Science of the Université Saint-Joseph, the CEMAM as well as the Orient Institut Beirut, the Ifpo Beyrouth and the Near East School of Theology; in Cairo, especially the Dominican Institute for Oriental Studies as well as the Franciscan Center of Christian Oriental Studies and the Netherlands-Flemish Institute; in Jerusalem, the National Library Givat Ram; in Amman, Ifpo Amman and the library of the University of Jordan. My deepest thanks to the Austrian Pilgrim-Hospice in Jerusalem.

I also had the honour of interviewing a number of persons to whom I am most grateful for their insight: George Sabra, Hareth Chehab, Mina Magdi, Fadi Yusuf, Jayson Casper, Bishop Murqus, Hani al-Gazeri, Fr Rafiq Khoury, Raouf Abu Jaber and his son Marwan, Bassem Farraj, Fr Hanna Kildani, Bishop Maroun Lahham, Bishop Benedict, Amir al-Hafi and Jiryis Habash.

Later on, I benefitted from the institutional support of Princeton University where the Firestone Library was most useful.

As this dissertation took shape and later on turned into a book, this would not have been possible without the help and suggestions of a number of people. I would like to express my deepest thanks to Thom Sicking, Rüdiger Lohlker, Bernard Haykel, Jack Tannous, Roel Meijer and Joas Wagemakers. I am especially grateful to Catherine Mayeur-Jaouen and the anonymous reviewers whose comments have been crucial. They are all blameless if this book eventually took a different direction. I am especially thankful to Emma House, Louise Hutton, Isobel Birks and Eddie Clark at EUP, and copy-editor Nina Macaraig, for guiding and supporting me through this process.

Finally, as life goes on while a book comes to fruition, I am most indebted to my partner Alexander, my parents and my in-laws for their invaluable help and support. Merci. Danke.

TRANSCRIPTION, TRANSLITERATION AND ABBREVIATIONS

Note on Transcription

Following house style, Arabic names and terms have been transliterated according to a simplified version of the IJMES guidelines (no diacritics in the main text). Names of persons and places for which there is an English version have not been transliterated.

Note on Translations

All translations from Arabic, French and German into English are mine.

Abbreviations

FJP: Freedom and Justice Party
FPM: Free Patriotic Movement
IAF: Islamic Action Front
IS: Islamic State
MP: Member of Parliament
MYU: Maspero Youth Union
POC: Proche-Orient Chrétien
SCAF: Supreme Council of Armed Forces
SSNP: Syrian Social National Party

INTRODUCTION
REVISITING CHRISTIAN–MUSLIM RELATIONS THROUGH A MINOR CONTROVERSY

In early September 2012, Coptic individuals living in the US caused an uproar in the Middle East with the publication of a poorly made thirteen-minute video in Arabic on YouTube. The first part of this video, titled 'The Innocence of Muslims' (*'barā'at al-muslimīn'*), depicted a presumably Muslim group attacking Copts in Egypt and looting their property. The second part discussed the alleged ultimate cause of this violence: the life and character of the Prophet Muhammad. Reactions in the Middle East considered the video offensive because it depicted Muhammad as a ruthless killer, child molester and violent warlord. On 11 September 2012, in reaction to the video, protesters tried to storm the US embassy in Cairo. During another protest in Cairo, a Salafi preacher burned a copy of the Gospel and called on protestors to urinate on the Bible.[1] Clashes between the police and protestors also occurred in Tripoli, Lebanon.

This controversy constituted a very dangerous moment for Christians in the region, especially for Copts in Egypt, who constitute 5 to 6 percent of the population according to the state census.[2] The Egyptian media quickly connected 'The Innocence of Muslims' to a handful of Coptic migrants living in the United States. As a result, several Salafi figures in Egypt called on their fellow Christians, especially the Coptic Orthodox Church, to distance themselves from the video, thus creating an atmosphere of tension and suspicion. In the past, similar 'offences' had often resulted in a backlash against Christians and their symbols in the Middle East. In 2005–6, the publication of cartoons depicting the Prophet Muhammad by a Danish newspaper provoked anger across the Middle East. In February 2006, a protest was held in front of the Danish embassy in Beirut, which turned violent, and a nearby Maronite church was attacked.[3] A couple of months later, following a controversial lecture by Roman Catholic Pope Benedict XVI in Regensburg, churches in Nablus and Tulkarem in the West Bank and in Gaza were firebombed.[4] Furthermore, Egypt was in the midst of an uncertain post-revolutionary phase after the Arab Spring, with Islamist forces gaining in the parliamentary and presidential elections. A former Muslim Brother, Muhammad Mursī, had been elected president in June 2012. At the same time, incidents of violence between Copts and Muslims had dramatically increased after the 2011 revolution. The Arab Spring had also affected the wider region, with the war in Syria causing waves of refugees to Lebanon and Jordan and a deeper polarisation of Lebanese politics. Consequently, a Coptic Orthodox priest wondered in reaction to the attempted storming of the US embassy in Cairo: 'Are we to expect a terrorist act against the Church in Egypt, especially on this coming Friday?'[5]

Yet, instead, in several parts of Egypt, joint Christian–Muslim protests took place after Friday prayers, followed by more joint protests on the following Friday, as well as in several parts of Lebanon, until early October 2012. In addition, a diverse set of actors across the region stepped in to condemn the video: not only Islamists and Salafis in Egypt, Jordan and Lebanon, but also actors of official Islam such as al-Azhar, the Sunni muftis, the Lebanese Higher Islamic Shi'a Council, as well as non-religious actors, such as the professional associations in Jordan. Crucially, Churches and Christian associations and figures in Egypt, Jordan and Lebanon issued strong condemnations of the video. In some instances, they were the ones to initiate the joint Christian–Muslim protests or conferences against 'The Innocence of Muslims'.

The uproar over 'The Innocence of Muslims' has attracted some scholarly attention.[6] For Yvonne Yazbeck Haddad and Joshua Donovan, '[t]his crisis highlighted the clash over the representation of the true "voice of the Copts" in diaspora that has been going on since the 1980s [. . .] As the video demonstrates, the actions of the few in diaspora can have real consequences for Copts in Egypt'.[7]

Yet, unlike this earlier scholarly approach, this study will look at the wealth of Muslim and Christian reactions to the video on their own terms. Paradoxically, all these condemnations were about a video no one had actually seen, was hardly ever named and whose content was rarely even discussed. I therefore chose to cut the video from the background of its original Coptic context and content and use this short-lived, intense crisis as an entry point for a study of Christian–Muslim relations in Egypt, Jordan and Lebanon in the context of the Arab Spring. This book will discuss the reactions of Christian and Muslim actors and institutions – including such joint reactions as statements, protests and conferences – in Egypt, Jordan and Lebanon and argue that these offer insights into the mechanisms and materiality of these relations. Instead of being an occasion for inter-communal violence, this controversy instead highlighted how both Muslim and Christian figures and institutions in these countries first amplified the outcry, but then, together as a society, found a way out. They managed to channel the potential violence and turn it into an occasion to strengthen Christian–Muslim relations and, crucially, their own positions. This requires us to radically posit the agency of Christians as vocal, visible and assertive actors, while highlighting the constraints to which Muslim, Salafi and Islamist actors were actually subject. This book seeks to be a contribution to the study of Christian–Muslim relations in the Middle East, by offering a thorough comparison of the reactions in three countries – Egypt, Jordan and Lebanon.

The situation of Christians in the Middle East and, as a result, of Christian–Muslim relations differ significantly in these three countries. At the time of the controversy, Christians numbered approximately 5 to 6 percent of the population in Egypt, 5.5 percent in Jordan and 36 percent in Lebanon.[8] The dwindling proportion of Christians compared to the general population was a major concern among them across the region, even though they have increased in absolute numbers in the twentieth century. Besides the Christian–Muslim divide, these three countries have different demographic make-ups. While Egypt grew increasingly homogenous after the departure of the Syro-Lebanese, Europeans and Jews who used to play a significant cultural and economic role, Lebanon has always been known for its diversity (eighteen communities are recognized, and the Shi'a now play an important demographic and political role). In Jordan, the divide between 'East Bank'

Jordanians of tribal heritage and Palestinian Jordanians, with Christians on both sides, has been a constant feature of Jordanian politics in the realm of the Hashimite monarchy.

These demographics have found different translations in the political system. Egypt did not introduce a quota system in parliament (until 2014), and it became increasingly difficult for Christians to get elected in the later years of the Mubarak regime. In Lebanon, all communities are allocated a specific number of seats in parliament, the state and the ministries, depending on their demographic weight as notified in the 1932 census. The president is Christian Maronite, the prime minister is Sunni Muslim, the speaker of parliament Shiʿa Muslim and the deputy speaker Greek Orthodox. In Jordan, Christians benefit from a quota system that guarantees their over-representation in parliament, and every government usually numbers one to two Christian ministers. The socioeconomic situation of Middle Eastern Christians is extremely varied: in Egypt, one can find Christians of a status ranging from the billionaire Naguib Sawiris to poor peasants in Upper Egypt, whereas Christians in Jordan as a whole play an important economic role. Finally, Middle Eastern Christianity is first and foremost charactised by an extraordinary diversity in terms of Churches – from the Oriental Orthodox (such as the Coptic Orthodox Church and the Armenian Apostolic Church), over the Greek Orthodox tradition, to the Eastern Catholic traditions (such as the Maronite Church), as well as many Protestant Churches. All these various aspects will be discussed in more detail below.

Violence against Copts in Egypt was the *raison d'être* of 'The Innocence of Muslims'. It has often been the starting point for investigating Christian–Muslim relations[9] in the Middle East and Christian communities in Middle East.[10] As Laura Robson notes when it comes to the latter:

> This sudden upsurge of scholarly interest has emerged alongside increased media coverage of Christian communities in the Middle East – focused especially on the plight of the Christians of Iraq as their nation disintegrated in the aftermath of the American invasion, but also including coverage of the Arab Christian communities of Palestine/Israel, Syria and Egypt.[11]

Discussing violence in connection with religion, however, is a more complex issue. A roundtable discussion in the *American Historical Review* (AHR) observed: 'This is the assumption that religious violence is really not fundamentally about religion – that other interests, claims, or identities of an economic, ethnic, political, or even psychological nature are at stake'.[12] There have been farther-reaching reflections on these instances of violence; Angie Heo in her book *The Political Life of Saints* says: 'Rather, I seek to broaden our notion of violence beyond discrete acts of bombing and torching, shifting our sights to the less punctual and more permanent structures of repression, dispossession, and seclusion that have defined Coptic experiences of suspicion, fear, and rage'.[13]

There have been attempts to approach violence upside down, as something beneficial for society. As Élizabeth Picard points out in her study on Christian militias during the Lebanese Civil War:

> Throughout the centuries these societies not only developed avoidance behaviour coded by highly subtle customs, but they are capable of inverting or controlling the effects of hostile relations by rules of hospitality, asylum, and, more generally, neighbourhood, whose security virtues compete with those of armed protection.[14]

This ambiguous nature of violence has found its way into the study of Peter Makari's *Conflict and Cooperation: Christian–Muslim Relations in Contemporary Egypt*, in which he emphasises that 'cooperation [occurs] even in the context of conflict;'[15] '*in the midst of tension and actual conflict, numerous examples of cooperation can be found* [italics in the original]'.[16] 'The Innocence of Muslims' is a story about that: how in the midst of an intense crisis, there were numerous instances of Christian–Muslim cooperation. But, unlike Peter Makari, who sees in 'the rhetoric expressed in official oration and the texts published for public consumption encourage[ment] and attempt[s] to foster a vibrant spirit of tolerance',[17] I will show here that this rhetoric was actually a means to build pressure on the other community. This book further introduces the notion of agency to the study of violence. 'The Innocence of Muslims' was a story about how violence was avoided – by choice, not chance. Therefore, I believe, there is a need to think about the possibility of agency in connection with violence. This allows us to produce a counter-example to the observation made by Philip Benedict that, '[u]ntil very recently, historians have been busier trying to understand the logic of religious violence than cases where it was prevented'.[18]

Agency is another notion that has gained wider traction in the study of Middle Eastern Christians, as a way to correct earlier scholarship, as Paul Rowe notes:

> In histories of the Middle East, Christians have often been portrayed as either protected, tolerated, or persecuted minorities in Arab and Islamic environments. Condescension to the toleration of Christians in Islamic societies is the boast of the Muslim apologist.[1] To Christian and Western polemicists, this treatment contributes to a pathology. Christians and Jews alike are confined to 'dhimmitude,' according to the controversial work of Bat Ye'or.[2] In other studies, Christians are objectified as fifth columns or pawns of Western interests. Historical pieces deal with the way that the various imperialist powers and the Ottoman capitulations, coupled with Western intellectual developments, altered the status of Arab Christians.[3][19]

Violence and agency thus seem closely connected. As much as scholars agree on the need to 'restore' the agency of Middle Eastern Christians, there is a need to rethink our understanding of agency. As Anh Nga Longva notes, considering Copts as 'whole persons and social agents and not only as victims allows us to better understand their dilemmas and appreciate the resourcefulness they display in facing these dilemmas'.[20] Agency, consequently, is often understood in terms of resistance, subversion and an outspoken language against domination. But as Saba Mahmood criticises in *Politics of Piety: The Islamic Revival and the Feminist Subject*, there is a 'tendency among scholars to look for expressions and moments of resistance that may suggest a challenge to male domination'.[21] Instead, she emphasises the need that 'the meaning of agency must be explored within the grammar of concepts within which it resides'[22] and that it is necessary to understand '"agency" not simply as a synonym for resistance to social norms but as a modality of action'.[23]

Based on Saba Mahmood's reflection, I am therefore making two claims in this book. First, that agency can be and needs to be conceptualised in connection to ambiguity. In *Die Kultur der Ambiguität: Eine andere Geschichte des Islams*, Thomas Bauer developed a theory of ambiguity or tolerance of ambiguity (*Ambiguitätstoleranz*) that emerged in the field of psychology: 'There is a phenomenon of cultural ambiguity if *two antithetic or at least two competing and clearly deviating meanings* are ascribed to a term, an action or an object over a longer period of time and *at the same time* [my emphasis]'.[24] The concept of ambiguity thus helps us transcend ideas of domination and opens up the full potential of Christian agency as well as the potential limits of Muslim agency. Simply put, Christians may have condemned 'The Innocence of Muslims' out of fear of a backlash, but *at the same time*, they managed to exert subtle pressure on Muslims through claims of intercommunal unity in order to negotiate the terms of Christian–Muslim relations. In the context of this controversy, agency worked as a mode of engaging in Christian–Muslim relations through claims of proximity to the other community, rituals of reciprocity and a language of denial and avoidance. A basic question in this regard was whether Christians condemned the video *as* Christians. Géraldine Chatelard notes:

> [T]he issue here is not to say who is Christian, but in what kind of interactions it is preferable to identify as Christian, in which cases one is solely considered Christian [. . .] and finally in which cases one can credibly identify with other belongings and which ones [. . .]. Being Christian is to identify or being identified as such. This also applies to any other type of social identity.[25]

The first question of agency is the choice whether or not to endorse an identity. The controversy offered a diversity of Christian positionings in this regard.

My second claim concerns the need to question the agency of Islamist and Muslim figures, especially in the context of a seemingly unstoppable triumph of Islamists in post-revolutionary Egypt. The post-Arab Spring phase in Egypt meant that movements like the Muslim Brotherhood, *al-Daʿwa al-Salafiyya* (through its political arm, the Nur Party) and the formerly violent *al-Gamāʿa al-Islāmiyya* entered the political game. By contrast, the Lebanese Shiʿi militia Hezbollah and the Jordanian Muslim Brotherhood (and its political arm, the Islamic Action Front) had a longer experience of politics and thus displayed a more mature political attitude. The way in which all these actors carried themselves during this controversy was an illustration of the 'inclusion-moderation hypothesis', according to which 'political actors will become more moderate if they are allowed to participate in legitimate competitive political processes, such as democratic elections, a free civil society, legal protests and demonstrations, and so on'.[26] Yet, despite their shared features as 'Islamists', these actors engaged in the controversy very differently. The Egyptian Salafi Nur Party quickly antagonised local Christians, whereas *al-Gamā'a al-Islāmiyya* managed to increase its political credentials by adopting a more moderate position towards local Christians. In this study, I will therefore show that for Islamist and Salafi figures Christians are useful political tools and therefore accommodating the latter was necessary to prove their political credentials and statesmanship. I will thus push the discussion on the 'inclusion-moderation hypothesis' further, arguing that the most powerful factor moderating Islamist attitudes was their fear of *fitna* – that is, chaos, strife – or not (depending on what or whom Islamist and Salafis considered the cause of *fitna*). *Fitna* has experienced an expansion of its meaning since the nineteenth century to include sectarian strife, as I will discuss below.

By the same token, this book is a contribution to the topic of the attitude of Islamists towards Christians, which has attracted a number of studies, especially when it comes to contemporary Islamist discussions of the *dhimma* and their vision of Christians' status.[27] But this approach often tends to reduce Christians to the status of passive bystanders, overlooking their voices and attitudes, even though, as Gudrun Krämer emphasises, '[i]t is the non-Muslims' behaviour towards Muslims that determines their status and treatment'.[28] Also, official Islam has largely been neglected, although it constitutes several important voices of Islam. David Grafton notes: 'To the extent that recent scholarship on Lebanese Islam has focussed upon these militant Islamic views, it has neglected a methodological review of moderate Lebanese Muslim religious political thought which has argued [. . .] for the maintenance of a pluralistic government in Lebanon',[29] who in the present context happen to be mostly representatives of official Islam. There now exist a few studies on the relations that official Islam has with Christians.[30] Yet, 'The Innocence of Muslims' presented them with an opportunity to strengthen their own positions in contrast to Islamist forces.

All of this suggests a need for a more non-deterministic and more thorough approach. Two key features of this book are therefore its character as micro-history and its comparative approach, through the lens of agency as an ambiguous mode of behaviour and expression. The non-deterministic approach is achieved by adopting a method inspired by micro-history – that is, looking at how the materiality and mechanisms of Christian–Muslim relations emerged within the span of two to three weeks of intense controversy, while at the same time opening up the geographical scope to include Egypt, Jordan and Lebanon, as well as a diverse set of institutional and non-institutional Christian and Muslim actors. A fascinating aspect of the controversy was that it compelled both nationally famous and minor local figures to react. As Roger Chartier notes about *The Cheese and the Worms*, 'it is on this reduced scale, *and probably only on this scale*, that we can understand, without deterministic reduction, the relationships between systems of beliefs, of values and representation on one side, and social affiliations on another'.[31] Focusing on such a short, albeit tense moment has its benefits, as Angie Heo observes regarding the shift away from the spotlight: '[t]his book approaches the quieter corners of divine intercessions to deprivilege the sensationalizing' for a broader understanding of violence.[32]

Radically reducing the chronological scale, I chose to open the geographic scope, including Lebanon and Jordan, where the video also made waves, to tackle the various questions raised so far. Laura Robson observes:

> Studies of Arab Christianity have until now been largely atomized by nation and denomination; it may be useful in the future to consider a broader and perhaps a more explicitly comparative approach. There are important comparisons to be made among the many varieties of Christian experience throughout the Middle East.[33]

The need for a comparative approach applies on many levels, all of which the controversy actually addressed. There is, first, a need to compare Christian–Muslim relations in different countries. However, 'The Innocence of Muslims' presented these countries with the same questions and issues, and each country either responded differently or displayed similar features. Second, the video also allows for more comparisons to be made between the Christians of each country, between Christians and Muslims, as well as, more importantly, between different types of actors: the Churches, al-Azhar, the Muslim Brotherhoods and parties, Jordanian professional associations, the Coptic youth organisations that emerged after the Arab Spring, Christian members of parliament (MPs) and so on, who were all motivated by similar desires: to genuinely condemn the video, defend Islam and pursue their own interests. But, due to their different positions, authority and outlook, as well as other causes, they engaged rather differently in this crisis. Strikingly, the same ambitions led the Nur Party to polemics with Copts, but helped its minor partner, the formerly violent *al-Gamā'a al-Islāmiyya* strengthen its relations with local Copts and appear as a serious political contender. Here we face a paradox: the Churches were more powerful than their counterparts of official Islam, which often lacked the power, authority and charisma of Islamist movements.

So far, I have used terms such as the 'mechanisms' and 'materiality' of Christian–Muslim relations. Based on the experience of Lebanon, George Sabra posits three different levels of Christian–Muslim dialogue: first, the 'existential dialogue' of everyday life; second, the 'dialogue of life' in which Muslims and Christians 'come together to discuss and exchange views;' and third, the 'dialogue of truth', which is the theological and accordingly the most complicated level.[34] In this book, however, I will show how religion is an area where negotiating Christian–Muslim relations is possible and, crucially, where it is possible to exert the most pressure. For if solidarity when Islam is offended implies reciprocity when Christianity is targeted, then Islam and Christianity are *equally* to be defended and protected – in short, they are *equal*. Amal Khoury suggests a similar model, with a fourth level: '[t]he ritualistic and ceremonial interfaith dialogue model, in which religious leaders participate in each other's religious ceremonies, or laypeople collaborate in organizing their religious festivities, such as *iftār* dinners, and so on'.[35] Condemning 'The Innocence of Muslims' was seen by many as engaging in a ritual of Christian–Muslim relations. This study will not tackle this aspect as the extension of social practice or popular religion, but as an expression of *realpolitik*, in which Islamists and Salafis also had to engage if they wanted to succeed on a national political level.

The analysis is almost exclusively based on Arabic and local French-speaking sources gathered through extensive research in various institutions in Beirut, Cairo, Jerusalem and Amman, as well as Princeton University.[36] I rely on official statements and comments by key actors and institutions that are to be found in specialised magazines (published by Churches, al-Azhar and so on), websites[37] and newspapers. We could all too easily dismiss these condemnations as shallow, ritualised displays of solidarity and collective condemnation. Yet, precisely their ritualised elements and the low-ranking audience that they addressed make them interesting. The repetitions, the mundane, the sensationalistic outside the fora of inter-religious dialogue shed light on the different mechanisms of Christian–Muslim relations.

Another set of sources which I use are the qualitative interviews I conducted during my fieldwork in 2015 for my doctoral research, foremost with Christian key actors (bishops, activists), to achieve a better understanding of the Christian motivations (the issue of fear) and to gather missing information on Christian communities, especially in Jordan.

Chapter One will introduce the political context of 2012 in more detail and the uncertain impact of the Arab Spring. In particular, Islamists in Egypt, Hezbollah in Lebanon and some protest movements in Jordan used the controversy as a foil against which local issues were acted out. Chapter Two takes the *raison d'être* of the video – Coptic–Muslim violence in Egypt – as the starting point for a bolder discussion of violence, arguing that fear did not prevent Christians from pursuing other motivations during the controversy and the need to examine where actors in the region actually located violence, something that partly explains why the controversy took a positive turn. Chapter Three explicates the political and legal foundations of being Christian or Muslim, introducing other key actors in the region: official Islam and the Christian laity. It is not until Chapter Four that I will discuss the Islamic foundations of Christians' status, the *dhimma* – a topic with which any study on Christians in the Middle East usually begins – in order to explore the search for proximity to the other community. Chapter Five, by contrast, is concerned with the behaviour of avoidance and the many rituals entailing the expectation of reciprocity. I argue that rituals constitute a powerful tool used by both Christians and Muslims to exert pressure on the other community. Chapter Six, finally, looks at the claims of unity as a means to renegotiate the terms of Christian–Muslim relations.

1

BEYOND THE CONTROVERSY: ISLAMIST MOVEMENTS AND THE CONSTRAINTS OF THE POLITICAL GAME

Introduction

'The Innocence of Muslims' condemned a specifically Egyptian situation: violence against Copts depicted as perpetrated by Islamists while the state stands by, not intervening to protect them. According to the video, the reasons for this are to be found in the life and teaching of the Prophet Muhammad, to whom the second part of the video is dedicated. A genuine condemnation of what was deemed offensive swept through the Middle East. Yet, it was not the first time that the 'offence' against religious content and symbols had attracted anger. The few studies discussing similar events have centred on the issue of freedom of speech versus the sanctity of religious content.[1] While alleged offences against Islam have made international headlines, similar 'offences' against Christian religious contents have attracted condemnation, too. For example, the acclaimed novel *Azazeel* by Egyptian Muslim author Yusuf Ziedan (2008) attracted the ire of the Coptic Orthodox Church.[2]

However, looking closer at the many voices condemning the poorly made video 'The Innocence of Muslims' in September 2012, one can see that they actually hinted at local issues and illustrated the ongoing upheavals of the Arab Spring in the region. Egypt, where the protests toppled the regime, has attracted more attention than Lebanon and Jordan, where the Arab Spring also had an impact, something the widespread condemnation of 'The Innocence of Muslims' made clear. In this chapter, I seek to show that, while there was a genuine condemnation of the perceived offence against Islam, actors in the region – including Christians – used it as a foil against which local issues were acted out to strengthen their own positions. These issues relate to the Islamic shift in Egypt following the revolution of 25 January 2011, the contested position of Hezbollah in Lebanon and ongoing dissatisfaction with the regime in Jordan. Islam was a paramount issue in all three countries. The recent electoral successes of the Muslim Brotherhood in Egypt and Tunisia had strengthened its branches in Lebanon.[3] This chapter, however, will show that, even though the Muslim Brotherhood was successful, it faced fierce competition from other Islamist and non-Islamist actors in Egypt, Lebanon and Jordan. At the same time, the controversy offered insights into how the various Islamist and Salafi movements navigated the political game, with some having a longer political experience such as Hezbollah, while others were complete newcomers. A tremendous number of actors – including Christians – stepped in to defend Islam against the video. In some cases, however, the ambition to defend Islam led to antagonising local Christians.

Egypt: Claiming the Islamic Leadership

In September 2012, when the video 'The Innocence of Muslims' caused outrage in Egypt, the country had just witnessed its first free presidential elections resulting in the victory of the former Muslim Brother Muhammad Mursī. Even though the Muslim Brotherhood, in common with other main Islamist or Salafi movements, had not played a major role in the early days of the 25 January 2011 revolution, they subsequently became more conspicuous. On 29 July 2011, the Muslim Brotherhood and other Islamist actors staged a protest on Tahrir Square, chanting: 'Raise your head high, you are a Muslim'.[4] A few months later, the greatest surprise in the parliamentary elections was the success of the Salafi Nur Party and its alliance, which won more than 120 of 508 seats.[5] Islamist forces also dominated the Shura Council of the parliament: the Freedom and Justice Party (FJP), the political arm of the Muslim Brotherhood, controlled 58 percent of the seats and the Salafi Nur Party 25 percent, whereas the secular forces held barely more than 10 percent.[6] In the constituent assembly, the Muslim Brotherhood controlled half of the seats and the Salafis twelve seats out of fifty.[7] Yet, in June 2012, the Supreme Council of Armed Forces (SCAF) dissolved the newly elected parliament because the Supreme Constitutional Court considered its elections unconstitutional, meaning that 'the next president of Egypt would have both executive and legislative powers concentrated in his hands'.[8] The 'Islamisation' of Egypt thus seemed inexorable.

The controversy surrounding 'The Innocence of Muslims' therefore illuminated the fierce debates over Egypt's identity and its Islamic leadership, for which not only the Muslim Brotherhood and the Nur Party but also figures of official Islam and minor Islamist and Salafi movements were competing. Although Islamists had steadily conquered state institutions after the revolution and dominated public discourse, this was by no means a united front standing behind the Muslim Brotherhood. On the contrary, its leadership was challenged by the Salafi Nur Party from the outset, something that was very much evident in September 2012 and had a destabilising effect on Christian–Muslim relations.

The (temporary) weakening of the authoritarian state in 2011 opened the door to the best-organised forces in Egyptian society: the Muslim Brotherhood and the myriad of actors issuing from the Islamic Awakening (*al-sahwa*) of the late 1960s. Established in 1928 in Ismailiyya by the teacher Hasan al-Bannā, the Muslim Brotherhood (*Gamā'at ikhwān al-muslimīn*) is of the earliest and most successful proponents of 'those ideologies and movements that strive to establish some kind of an "Islamic order" – a religious state, shari'a law, and moral codes in Muslim societies and communities'.[9] According to Gudrun Krämer, Hasan al-Bannā was not an original thinker, but combined elements of Islamic reformist discourse with ideas from Muhammad Rashīd Ridā, the attitudes of Egyptian Sufism, especially its hierarchical structures, and the mass movement approach of fascists movements in the 1930s, all mixed with a strong anti-Western outlook.[10] The core of the Muslim Brotherhood was its organisation, the *gamā'a*, even more so when Gamal Abdel Nasser, having initially formed an alliance with them against the monarchy, then cracked down on them, driving the Brotherhood into exile or underground. Under al-Sadat, the group slowly re-emerged; under Mubarak, they participated in the political process through independent candidates. In this context, the Muslim Brotherhood tried to present a moderate attitude toward Christian Egyptians. In 2000, the movement attempted to enrol a Christian candidate.[11]

By contrast, the Salafi Nur Party and *al-Gamā'a al-Islāmiyya*[12] arose from the Islamic Awakening of the late 1960s. This 'revival' alludes 'more broadly to a religious ethos or sensibility' 'in response to the perception that religious knowledge, as a means of organizing daily conduct, had become increasingly marginalized under modern structures of secular governance'[13] and came about partly in reaction to the humiliating defeat against Israel in 1967 and partly as it was supported by the new president Anwar al-Sadat (1970–81) to counter Nasserist remnants. It is noteworthy that Mubarak's efforts to control Islam 'paradoxically further bolstered its pregnancy in Egyptian society'.[14] However, the turn towards a greater Islamisation of the state and society had already started under Nasser, under whose rule Christian Egyptians were barred from some professions (Arabic teacher, gynaecologist) and teaching the Qur'an in private schools became mandatory.[15] Bernard Haykel describes Salafis as 'first and foremost religious and social reformers'.[16] As Richard Gauvain notes, the idea of purity – the purity of the doctrine, practices and behaviour – is a key characteristic of this movement,[17] of which the Nur Party was a prime example. It was the political arm of *al-Da'wa al-Salafiyya*, which emerged in Alexandria in the 1970s and focused on teaching and promoting a purified form of Islam:[18] 'Their quest for purity refers to their conviction that an uncorrupted Islamic reality may be achieved through the correct education and training [. . .] Such purity, ultimately, is doctrinal and ideological'.[19] Established in the late 1970s, *al-Gamā'a al-Islāmiyya* was a violent radical Islamist group that targeted the regime and Copts. Several of its leaders were imprisoned, among them Tāriq al-Zumur and 'Abbūd al-Zumur, for plotting to assassinate President Anwar al-Sadat. While in prison, they announced an end to all violence in 1997.[20] During his incarceration, Tāriq al-Zumur earned a doctorate in constitutional law.[21] After their release, the leadership of *al-Gamā'a al-Islāmiyya* founded a political party, the Building and Development Party, and formed an alliance with the Salafi Nur Party during parliamentary elections, winning thirteen out of 508 seats.[22]

The Muslim Brotherhood, the Nur Party and *al-Gamā'a al-Islāmiyya* were the most prominent and most powerful actors of the Islamist and Salafi movement and chose to establish political parties: in April 2011, the Muslim Brotherhood founded the Freedom and Justice Party (*Hizb al-hurriya wa-l-'adāla*);

in June 2011 *al-Daʿwa al-Salafiyya* set up the Nur Party (*Hizb al-nūr*);[23] and in June 2011 *al-Gamāʿa al-Islāmiyya* created the Building and Development Party (*Hizb al-binā' wa-l-tanmiya*). But from the onset there were tensions between the mother organisations and their political branches. In the case of the Muslim Brotherhood, '[t]here was a faction within the movement that endorsed the idea of a clear separation of roles between *daʿwa* (the remit of the MB) and political work (the remit of the party)', but 'leaders held multiple hats in both the MB and the FJP and because the movement's guidance bureau continued to serve as the higher decision-making power on all matters, including those pertaining to the FJP'.[24] Likewise, the Nur Party was torn between its ideological stances and political requirements. In particular, the then secretary general of the Nur Party, ʿImād ʿAbd al-Ghaffūr, showed extensive political pragmatism, claiming that, 'as the secretary of the Nur Party, I have strong relations with all political parties and different streams, as we have come to have now relations with all the communities and Islamist streams as well as the non-Islamist streams'.[25] He formed a group of experts to draft a political programme, including a number of non-Salafi experts.[26] As there was no clear divide between the political party and *al-Daʿwa al-Salafiyya*, tensions increased over time and were very perceptible in September 2012.[27]

The move of *al-Daʿwa al-Salafiyya* into politics seemed to contradict the earlier 'apolitical' etiquette, thus at least implicitly in part endorsing the democratic system. Esen Kirdiş puts it down to the fact that a decision on 'whether or not to participate is foremost shaped by the "political opportunity and threat structures"'.[28] Prior to the revolution, it had remained politically aloof.[29] I believe that there is a need to reflect more deeply on these movements' attitude towards the state and violence, and on the close connection between the state and violence, rather than simply looking at violence and Islamism (or Salafism). Second, the issue of politics needs to be considered in light of what these actors consider necessary as opposed to contingent or contextual. The 'apolitical' position thus seems rather contextual. *Al-Gamāʿa al-Islāmiyya* leader ʿIsām Darbāla illustrated this point in May 2011 when he justified the movement's past use of violence by the fact that 'the state did not respect the law it had established'.[30]

All of the Islamist actors discussed here considered 'The Innocence of Muslims' an opportunity to demonstrate their commitment to defend Islam while using it as an opportunity to strengthen their political positions. The Muslim Brotherhood, the FJP, the Nur Party, *al-Da'wa al-Salafiyya* and *al-Gamā'a al-Islāmiyya* condemned the video on numerous occasions. But the controversy was soon tarnished by the attempted storming of the US embassy in Cairo on 11 September 2012, which seriously hindered the ability of Muhammad Mursī and the Muslim Brotherhood to respond to the video and mobilise its followers. The spokesman of the presidency issued a statement on 12 September 2012, one day after the failed storming of the US embassy in Cairo.[31] Security forces struggled to maintain control over downtown Cairo after the incident at the US embassy: clashes continued on Friday, 14 September, and through the night from 15 to 16 September.[32] Security forces only regained control over Tahrir Square on 16 September 2012.[33] On an international level, the controversy damaged Egypt's relations with the United States. US President Barack Obama said on 13 September 2012: 'I don't think we would consider them an ally but we don't consider them an enemy'.[34] In response, Khayrat al-Shāṭir, the deputy Supreme Guide of the Muslim Brotherhood, published a letter in the *New York Times* on 13 September 2012, in which he emphasised that 'we do not hold the American government or its citizens responsible for the acts of a few who abuse the laws protecting freedom of speech'.[35] Still, he believed that Egyptians did have a right to demonstrate in this new, democratic Egypt.

As a result, even though the Muslim Brotherhood initially called for peaceful protests in several parts of the country for Friday, 14 September 2012,[36] following the violent clashes in the area of the US embassy, it decided to scale back its mobilisation to avoid jeopardising its aura of statesmanship and participated only in a symbolic protest on Tahrir Square.[37] In Suez, the Brotherhood marched in cooperation with 'Salafi movements' and 'liberals'; in Damietta and al-Fayyum, it marched with *al-Da'wa al-Salafiyya* and other political forces.[38]

By contrast, as the biggest opposition force, the Nur Party and its mother organisation *al-Da'wa al-Salafiyya* used the controversy as an opportunity to pressure President Muhammad Mursī to take a firm stance towards the United States and suspend relations with them.[39] The first speaker of the Shura-Council, 'Abd Allāh Badrān of the Nur Party, emphasised the parliament's demand to stop all relations with the United States, especially since 'we now have a Muslim president'.[40] However, the virulent stance of the Nur Party brought great turmoil, as it antagonised local Christians.

The eagerness to defend Islam was thus seriously hampered by two factors: statesmanship and efforts to accommodate Copts. The seemingly inexorable rise to power of Islamists and, with that, their agency was actually limited in post-Arab Spring Egypt.

The Risks of Antagonising Copts

In their attempts to defend Islam and use the controversy as an opportunity to assert their own positions, some Islamists started to antagonise local Christians, contributing to an atmosphere of tension that could have had dangerous consequences. Yet, as I will discuss here, other actors also contributed to this atmosphere. As a result, representatives of the Islamist movements and official Islam navigated the controversy between denouncing the video and de-escalating the tension, to varying degrees of success. These figures' ability and claim to speak for Islam were thus significantly limited, despite the extraordinary opportunities provided by the post-revolutionary phase.

Before the attempted storming of the US embassy, prominent Islamist figures called on the Coptic Orthodox Church to officially condemn the video in a display of loyalty. In a declaration published by *al-Yawm al-Sābiʿ* on 7 September 2012, Wisām ʿAbd al-Wārith, preacher on the channel *al-Hikma*, called on 'the Church to make her position clear, either she distances herself from those individuals who produced this film or she remains silent, and this means she assents to this'.[41] A famous Salafi preacher known as Abū Yaḥyā, who in May 2011 had played a role in the inter-communal clashes in Imbaba in the governorate of Giza,[42] demanded that 'the Church distances herself from the producers and the promoters of the film'; he supported measures regarding the citizenship of the producers in order to prevent 'strife between Muslim and Coptic Egyptians'.[43] The most spectacular anti-Christian reaction in connection to 'The Innocence of Muslims' was the burning of pages of a Bible copy by the Salafi preacher Ahmad ʿAbd Allāh, nicknamed 'Abū Islām'.[44] But even secular figures such as ʿAmr Mūsā, former minister of Foreign Affairs and secretary general of the Arab League, contributed to the tensions, calling on 'all intellectuals and followers of different religions to take a clear position' against the video.[45] Strikingly, the media did much to nurture this atmosphere of suspicion by systematically establishing a connection between 'The Innocence of Muslims' and local Christians, as illustrated by the fact that *al-Yawm al-Sābiʿ* published the call of Wisām ʿAbd al-Wārith to the Coptic Orthodox Church on 7 September 2012 – that is, four days before the video achieved wider relevance through the clashes around the US embassy. On 8 September 2012, in a similar article, *al-Yawm al-Sābiʿ* described the controversy as follows:

> *A number of Copts of the diaspora* [*aqbāt al-mahjar*] [my emphasis], and their head, ʿIsmat Zuqlama, who called for the partition of Egypt and is president of the so-called Coptic state, and Morris Sadek, who cannot refrain from attacking Egypt in all international forums and turning foreign countries against her, [. . .] have announced the production of a film about Muhammad (PBUH) which contains heinous offences and serious insinuations against the noble Messenger [. . .].[46]

The article suggests that those involved in this video are not limited to these three people but also comprise an unknown number of Copts, adding:

> At the same time, a *number of Coptic Egyptian leaders* [my emphasis] condemned the film [. . .] refusing any offence against the noble Messenger and condemning the production of a film which offends one of the prophets of God, as it offends Islam.

The phrases 'a number of Copts of the diaspora', on the one hand, and 'a number of Coptic Egyptian leaders', on the other hand, raise the following question: what did the majority of Copts in Egypt think? The article thus establishes a dichotomy between 'good' Copts showing their solidarity with Muslims and 'bad' Copts participating in this 'offence'.

The Islamist actors, discussed in the previous section, navigated these political white-waters unevenly. The Nur Party, in particular, participated in this turmoil and jeopardised its political credentials. Some vitriolic reactions included its spokesman Yusrī Hammād criticising Muslims for their alleged passivity:

> Where are your loud voices now? You are now silent like the dead, and you remain quiet [about] the Copts of the diaspora who were announcing that

God is love; and when they left your country, they declared enmity for you and abuse your religion and your Prophet.[47]

The question here is: did Hammād mean that Copts had declared war on Muslims upon leaving the country, or had this enmity already been there? In the public mind, the Nur Party became so entwined with the controversial Salafi Front and other movements that Nādir Bakkār, the Nur Party's media spokesman, felt obliged to publicly reject allegations that the Salafis had agitated against Copts, claiming instead that the Salafis had protested with 'liberals and Copts'.[48] A couple of days earlier, a Coptic Orthodox priest named Salīb Matā Sāwirīs had called out Bakkār because a small Salafi group, the Salafi Front, had identified him on their Facebook page as 'Āb Yūtā', a controversial Coptic cyber-activist,[49] something he denied.[50]

The atmosphere became so tense that the leaders of the Nur Party and the Muslim Brotherhood even felt the need to dissociate local Christians from the video. In a sermon delivered on Friday, 14 September 2012, in a mosque in Alexandria, 'Imād 'Abd al-Ghaffūr, the secretary general of the Nur Party, condemned the burning of the Bible by Abū Islām, reminding his audience that 'God and His Messenger forbade the offence of the other religions', insisting on the 'need not to punish the Christians of Egypt for the crime of the producer of the film'.[51] His condemnation was backed by a fatwa by the deputy secretary general of *al-Da'wa al-Salafiyya*, Yāsir Burhāmī, who condemned the burning of the Bible.[52] As the biggest opposition force, the Nur Party's opportunity to challenge the Muslim Brotherhood thus went off course when it drifted into polemics against local Christians. The party faced a difficult dilemma: remaining loyal to its ideology or proving statesmanship. Similarly, in his weekly letter, the Supreme Guide of the Muslim Brotherhood, Muhammad Badī', warned that 'it is fair not to make our Christian brothers bear the sin of a group of idiots animated by hidden fingers'.[53] Unlike the Muslim Brotherhood and the Nur Party, *al-Gamā'a al-Islāmiyya* and its political arm navigated these political white-waters more easily. As will be discussed in Chapter Four, it managed to publicly defend Islam without antagonising local Christians and consequently to strengthen its positions.

However, Christian Egyptians did not remain passive during this controversy, a stance that will emerge throughout this book. For the time being, it suffices to say that many Christian clerics and lay figures did react, although their tone varied greatly. For the Coptic Orthodox Church, to which the majority of Christian Egyptians belong, the controversy occurred in a difficult period, as Patriarch Shinūda III (1923–2012, in office 1971–2012) had died in March 2012, and Patriarch Tawādrūs II had been elected two months later, in November 2012. In the meantime, in September 2012, Bishop Bākhūmyūs, the bishop of al-Buhayra, was the patriarchal caretaker. Overall, the Coptic Orthodox and Protestant Churches in Egypt were concerned with dissociating local Christians from the controversy. The Coptic Orthodox Church issued an initial statement on 9 September 2012 and a second one three days later. It gathered a third time on 21 September 2012, for an urgent meeting to counter the accusations made by the above-mentioned Salafi Front.[54] On 22 September 2012, Bishop Bākhūmyūs weighed in, again to emphasise the condemnation of the video by the Church.[55] In addition, fifteen of the forty-nine bishops in Egypt reacted at least once in comments to the press or official statements, as well as by joining protests and conferences. The initial statement by the Coptic Orthodox explained: '[T]he Church has learnt that some Egyptians living in foreign countries work on spreading disunion between the children of the united nation (*abnā' al-watan al-wāhid*) by offending (*isā'a*) Islam and its noble Prophet'.[56] The reactions of the Coptic Catholic Church differed significantly in terms of tone and content: it explained the reason for issuing a statement on 11 September 2012 as a result of 'what the media have published about the showing of a film offending Islam',[57] thus implying that its statement was not prompted by the video itself, but by the *media's mention of the video*. In addition, many Christian Coptic lay organisations and figures also entered the controversy (see Chapters Three and Five).

The video 'The Innocence of Muslims' quickly provoked a controversy in Egypt in which Islamist and Salafi actors saw an opportunity to further their personal interests. Yet, the Muslim Brotherhood and the Nur Party were quickly limited in their endeavour, both by the requirements of statesmanship and by their contribution to an atmosphere of suspicion towards Christian Egyptians, which compelled the Churches to react. However, Christian reactions in Egypt were not solely motivated by the fear of a backlash.

Lebanon: Contesting Hezbollah's Islamic and Lebanese Leadership

On Friday, 14 September 2012, the same day as the protests in Egypt, the Roman Catholic Pope Benedict XVI began a three-day visit to Lebanon. As soon as he left the country on Sunday, 16 September 2012, Hasan Nasr Allāh, leader of the Lebanese militant Shi'i party Hezbollah, delivered a forty-minute speech on *al-Manār*, the party's TV channel, in which he insisted on the threat that the video posed to Islam and Christian–Muslim relations, aiming to produce 'strife between Muslims and Christians' and push them into a 'a bloody religious, sectarian conflict'.[58] Muslims would be expected to attack churches and Christian holy sites. The following day, Hezbollah and its political ally, the Shi'i Amal Movement, mobilised their followers in peaceful protests in the southern suburb of Beirut, which continued in Tyre (19 September), Baalbek (21 September), Bint Jbeil (22 September) and Hermel (23 September 2012). These protests attracted 10,000 followers of both movements,[59] including high-ranking Christian and Sunni Muslim figures.

How could a poorly made video which denounced a specific situation in Egypt make such waves in Lebanon? How was Hasan Nasr Allāh able not only to mobilise his followers, but also to attract high-ranking political and religious Christian figures, as well as Sunni MPs? To put it simply, Hasan Nasr Allāh *manufactured* this controversy but, unlike the Nur Party in Egypt, he carefully crafted his condemnation of 'The Innocence of Muslims' in such a way that he was able to reconcile Hezbollah's politicised Shi'i Islamist ideology and his claim for Islamic leadership, while also claiming proximity to local Christians. He managed to fashion himself as a cross-sectarian Islamist *and* Lebanese leader. Thus, to a certain extent, Hezbollah illustrates a more mature stage of Islamist involvement in politics. Yet, Nasr Allāh's claim did not go unchallenged by his opponents, who accused him of trying to divert attention from the movement's involvement in Syria on the side of the regime of Bashar al-Assad, something which became undeniable in May 2013.

The manner in which the controversy around 'The Innocence of Muslims' unfolded reflected the mounting polarisation taking place in Lebanese politics after the Civil War, which reached another level with the conflict raging in neighbouring Syria after March 2011, in which some Lebanese parties became involved. In 1989, the Taef Agreement finally put an end to the Civil War. It maintained the confessional system and the Christian Maronite hold over the state, although it decreased the power held by the president. It ordered the disarmament of all militias, except for Hezbollah,[60] since it was considered part of the 'national resistance' against the Israeli occupation in the south; this ended in 2000. The introduction of UN Resolution 1559 in September 2004, which demanded the disarmament of all militias – including Hezbollah[61] – and the assassination of Prime Minister Rafīq al-Harīrī on 14 February 2005 upset and deeply polarised the Lebanese political landscape. The subsequent Cedar Revolution led to a withdrawal of Syrian troops from Lebanon, which had numbered up to 30,000 men.[62]

The March 14 Alliance and the March 8 Alliance emerged with competing strategic outlooks and alliances. The more Western-orientated and increasingly anti-Hezbollah March 14 Alliance was made up, as of 2012, of the al-Harīrī family's Future Movement, the Christian Lebanese Forces, the Christian Phalange Party or Kataeb (*Hizb al-katā'ib al-lubnāniyya*) and the Lebanese branch of the Muslim Brotherhood, *al-Jamā'a al-Islāmiyya*.[63] Following his release from prison, Samīr Geagea, the leader of the Lebanese Forces, became one of the main figures in the March 14 Alliance. The March 8 Alliance comprised, as of 2012, Hezbollah, the Shi'i Amal Movement, the Christian Free Patriotic Movement (FPM) of Michel Aoun, the Christian Marada Movement, the anti-sectarian Syrian Social National Party (SSNP), and smaller Alawi and Druze parties. This very heterogeneous alliance was united by an anti-Israeli, pro-Syrian and pro-Iranian outlook. The mid-2000s alliance that Hezbollah made with the SSNP and the Christian Free Patriotic Movement illustrated Hezbollah's political maturation without forsaking its politicised Twelver Shi'i identity.

Since its establishment during the Civil War in the early 1980s, Hezbollah has identified with the *vilāyat-i faqīh*, the rule of the jurist, the official doctrine of the Islamic Republic of Iran, which was elaborated by Ayatollah Ruhollah Khomeini; unlike other leading Shi'i figures in Lebanon, in 1995 it recognized the religious reference (*marja'*) of Ali Chamenei.[64] Over time, its rhetoric also changed. In 1992, the movement still defined itself as a 'jihadi movement created in the wake of the Israeli invasion of 1982'.[65] Yet, in 2009 Hezbollah issued another manifesto in which it scaled back its Islamist language and emphasised the dangers of 'US hegemony'.[66] The liberation of southern Lebanon in 2000 increased Hezbollah's popularity in Lebanon. In his 'victory speech', Hasan Nasr Allāh stated: '[Hezbollah] fought for Lebanese territory, defended Lebanese citizens and confronted an enemy behaving aggressively against the Lebanese people'.[67] During the war against Israel in July 2006, which resulted in thousands of deaths and almost a million displaced people,[68] Hezbollah was at the climax of its national and regional popularity. Nasr Allāh was even popular among Christians in the region, including in the Palestinian Territories.[69]

But Hezbollah's seemingly unchecked power increasingly unsettled the Lebanese Sunni population, which suffered from a lack of charismatic leadership after the murder of Rafīq al-Harīrī. In May 2008, when the government decided to end Hezbollah's secret communication networks, Hezbollah deployed in Beirut.[70] A small-scale civil war ensued between the pro-Hezbollah alliance and its opponents, with over a hundred deaths or wounded in Beirut and its hinterland.[71] By 2012, the Sunni political leadership claimed by Saʻad al-Harīrī, son of Rafīq al-Harīrī, was basically non-existent, since he had left the country following the collapse of his government in 2011. The new Prime Minister Najīb Mīqātī, who came into office with the backing of Hezbollah, had a certain level of autonomy.[72] Instead, an unknown Salafi preacher from Sidon, Ahmad al-Asīr, sought to claim the Lebanese Islamic leadership (see Chapter Four).

The relentless support for Hezbollah results from its having provided support to the population in the south since the Civil War.[73] However, one of its greatest successes is perhaps the growing assertion and self-confidence of a formerly weak and marginalised Shiʻi Lebanese community, the 'deprived' (*mustadhʻafīn*). Nasr Allāh, in particular, has come to embody the party. As Sabrina Mervin puts it, 'he changes the eternal losers of history into winners and, with him, it is no longer a spiritual or symbolic [. . .] victory, but a real victory by arms, won by the Hezbollah (in 2000 and 2006) thanks to the endurance of its supporters'.[74]

This politicised Shiʻi discourse is still very much part of Hezbollah's discourse, especially when cultivating a connection with its followers. During the protest in Beirut in September 2012, Nasr Allāh switched between Modern Standard Arabic and colloquial Arabic to display his proximity to his supporters. He mingled his call for resistance with a politicised form of Twelver Shiʻi, haranguing the audience in Beirut:

> Nasr Allāh: Oh Messenger of God (*yā rasūl Allāh*)!
> The audience: Oh Messenger of God!
> Nasr Allāh: At your service, Messenger of God (*fidāk yā rasūl Allāh*)!
> The audience: At your service, Messenger of God!
> Nasr Allāh: My soul and my blood!
> The audience: My soul and my blood!
> Nasr Allāh: And my father and my mother!
> The audience: And my father and my mother!
> Nasr Allāh: And my family and my children!
> The audience: And my family and my children!
> Nasr Allāh: And all my wealth!
> The audience: And all my wealth![75]

The protest against 'The Innocence of Muslims' thus became a re-enactement of the Battle of Kerbala, the founding myth of the politicised Shiʻi community introduced in the 1970s in Lebanon.[76] Instead of being at the margins of Islam and Islamist discourse, Hezbollah's Islamic and Islamist identity, albeit a Shiʻi identity, is framed as being at the heart of the broader Islamic narrative. In his move against the video, Nasr Allāh claimed to embody Islamic leadership, criticising the rulers in the Muslim world at length, claiming that had this video offended 'the kings, the princes, the presidents and the leaders in the region', they would have reacted differently: 'This is your Islam! This is your religion! This is your *umma*!'[77] In his speeches on *al-Manār* TV as well as in Beirut, he addressed all Muslims in general and, in doing so, tried to transcend the divisions between Muslims, stating that it was not merely the responsibility of one 'confession (*madhhab*)', or the March 8 and the March 14 Alliances, to react.[78]

Unlike the Nur Party in Egypt, Nasr Allāh's claim to leadership did not antagonise local Christians. Rather, he made them an integral part of his condemnation of the video. High-ranking Christian figures such as the Maronite bishop Samʻān ʻAtāʼ Allāh and the Greek Catholic MP and vice secretary general of the SSNP, Marwān Fāris, featured prominently in the Hezbollah/Amal protests, something that turned the protests into joint Christian–Muslim efforts. The claims to Islamic and Lebanese leadership reinforced each other. Presenting himself as the standard-bearer for the whole Islamic community, Hasan Nasr Allāh articulated his response in the context of 'Christian–Muslim coexistence': 'I thank the 'ulamā', whether Sunni or Shi'i, the representatives of the Christian leaders and of the Lebanese and national parties, and I feel grateful for our brothers, the leaders in the Amal Movement', present at the protest in Beirut.[79] He linked the mobilisation to the pope's visit: 'On the contrary, Lebanon has presented us with a model [. . .] of coexistence between Muslims and Christians', for 'Lebanon is always bigger than its size in issues of civilisation and values'.[80]

But these claims did not go unchallenged. The March 14 Alliance was critical of Hezbollah's outcry over a poorly made video. The (mainly) Maronite National Liberal Party accused Hezbollah of trying to distract attention 'from the crimes of the Syrian regime'.[81] During a press conference, the Maronite leader of the Kataeb, Amin Gemayel, questioned: 'Against whom is Nasr Allāh protesting?' Therefore, 'we don't know where this mobilisation can possibly lead'.[82] The Salafi preacher Ahmad al-Asīr, briefly mentioned above, sought to create a Sunni counter-weight (see Chapter Four). By 2012, the war in Syria was already having an effect on Lebanon. Several political forces were deeply involved in the conflict, either on the side of the Syrian regime or on the side of the opposition. Weapons were shipped to Syria via Lebanon.[83] The Central Beqaa Valley in Lebanon served as the 'primary logistical hub for arms procurement' for rebels operating in Syria.[84] In September 2012, Hezbollah's rivals denounced the party for its involvement in the war, an accusation that it consistently denied or silenced, but its support of the Syrian regime finally became undeniable during the Battle of al-Qusayr in May 2013.[85] The effects were evident in Lebanon, in Tripoli, where in February 2012 the mainly Sunni neighbourhood of Bab al-Tabbaneh was pitted against the Alawi-dominated neighbourhood of Jabal Mohsen,[86] both poor areas. However, these violent clashes were not only a consequence of the war in Syria since they also reflected the ongoing impact of the Lebanese Civil War.[87]

But the party's ubiquity overshadowed the other events taking place in Lebanon: first, the visit of Pope Benedict XVI; second, the video even caused clashes in the northern city of Tripoli; and third, there were many other joint Christian–Muslim protests throughout the country. Finally, for some actors in Lebanon, such as the Churches, 'The Innocence of Muslims' was irrelevant, even though Church representatives were instrumental in the joint Christian–Muslim responses to the video, both higher-up and at lower local levels. Fr Antoine Daw and Bishop Samʿān ʿAtāʾ Allāh participated in a Hezbollah/Amal protest, and Greek Orthodox Bishop Bāsīlyūs Mansūr joined a conference in the northern governorate of Akkar (see Chapters Four and Five).

Jordan: Dissatisfaction with the Regime

As in Egypt and Lebanon, 'The Innocence of Muslims' attracted widespread condemnation in Jordan, where it was likewise used to demonstrate Islamic credentials and, more importantly, to express dissatisfaction with the regime. But the Jordanian case differed significantly from the Egyptian and Lebanese contexts. First, although there were many Christian reactions, there were no (explicit) joint Christian–Muslim reactions. Second, the condemnations of the video hardly ever connected it to local Christians. Third, Islamist forces dominated neither among the voices of condemnation nor in the organisation of the mobilisation, but professional associations were far more powerful. Moreover, the Islamic Action Front (IAF), the political arm of the Jordanian Muslim Brotherhood, did not act independently. Fourth, the Jordanian monarchy plays a key role in Jordan, impacting both Islam and Christian–Muslim relations. All these factors make Jordan a salient addition to our study.

The controversy over 'The Innocence of Muslims' shed light on an ongoing Arab Spring in Jordan. Even though it had taken place on a small scale, it had been a potentially dangerous moment for the monarchy, since its traditional pillars – the tribes and the army – were key actors in the protests. The protests subsequently included the Jordanian Palestinians, Islamists and unaffiliated young people, all united by the same demand to end corruption and implement a new electoral law.[88]

Interestingly, in the context of the video, the Muslim Brotherhood was just one of many actors. Founded in 1946 in Palestine, it has had a history of good relations with the monarchy, which allowed the former to be involved in social services and to refrain from discussing internal Jordanian politics.[89] The Muslim Brotherhood adopted the strategy of a 'march through the institutions' and began to infiltrate the Ministry of Education in the 1960s.[90] Following the legalisation of political parties, the Muslim

Brotherhood established the Islamic Action Front (IAF, *Jabhat al-ʿamal al-islāmī*) in 1992.[91] The monarchy changed the electoral law after the success of the Muslim Brotherhood at the first free elections in 1989.[92] As a result, the Jordanian Muslim Brotherhood boycotted the elections in 1997[93] and 2010.[94] Yet, there was no agreement within the movement and the party over this boycott.[95] Furthermore, relations with the monarchy started to deteriorate after King Abdullah II 'tended to view the Muslim Brotherhood through the prism of security, rather than politics'.[96] This further deteriorated after the Arab Spring, when the king described the Muslim Brotherhood as 'Masonic cult [. . .] run by wolves in sheep's clothing' and when the headquarters of the movement were besieged.[97] Nevertheless, the situation of the Muslim Brotherhood and the IAF contrasts with their counterparts in Egypt, because members in Jordan searched for cooperation outside the Islamist movement in the context of the Arab Spring in order 'to solve the kingdom's problems in a broad-based – rather than Islamist – way'.[98]

This approach was also adopted in reaction to 'The Innocence of Muslims'. The bulk of the protests took place in the northern governorates, where the IAF marched together with local reform movements. In the governorate of Jirash, on Friday, 14 September 2012, following prayers, the Muslim Brotherhood marched together with the Coalition of Jirash for Reform (*I'tilāf Jirash li-l-islāh*). According to the pro-monarchy newspaper *al-Dustūr*, they chanted Islamic slogans.[99] *Al-Ghad*, however, reported that they also demanded the protection of freedom and expressed their rejection of restrictions on freedom of speech and of the imprisonment of those participating in sit-ins.[100] Kirdiş notes that, after that time, 'new laws limiting the press and online media freedoms were introduced, and the new electoral law was altered to be more restrictive so that "no party [was] permitted to take more than five seats"'.[101] In the governorate of ʿAjlūn in the locality of Kufranja, on 14 September 2012, representatives of the IAF led a march together with the Popular Movement of Kufranja for Reform and Change (*Hirāk Kufranja al-shaʿbī li-l-islāh wa-l-taghyīr*) and other local movements.[102] All condemned 'The Innocence of Muslims' but used it as an opportunity to criticise the regime.

'The Innocence of Muslims' also presented the monarchy with an opportunity to emphasise the country's role in promoting a positive image of Islam, especially given the Hashimite monarchy's claim to Islamic legitimacy. In its official reaction on 13 September 2012, the government's spokesman insisted on the 'Amman Message' which displayed 'the wisdom of its leadership that moderation (*wasatiyya*), in its true concept, contributes to combatting extremism in all its forms'.[103] The Amman Message was released in 2004, in the month of Ramadan, by King Abdullah II himself, to promote inter-Islamic dialogue and tolerance.[104] The Amman Message was also mentioned by the minister of Islamic Endowments, Islamic Affairs and Sacred Places (*muqaddasāt*), 'Abd al-Salām al-'Abādī, who defined Islam as 'the religion of mercy, humanity, tolerance, moderation and balance, the religion of justice and peace, a religion that condemned the contemporary meaning of terrorism',[105] using slogans similar to the government's.

Yet, the bulk of the condemnation and mobilisation was undertaken by non-religious actors – professional associations and two tribal confederations – something that sets Jordan apart from Egypt and Lebanon. Most of the professional associations were established in the 1950s, under government supervision.[106] But unlike trade unions, which were subject to repression, professional associations were able to assert their independence,[107] due in part to their strong – compulsory – membership and the outlawing of political parties.[108] In the mid-1990s, they numbered 70,000 members and, despite a reduced role, they have retained their influence.[109] They continue to be seen as a substitute for political parties.[110]

Professional associations across the country issued condemnations and dominated the protests. The association of agricultural engineers staged a sit-in in front of the building of the Counsel of Professional Associations,[111] and the imams and employees of the Ministry of Islamic Endowments staged a protest in the greater area of Amman on 17 September.[112]

By contrast, unlike in Egypt or Lebanon, no Islamist or Salafi force managed to lay claim to or actually take the lead. It is true that the IAF protested together with local reform movements and voiced criticism towards the government, but the party's official statement was moderate, asserting the importance of 'peaceful and civilised' reactions. Moreover, it called on the US government and on other countries to issue laws condemning such acts, as well as on Arab and Islamic governments to take a firm stance.[113] Salafi(-Jihadi) protests took place in Amman and in Ma'ān, a traditional hotbed of Islamism on Friday, 14 September 2012, after prayers.[114]

As a result, even though a diverse number of Jordanian actors and institutions harshly condemned the video – including sectors of the Jordanian government, the minister of Islamic Endowments, Islamic Affairs and Sacred Places, the Fatwa Council, both the Lower House[115] and the Senate,[116] and, on the local level, the municipal council of Greater Tafila[117] – neither representatives of official Islam nor leaders of Islamist and Salafi movements dominated among the voices condemning 'The Innocence of Muslims'.

The Jordanian case presents a methodological challenge because the absence of explicit joint Christian–Muslim reactions did not necessarily imply the absence of the Christian element, given the economic and political role of Christians (see Chapter Three). Out of ten reactions, only two professional associations and one political party, the Arab Islamic Democratic Movement (*Hizb al-duʿā*), implicitly alluded to Christians – probably because they had Christians in their ranks.[118] *Hizb al-duʿā* warned against 'violating Islamic and Christian revealed beliefs [. . .] because the followers of the revealed religions are an integral part of our Arab nation (*umma*)'.[119] The professional association asserted in its statement on 13 September 2012 that Christians had condemned the video before Muslims did and that it also rejected any generalisation concerning Christians and Muslims based on a single act by an extremist.[120]

Moreover, much like in Egypt and Lebanon, a broad range of Churches, Christian associations and individual figures weighed in to condemn the video. As in Egypt, Protestant actors expressed a stronger sense of concern and displayed efforts to dissociate local Protestant Christians from the issue.[121] The statement issued by the Council of the Heads of the Churches (subsequently 'Council of Churches') on 14 September 2012 is particularly interesting and will be carefully discussed in the course of this book. This council had been established in 1999 by the four bishops of Amman: the Greek Orthodox Bishop, the Latin Bishop, the Greek Catholic Melkite Bishop and the Armenian Apostolic Bishop.[122] It was recognized by the government as the body that would officially deal with Christian matters.[123] Its then secretary general, Hannā Kildānī, a Latin priest in the suburb of Marj al-Hammam, published a long statement,[124] which was partly reproduced in the newspapers *al-Raʾy* and *al-Dustūr*.

Thus, despite the absence of explicit Christian–Muslim reactions against the video, several aspects of the controversy in Jordan produced the impression that condemning the video was a joint Christian–Muslim effort.

Conclusion

A brief controversy over a poorly made video thus offered glimpses into larger issues that the region was facing after the Arab Spring: claims to speak for Islam and, thus, the place of Islam in the polity, as well as the place of Christians, who were quickly targeted by suspicions. Moreover, this chapter has shed light on the various degrees of political maturity, which was evident in the way in which the Islamist movements introduced here navigated the controversy. They needed to strike a subtle balance between their ideological stance and the political requirements of statemenship; as we will see, Christians played a role in both of these aspects. While Hezbollah leader Hasan Nasr Allāh was able to reconcile the party's politicised Shi'i Islamist ideology and fashion himself as a cross-sectarian Islamist *and* Lebanese leader, the Egyptian Salafi Nur Party, as the strongest opposition force in Egypt, quickly entered polemics with Christians, which jeopardised its political credentials. In Jordan, the Muslim Brotherhood and the IAF displayed political maturity and cooperation with non-Islamists. All of this shows the subtle limits imposed on the agency of Islamist and Salafi actors in the political game.

2

ANOTHER UNDERSTANDING OF VIOLENCE: FROM COPTIC–MUSLIM VIOLENCE TO A FAR GREATER DANGER

Introduction

Following the attempted storming of the US embassy in Cairo on 11 September 2012, the Coptic Orthodox priest Father Fīlūbātir Gamīl 'Azīz[1] wondered: 'Are we to expect a terrorist act against the Church in Egypt, especially on this coming Friday?'[2] There were many more causes for fear besides the attack on the US embassy. The first chapter has shown how, in their eagerness to speak for Islam, some Salafi figures in Egypt, especially the Nur Party, entered dangerous waters and nurtured suspicion towards Christian Egyptians. Tensions were so high that Muhammad Badīʿ, the Supreme Guide of the Muslim Brotherhood, and ʿImād ʿAbd al-Ghaffūr, the secretary general of the Nur Party, warned about a backlash against local Christians.

Fears of violence were legitimate, as in the past responses to similar events of 'offence' had often resulted in backlashes against local Christians. In 2006, a protest in reaction to the 'Danish cartoons' held in front of the Danish embassy in Beirut turned violent, and a nearby Maronite church was attacked.[3] Following Benedict XVI's lecture in Regensburg in September 2006, churches in Nablus and Tulkarem, in the Palestinian Territories, and in Gaza were firebombed.[4] In the context of 'The Innocence of Muslims', violence indeed erupted quickly. A protest in Cairo on 11 September 2012 tried to storm the US embassy. A couple of days later public anger targeted the homes and family members of the video's producers (something to be discussed in this chapter).

The journal *Proche-Orient Chrétien* (POC) reported a total of two deaths and 250 injured in clashes between security forces and protesters in Egypt.[5] More importantly, as we will see in the present chapter, sectarian violence had dramatically increased in Egypt in the aftermath of the Arab Spring. Violence also affected Lebanon (see further below).

Yet, on that Friday, instead of a much-feared backlash against local Christians, joint Christian–Muslim protests took place in several parts of Egypt, followed by more joint protests on the following Friday, this time in Lebanon as well, including the large-scale protests orchestrated by Hezbollah and the Amal Movement. The controversy of 'The Innocence of Muslims' was not so much a story about violence against Christians, but rather a story about how this potential violence was avoided, prevented and, in the end, turned into an event that paradoxically strengthened local Christian–Muslim relations.

This chapter is concerned with violence in connection to this controversy: the actual violence, its targets, the potential violence and, more importantly, how Muslim and Christian figures anticipated violence and channelled it into a positive outcome. I will explore other dimensions of inter-confessional violence, which have often been depicted as almost inevitable. I am making the case here that, instead of viewing Muslim and Christian actors in Egypt, Lebanon and Jordan as passively awaiting the outbreak of a cycle of violence, they both must be considered actors taking an active part in shaping it. Paradoxically, both Muslim and Christian actors increased the event's significance, viewing it as an opportunity to strengthen their relations and, more importantly, their individual positions. If one introduces the possibility of agency when facing violence, one is also able to question these various actors' take on violence. Simply put, if the assault on the US embassy in Cairo was an act of violence, this does not mean that the actors also saw it as an act of violence. Rather, Christian and Muslim figures who condemned the video located violence somewhere else.

This chapter will first locate the video in the context of inter-communal violence in Egypt, then explore Christian fear as something more complex. I will then look at the targets of violence in September 2012 and the various actors' take on them, while finally shifting the focus to where these actors mostly located violence: the *potential* violence that they managed to avoid.

The Starting Point: Sectarian Violence in Egypt

Violence against Christians in Egypt was the actual *raison d'être* of 'The Innocence of Muslims'. Its first part depicts a typical incident of sectarian strife in Egypt.[6] A – presumably Coptic – doctor dressed in western style witnesses how an 'Islamist mob' – that is, a group of men dressed in traditional Egyptian dress and wearing head coverings – attacks Copts and Coptic property, while the police do not interfere. The Coptic physician then comes home and tells his two daughters: 'The Islamic Egyptian police arrested 1,400 Christians, tortured them and forced them to confess to the killings'. When asked by his daughters about the reason for this assault, the doctor takes a flip chart and writes the equation 'Man plus "x" equals Islamic terrorism. Islamic terrorism minus "x" equals man'. As for the meaning of 'x', the Coptic doctor tells his daughters: 'You need to discover it for yourself'. The video goes on to retrace the life of Muhammad. The makers of the video thus established a clear link between violence against Copts and Islam, but these connections are controversial in both academic literature and Egyptian public discourse. As Angie Heo notes, '[a]ccounts of religion's role in the politics of inclusion and marginalization invariably risk smuggling in assumptions about what "religion" is and what it does', resulting 'in a bewildering methodological impasse' about sectarian incidents as having '"everything to do with religion" and "nothing to do with religion at all"'.[7]

Attacks such as those described in the video are said to have begun in 1972, when an illegal church in Khanka, Upper Egypt, was assaulted by Muslims and a hundred priests protested in reaction, marking the beginning of clashes on church grounds.[8] However, Vivian Ibrahim and Sebastian Elsässer note that there had already been attacks on Copts in the 1950s and 1960s.[9] In the context of intense political turmoil, in January 1952 a church was burnt and several Copts attacked.[10] These are sudden, localised brutal outbreaks of violence, which often result from conflicts over church building and renovation, marriage, land and the disappearance of young Coptic women. Violence increased against the backdrop of demographic explosion in Egypt. The number of Copts doubled between 1950 and 1970, as well as between 1970 and 2010,[11] while the general population more than tripled between 1960 and 2012.[12] This led to the need for new churches and mosques. Migration to the cities has contributed to a stronger Coptic presence in regions such as the Sinai and the

Suez.[13] In Cairo, Copts mainly migrated to the suburb of Shubra al-Khayma, where there was no church until 1926.[14] In the 1930s, the suburb of Giza had only one church.[15] Catherine Mayeur-Jaouen sums up this new situation:

> [T]he architectural landscape has been the scene of exaggerated competition between Copts and Muslims as they try to occupy visual and sonic space all over the country, in both towns and villages. Church towers are becoming higher and minarets are becoming higher. Religious institutions have developed an obsession with building.[16]

At the same time, many more incidents occurred in Upper Egypt, a region which has a negative reputation and where violent Islamists operated.[17] Catherine Mayeur-Jaouen, however, notes that not all violence in Egypt has religious causes; quite often '[t]he problems with Muslims are conflicts of neighbourhood in the first place, that may quickly escalate, depending on the interpretation and the echo given to [such events] and in which [. . .] the police or the Security of the State play a defining role'.[18]

Besides its wrath, violence in Egypt is characterised by denial and lack of fair prosecution. Sectarian violence is called *fitna tā'ifiyya* in Arabic, but the term often seems to be a euphemism. For Angie Heo, it is 'more of an elastic, umbrella term, encompassing any act of "Muslim" violence toward a "Christian", and vice-versa'.[19] The Coptic Egyptian journalist and chief-editor of *Watanī*, Youssef Sidhom, rejects the very idea of 'sectarian strife' because it places the victim and the offender on the same level.[20] As Laure Guirguis puts it, '[d]enial [takes place] as the [very] denial of the existence of even tensions, disagreement or feelings of animosity between the "two elements of the nation".'[21] And the alleged mental illness of the offender or a conspiracy from abroad are usually put forward.[22] The role of the state is therefore crucial, as suggested above. During the first wave of sectarian violence between 1972 and 1997, the state was in fact complicit with radical Islamists.[23] Also, more often than not, the state denies the victims fair prosecution. Under Husni Mubarak, reconciliation took place between the victim and the offender, in which the former usually had to forgive the latter. Yet, according to Saba Mahmood, the 'Coptic Orthodox Church helps forestall legal investigation or prosecution of such crimes. Instead, in collusion with the government, Church officials force the victims to informally settle such conflicts through publicly staged "reconciliation meetings" (*jalsat al-sulh*) that allow the perpetrators to go free in exchange for issuing an apology'.[24] Following the killing of six people leaving Christmas mass in Nag Hammadi in January 2010, the bishop of the diocese, Kīrillus (who condemned 'The Innocence of Muslims' in 2012), refused to testify against the instigator of the attack, a former member of parliament from Mubarak's party.[25]

Reconciliation meetings under the pressure of the state have been counterproductive, as they have instead 'nurtured resentment and sowed the germs of future violence, as proven by the fact that skirmishes often repeat themselves in the same places'.[26] Reconciliation has been, however, a recurring method to restore peace, as Aïda Kanafani-Zahar notes in the context of Mount Lebanon after the Civil War. But she concedes that, for such reconciliation meetings to be sustainable, there is a need to designate the offender and hold him accountable, as only then victims may grant forgiveness.[27] By contrast, in Egypt, there was a lack of individual accountability on part of the offender, and the initiative for such reconciliation meetings was hardly ever local.

At the same time, the media have exhibited eager sensationalism. The liberalisation of the media in 2005 resulted in a more open discussion of inter-religious relations and clashes. As Elizabeth Iskander demonstrates, this became a 'hot topic' that increased sales, while still covering the issue in the context of national unity.[28] This explains the problematic coverage of 'The Innocence of Muslims' described in Chapter One. Some media sources systematically connected the video with local Christians. When they did not leave the reader wondering whether the majority of Coptic Egyptians actually agreed with the content of video, they made key Muslim figures question Christians' loyalty. For instance, in his interview with *al-Ahrām* on 21 September 2012, Mufti 'Alī Gum'a was at first very vague concerning the video's background. Nevertheless, *al-Ahrām* asked him about his 'satisfaction' with the Christians' reactions and positions, to which he responded: 'The brotherly relations between the children of the united nation, Muslims and Christians, are governed by respect and mutual brotherhood'.[29]

Such incidents dramatically increased following the 25 January Revolution; in 2011 they rose to a level a third above that of 2010 and double that of 2008 and 2009.[30] Most incidents took place in Cairo and Upper Egypt, particularly in al-Minya, Beni Suef, al-Fayyum, Aswan, Asyut, Sohag, Luxor and Qena.[31]

Under the rule of the SCAF, which lasted until June 2012, a church was burnt in Helwan, south of Cairo (and subsequently rebuilt).[32] In May 2011, rumours about a woman having converted to Islam and being detained in a church provoked the anger of Salafis in Imbaba, in the governorate of Giza.[33] The local Salafi preacher, Abū Yaḥyā, mentioned in Chapter One as having called on the Coptic Orthodox Church to take a clear position against 'The Innocence of Muslims', then reportedly 'instigated' an attack on the church in Imbaba.[34] But other Salafi figures harshly condemned the attack.[35] There are various figures regarding the casualties in Imbaba. According to Anthony Shenoda, two churches, ten houses and thirteen shops were burnt, twelve people were killed and 238 injured in Imbaba,[36] including Muslims, according to Richard Gauvain.[37] Youssef Sidhom stated that these attacks were foreseeable, but the police did not intervene to prevent them.[38] This highlights the critical role that the Salafis came to play after the Arab Spring. In the summer of 2012, there were more assaults in Dahshur (governorate of Giza), where Copts had to temporarily leave their homes, as well as in Asyut (Upper Egypt).[39] In Dahshur, a village near Cairo, clashes erupted after a Copt had burnt a Muslim's shirt while ironing it.[40]

Joint Christian–Muslim reactions against 'The Innocence of Muslims' in Egypt may thus seem to be a means of preventing a resurgence of sectarian violence in areas that had previously been affected by it. This was the case in Nag Hammadi, where in January 2010, as mentioned above, a man killed six people who were leaving Christmas mass. In 2012, the local bishop, Kīrillus, condemned 'The Innocence of Muslims' during a speech delivered at a festival for inter-religious understanding attended by a representative of *Bayt al-ʿāʾila* (House of the Family), which had been established by Shaykh al-Azhar Ahmad al-Tayyib in response to the terror attacks on the Coptic Orthodox Two Saints Church in Alexandria on 1 January 2011.[41] Similarly, the priest of Church Mār Mīnā in Imbaba, one of the churches attacked in May 2011,[42] joined a protest against 'The Innocence of Muslims' in the governorate of Giza on Friday, 14 September 2012, expressing his solidarity with Muslims but also the need for the protests to be peaceful.[43] Yet, the twelve Coptic Orthodox bishops (out of a total of forty-seven bishops in 2007, excluding the diaspora)[44] who reacted at least once in statements, comments to the press and speeches at conferences were largely from Lower Egypt, rather than from Upper Egypt where most violent incidents occurred. The connection between local violence and joint mobilisation is thus a tenuous one. Other factors and rationales played a role in the decision to initiate and participate in joint actions against 'The Innocence of Muslim'.

The same applies to Christian–Muslim reactions in Lebanon, which occurred in areas affected by past violence, such as the south during the Civil War (see Chapter Five) as well as in areas where inter-communal relations have been historically peaceful, such as the north (see Chapter Four). Similarly, in Jordan, many Christian actors condemned the video, despite the absence of sectarian violence.

Finally, the long list of sectarian incidents includes violence against Copts that were not seen as 'sectarian' but were either classed as 'terrorist' or were silenced, even though the end-result was the same: Coptic victims. More important, so notes Angie Heo, 'the Egyptian state decides which acts of violence are "terrorist" and which not'.[45] This results in the admission or withholding of justice. An attack defined as 'terrorist' was the bombing on a church in Alexandria on 1 January 2011, which triggered appeals to national unity by the president, the Coptic Orthodox Church and Shaykh al-Azhar Ahmad al-Tayyib, with *Majallat al-Azhar*, for instance, covering these responses extensively.[46] Unlike sectarian incidents, the victims in this context were recognized as martyrs of the nation. This recognition illustrates the following comment by Angie Heo:

> The distinction between 'sectarian' and 'terrorist' violence is significant for determining the value of Coptic deaths under the sign of Egyptian nationhood [. . .] their distinction from one another is vastly consequential, resulting in national heroes of commemoration on the one hand, and failures in obtaining legal enforcement or punishment on the other.[47]

A case of violence against Copts that was silenced consisted of the 'Maspero Massacre' in October 2011, during which mostly Coptic activists were killed by the army (see Chapter Three): 'What is striking today about the Maspero Massacre is the deafening silence that continues to surround its victims at the military's hands'.[48] By contrast, the outcry over 'The Innocence of Muslims' was unique, as the post-revolutionary phase offered a more democratic space for reflection on violence.

The Issue of Christian Fear

It is easy to assume that the Christian reactions were primarily motivated by the fear of a backlash. I am making the case here, however, that this fear was more complex and did *not exclude* other motivations – much like Muslim figures used the controversy as an opportunity to strengthen their own positions, so did Christians – and that this fear did not exclude criticism of Muslim reactions. This question illustrates the benefit of the concept of ambiguity and allows to expand Thomas Bauer's understanding of it: 'a phenomenon of cultural ambiguity [occurs] if *two antithetic or at least two competing and clearly deviating meanings* are ascribed to a term, a course of action or an object over a longer period of time and *at the same time* [my emphasis]'.[49]

Fear was especially evident in the case of the Coptic Orthodox Church and the Protestant denominations in Egypt. It is noteworthy that none of them mentioned the first part of the video showing an attack on Copts, and very few addressed the violent reactions to it. Often, if it were not for the context, it would be very unclear what the Coptic Orthodox bishops were actually condemning. They devised several strategies for countering the potentially damaging effects of 'The Innocence of Muslims', such as denying that it had any Christian foundation, dissociating local Christians from it and appealing to the Muslims' nationalist sentiment. By contrast, the Coptic Catholic Church and the Churches in Lebanon only seemed to display solidarity with Muslims; some Churches did not react at all. But even in those cases where the fear of violence was most evident, the reactions to the video were often ambiguous, being attempts to *both* dissociate local Christians from *and* criticise Muslim reactions to the video. In particular, references to the practices of Jesus Christ by Protestant figures in Egypt present cases of ambiguity: 'If someone offends us, we do not offend back', asserted Safwat al-Biyādī, president of the Evangelical Church, on 9 September 2012, when *al-Yawm al-Sābi'* asked several church representatives in Egypt for their opinion.[50] Other Christian reactions in Egypt were much more explicit. Fr Rafīq Garīsh, speaker of the Coptic Catholic Church, blamed 'the simpletons amongst the Muslims in Egypt' who 'have already been affected [by this]'.[51] A few days later, he accused the media of having 'indirectly made free propaganda'[52] – an idea on which the official statement by the Coptic Catholic Church elaborated. As for lay Christians, especially Coptic youth organisations, the tone was sometimes more virulent.

On 10 September 2012, the coordinator of the association Copts Without Restrictions vilified what he called the 'double standards' of Egyptian society, of the state and of the media, asking: 'Why are these voices not raised to condemn more extremist positions of institutions and media trumpets in Egypt against the Christians, their sacred items and symbols?'[53] The most explicit and high-ranking criticisms were formulated in Lebanon. Samīr Geagea, leader of the Lebanese Forces, stated: 'What bothered me was the way in which the insignificant persons behind this futile film were able to provoke the mobilisation of some groups of Muslims, something that would help confirm the negative image conveyed by this film'.[54]

It is noteworthy that fear did not necessarily result from the immediate experience of a local or even national context. Minā Magdī, activist of the Coptic Maspero Youth Union (MYU) told the author (in 2015) that he did not fear for himself but for Copts living in poor areas.[55] The case of Jordan is particularly interesting in this regard: Christian–Muslim relations there have been historically peaceful, and yet fear did play a role. Both Fr Hannā Kildānī, then secretary general of the Council of Churches, and the Latin Bishop of Amman, Mārūn Lahhām, discussed this issue with the author in 2015. Fr Hannā Kildānī said that he had been concerned about a potential backlash against Christians, although in the region generally and not specifically in Jordan.[56] Mārūn Lahhām stated: 'We condemn any action, any film, any report, any article that disturbs the peaceful coexistence between Christians and Muslims'.[57] Yet, neither the Greek Orthodox bishop of Amman, Bishop Benedict, nor Bāssim Farrāj, secretary general of the Orthodox Society in Jordan, mentioned this to the author.[58]

Christian reactions revealed many other motivations, as did Muslim reactions. Displaying solidarity with the latter was one key factor. This was the case in Lebanon, where the reactions of the Churches were infrequent and brief. Except for the Greek Catholic Melkite Church, none of the Churches in Lebanon issued an official statement: they promulgated their reactions as part of Holy Synod final statements or during press conferences. Yet, like Muslims, many Christian actors tried to exploit the outcry. An example of this can be found in the two statements by the Greek Catholic Melkite priest and director of the Jordanian Interfaith Coexistence Research Centre, Fr Nabīl Haddād. His second statement, published on 22 September 2012, very strongly dissociated Christian faith from the video. But, at the same time, he took the opportunity to emphasise the role that he himself and his centre had played in inter-religious dialogue, noting that it had been one of the first to promote the 'Amman Message' initiated by King Abdullah II abroad and claiming that his centre was one of the first to invite high-ranking Islamic leaders, such as 'ulamā' from al-Azhar.[59]

Taking account of these nuances when considering Christian fear helps to put Christian reactions on a more equal footing with Muslims in terms of their approach to violence.

The Hierarchisation of Targets and Victims

Having established a more complex understanding of Christian motivations in the region – where fear, solidarity with Muslims and personal interests coexisted – I now would like to place Christian and Muslim reactions side by side in their understanding of 'violence'. This seems counter-intuitive, because the controversy over 'The Innocence of Muslims' posed a real threat to Christians, especially in Egypt. But it turned out to be a moment in which violence in its sudden, brutal flare-ups known as *fitna tā'ifyya* did not occur. Violence did occur, but it was contained and limited. It targeted the US embassy in Cairo, and there were clashes in the northern city of Tripoli. In Egypt, family members of the video's makers as well as Christian religious objects were targeted. But these various targets attracted very different reactions from Christian and Muslim actors who appeared to have in mind a hierarchical ranking of the targets' value. As Philip Benedict observes, 'one helpful approach to label something as religious violence is phenomenological: to look at the character of the violence and the people and objects singled out for attack'.[60] But when shifting attention to how both Christians and Muslims envisioned violence and where they located it, it becomes apparent that they fundamentally agreed. Crucially, even if Christians feared a backlash, this did not prevent them from navigating the crisis for their own benefit.

First, violence targeted Western symbols. The most spectacular moment of the controversy was the storming of the US embassy in Cairo on 11 September 2012, which made the headlines worldwide. Although, prior to the event, the Salafi Nur Party and *al-Daʿwa al-Salafiyya* had been reported to be involved in its organisation,[61] on the actual day, secular revolutionary organisations, some Coptic organisations and the soccer clubs Zamalek and Ahli joined in the protest,[62] which grew to several thousand participants.[63] The British newspaper *Guardian* stated that 'Islamists' in particular had climbed the walls of the embassy to replace the US flag with the so-called black Islamist flag.[64] But Jayson Casper, a researcher at the Arab West Foundation located in Cairo, witnessed the protest on 11 September 2012 and stated that it was, in fact, football hooligans who had attempted to climb the walls of the embassy, while the police appeared to be depending on the Salafi protesters to de-escalate the situation.[65] Besides the protest's diverse composition, the slogans on display revealed a tension between an Islamist, even radical, Salafi-Jihadi outlook and an Egyptian nationalist outlook. The Salafi-Jihadi slogans included: 'We are all Osama bin Laden'.[66] By contrast, a number of banners emphasised Christian–Muslim coexistence in colloquial Egyptian Arabic, such as 'Muslims and Christians say "no" to Americans and to offending Islam'[67] and 'Muslim and Christian are strongly united'.[68] In the following days, tensions remained high, compelling the Coptic Orthodox priest Fr Fīlūbātir Gamīl ʿAzīz, quoted in the introduction, to wonder: 'Are we to expect a terrorist act against the Church in Egypt, especially on this coming Friday?'[69] As mentioned in Chapter One, security forces struggled to maintain control over downtown Cairo. In Lebanon, too, tensions were building, especially ahead of the visit of Pope Benedict XVI. Branches of Kentucky Fried Chicken and Hardees were attacked, and pictures of Pope Benedict XVI were reportedly burnt.[70] Protesters also tried to storm the seat of government in Tripoli.[71] But here again, the protests of 14 September 2012, which initially had been organised by Islamist organisations such as Hizb ut-Tahrir, were soon joined by youth and escalated.[72]

Second, violence included attacks on family members of the video's makers, a fact which attracted almost no attention. On 18 September 2012, the house of Jūzīf Nasr Allāh in Giza was attacked by followers of *al-Daʿwa al-Salafiyya*,[73] and the house of Morris Sadek was also reportedly targeted, without police interference.[74] On 19 September 2012, roughly 200 'people' attacked the house of Niqūlā Bāsilī Niqūlā's mother, and the police had to intervene to protect her.[75] The police also arrested an inhabitant of the slum Izbat al-Nakhl in Cairo, because he had posted a link to the video.[76]

A third type of targets included Christian religious symbols. I have already mentioned that, during a protest on 15 September 2012 in Cairo, 'Abū Islām', burned pages of a copy of the Bible.⁷⁷ In Tripoli, pictures of Pope Benedict XVI were burned.

All of these various targets attracted diverse responses. On the Muslim side, there were condemnations of the attempted storming of the US embassy, whereas in the case of the Coptic Orthodox Church, only one priest in the diocese of al-Minufiyya criticised the violence in connection to 'The Innocence of Muslims', claiming that 'it is necessary to behave wisely'.⁷⁸ By contrast, the targeting of Christian religious symbols attracted the greatest condemnation. In reaction to the burning of a copy of the Bible, thirty-five notifications were sent to the general prosecutor, among them one by *al-Gamāʿa al-Islāmiyya*.⁷⁹ A lawsuit was instigated against Ahmad ʿAbd Allāh and his son, as well as the journalist Hānī Yāsīn,⁸⁰ and in January 2013 Abū Islām was sentencec to eleven years in prison, while his son received a sentence of eight years,⁸¹ for 'crimes of despising the Christian religion' and the burning of a Gospel.⁸²

On the Christian side, there was a similar focus on Christian religious symbols. The Coptic Orthodox Church's condemnation of 'The Innocence of Muslims' did not differ in its wording from its condemnation by Muslims. Referring to *The Da Vinci Code*, Bishop Athanāsyūs of Beni Mazar, Upper Egypt, asserted in his criticism of 'The Innocence of Muslims' that Christianity had been likewise targeted in the past and that both works shared the same goal: 'A battle between humanity'.⁸³ The position of the Church was thus consistent with its position regarding the film *The Da Vinci Code* in 2006 and the novel *Azazeel* in 2008. In this regard, Laure Guirguis notes that the Coptic Orthodox Church has actively encouraged censorship.⁸⁴ *The Da Vinci Code* by Dan Brown depicts Jesus Christ as having a wife and children.⁸⁵ In response, the Churches in Egypt issued a statement condemning the film as 'propagat[ing] Zionist thought' that strove to establish 'a materialistic civilisation, devoid of a spiritual and religious pulse, of the meaning of life and of the eternal destiny of the human being'.⁸⁶ In 2008, the novel *Azazeel* published by Yusuf Ziedan provoked strong condemnation from the Coptic Orthodox Church.⁸⁷ The novel relates the dismay of a Coptic monk, Hiba, at the fanaticism and violence of the Coptic Orthodox Church in fifth-century Alexandria under Patriarch Kīrillus I (412–44).⁸⁸ While Ziedan claimed his 'right as a novelist to render [historical events] according to the protocols of literary production', the Coptic Orthodox Church sought to ban the novel for 'defaming the Christian religion'.⁸⁹

Other Churches in the Middle East held a similar position, and both the book and the film *The Da Vinci Code* were forbidden in Jordan and Lebanon.[90] In an interview with the author in 2015, the secretary general of the Council of Churches in Jordan, Hannā Kildānī asserted that the 'Danish' cartoons had likewise offended Christianity and that Christians had experienced a long history of offences, for example, in *Jesus Christ Superstar*.[91]

Besides persons and objects, there is a fourth type of potential target that Philip Benedict does not mention: persons who are turned into symbols and objectified, who are denied individuality and agency but nevertheless attract an outcry. There was no such case in the context of 'The Innocence of Muslims', but such targets have a high potential for escalation, as illustrated by the violence in Imbaba. For Saba Mahmood, the case of Wafā' Qunstuntīn, the wife of a Coptic priest, who disappeared in 2004 was '[t]he ur-controversy, the paradigmatic reference in these events'.[92] She had been married to a priest and seemingly converted to Islam in order to escape an abusive marriage. Yet, her whereabouts were unknown, and this stirred the anger of Islamist radicals. The alleged forceful conversion and/or kidnapping of Coptic women is a powerful trope that 'The Innocence of Muslims' illustrated with the screenshot of a dead young woman lying in the street. However, this often results from the women's own desire to escape stifling and dominating family structures.[93] Saba Mahmood explains: 'This gendered narrative of abductors (male) and abductees (female) seems emblematic of how women have often been treated as symbolic placeholders for broader struggles over cultural, identarian, and territorial claims throughout history'.[94] According to this view, women are completely denied agency, while a 'man's conversion to Islam is presumed to be a result of autonomous and individual will, the proper domain of civil rights, Qustuntin and Shehata's actions are seen as coerced, ultimately located within the ambit of the family, sequestered from civic life'.[95]

For the time being, it is worth remembering that the alleged offence of religious symbols ('The Innocence of Muslims', the burning of the Bible, *The Da Vinci Code*, the 'Danish' cartoons) attracted the most condemnation from both Muslims and Christians, whereas Muslim figures were more outspoken against the attempted storming of the US embassy, unlike the Coptic Orthodox Church. The families of the video's makers did not attract any attention. This differentiated approach at first glance seems to be a blatant hierarchisation of the targets' value, with religious symbols apparently more valuable than people. Yet, this hides more significant implications, as we will see in Chapter Five, and was actually a means of applying pressure.

The Greater Danger: *Potential* Violence

Surprisingly, condemning 'The Innocence of Muslims' was more than often a reflection on the *potential* violence that the video could have caused. Hasan Nasr Allāh's claim was paradigmatic for this viewpoint, which morphed into ideas of conspiracies (be they Western, Jewish, or Zionist) that proliferated across the region, often resorting to blatant anti-Semitism.[96] On *al-Manār* TV, he affirmed that the video aimed to produce 'strife between Muslims and Christians', propelling them into 'a bloody, religious sectarian conflict', while Muslims were expected to attack churches and Christian holy sites. By envisioning the video as a potential danger for much more violence, a new victim emerged: Muslims *and* Christians *together*. Christians and Muslims therefore created a shared enemy – despite the often-blatant anti-Semitic rhetoric. As Élizabeth Picard highlights, 'the cycle of aggression and retaliations between enemy segments contribute as much to the maintaining of the group's internal solidarity as to a demographic, economic, and hierarchic rebalancing between the groups. Violence is at the heart of kinship, clan, and community relations'.[97] In our case, this cycle of aggression and retaliation relates to the idea that 'The Innocence of Muslims' was seen as part of a series of similar offences. For Christians, however, the stakes were higher: Coptic individuals in the US had produced the video. On the one hand, Christian and Muslim figures magnified the video's relevance to strengthen intercommunal relations and push their personal interests. Yet, on the other hand, the road leading to that point was tricky, and Christians faced a constant risk of conflation and suspicion as well as alienation from the social and political fabric of these countries.

The fact that it was Coptic Egyptians who had migrated to the US who were behind this video posed a serious problem. At first, the name 'Sam Bacile' emerged in the US media, a self-described 'Jewish Israeli' real estate agent living in California, who had received donations from '100 Jewish donors' to produce a film on Islam worth five million dollars: he described Islam as 'a cancer, period'.[98] What was gradually revealed, however, was a very small and loose network dedicated to activism against Islam in the US. The Associated Press soon discovered that 'Sam Bacile' was in fact Niqūlā Bāsilī Niqūlā, a fifty-five-year-old Egyptian-born Coptic American with a criminal record,[99] while a non-profit Evangelical organisation run by a certain Jūzīf Nasr Allāh, Coptic Egyptian, had produced the video.[100] Niqūlā Bāsilī Niqūlā claimed to have connections with Morris Sadek,[101] the leader of the National American Coptic Assembly and a more prominent figure in Egypt. He proceeded with the very effective step of disseminating the video via social media: he sent it to an Arabic blog[102] and posted it on his own Twitter account.[103] Eventually, a few media outlets established a connection between these people and the controversial Coptic Orthodox priest Zakaryā Butrus, whose influence[104] on the video was indeed pervasive (see Chapter Four). Nevertheless, early on Egyptian media had already firmly established the video's 'Coptic background', and the protesters at the US embassy in Cairo on 11 September 2012 clearly referred to Morris Sadek as its producer.[105]

The extent to which the various reactions engaged with this Coptic background varied greatly. In Egypt, there was a clear move to silence it. At first, even the Coptic Orthodox bishops did not agree on how, or even whether, to mention it. The Church insisted on the Egyptian identity of the video's makers while silencing their Coptic belonging: '[T]he Church has learned that some Egyptians living in foreign countries work on spreading disunion between the children of the united nation by offending Islam and its noble prophet'.[106] Some did not mention it at all, yet others diverted the attention towards a 'Zionist' or 'Israeli' background. Bishop Būlā of Tanta, for instance, built on the reports discussing 'Sam Bacile' in the US media – something that was never an issue in Egyptian media – in the conference he initiated. During this conference, he claimed that the main character in the video was played by 'the son of a leader of Hamas who has converted to Christianity and has become an agent of the Israeli Mossad, and the promoter is an Evangelical priest', Terry Jones.[107] The 'agent of Mossad' was Musʿab Hasan Yusuf who first started to spy for the Shin Bet and then converted to Christianity. In his memoirs, *Son of Hamas*, he alludes to the defining influence of Zakariyā Butrus on his conversion.[108] This purported connection to 'Zionism' and 'Mossad' was a clear attempt at diverting attention away from Coptic involvement in 'The Innocence of Muslims'.

Similarly, the Egyptian minister of Islamic Endowments, Talʿat ʿAfīfī, clearly altered his position. At first, he was not only certain that Coptic Egyptians were involved in this video – stating that it had been 'the intention of a number of Copts of the diaspora to produce a film offending the Messenger (PBUH) in cooperation with the priest Terry Jones' – but certain that they were in the service of 'Zionism': '[T]hose who attempt to divide us or to disperse us, they follow the force of Zionism'.[109] On 11 September 2012, *al-Yawm al-Sābiʿ* published a statement in which the minister discussed the responsibility of Copts in the making of such an 'offence'; 'such affairs at the hands of the enemies of Islam are not unusual'.[110] ʿAfīfī distinguished between two types of Copts, the 'bad ones' who were involved in the production of 'The Innocence of Muslims' and the 'good ones', 'the Copts of Egypt [who] condemned this and [. . .] live with us in harmony and love'. Behind all this 'Zionist propaganda', there are 'some Copts in the diaspora who depict Islam as a terrorist religion to the world', an assumption supported by a long quote from Qur'an 8:36–37.[111] As a result, the Copts involved in the production of the video were associated with the 'unbelievers' whom Islam had fought at its beginnings. In contrast, in his two subsequent reactions, the minister was much more cautious and no longer mentioned Copts.[112]

In Lebanon, many actors were well aware of the Coptic background, yet systematically framed their criticism in the context of a fight against 'Zionism'. Again, Hasan Nasr Allāh's claim was paradigmatic. In his speech on *al-Manār*, he mentioned the Coptic background of the video: according to 'the media', 'Egyptian Copts' were behind it, but he put this information in the broader context of the 'Zionist movement', using 'apostate Muslims like Salman Rushdie or a Christian, as in the case of the burning of the Qur'an by the Christian cleric Jones'.[113] Likewise, a former MP and deputy speaker of parliament, the Greek Orthodox Elie Ferzli,[114] considered all these acts part of a series of offences that had started a decade ago to 'ignite the "clash of civilisations"', which he placed in the broader context of a clash of civilisations in the interest of Israel; 'the Zionist creature' with Israel sitting at the head of a war.[115] Elie Ferzli re-wrote the history of the twentieth century, starting with the Balfour Declaration that 'planted the Zionist creature in the region'. He believed that the collapse of the Soviet Union meant that the West was now searching for a new war between East and West. 'The Innocence of Muslims' thus particularly affected Christians, because it aimed to 'inflame Islamic feelings against the Christians in the region, especially the Copts in the region, in order to deepen the conflict and to destroy the Christians in the East'.

In Jordan, most reactions only discussed the background of the video very vaguely, but a few reactions did connect the video to a Zionist conspiracy. Here, again, there was confusion between 'Zionism' and 'Jewish products', which people were called on to boycott.[116] Yet, the Jordanian case also presented another aspect of this issue: since many reactions countered the video by emphasising the tolerant and peaceful message of Islam, they actually also referred to Judaism as a 'revealed message' recognized by Islam to back their claim. 'We as Muslims', claimed the Tribes of the Tafileh Governorate Demanding Reform, 'we do not complete our faith except through our faith in God, His books, His Messengers, where our brothers from the revealed religions lived and continue to live among us. To them that which is for us and upon them which is upon us'.[117] Interestingly, Christians weighed in to promote the idea of a Jewish or Zionist conspiracy, as illustrated by the Council of Churches: 'Some Americans and Jews want us to leave and descend from their summits [of peaceful coexistence] into the valleys of their loathing and the production of hate'.[118] The statement clearly works by holding up a mirror to compare the 'supporters of strife (*ashāb al-fitna*)' and the 'the followers of the revealed messages (*ashāb al-risālāt al-samāwiyya*)', giving the Council of Churches the opportunity to establish Jordan as a model of Christian–Muslim relations.

As appealing and useful as the shared Jewish/Zionist/Israeli bogeyman was, this distracting conspiracy theory was double-edged and potentially dangerous. The comments by Tal'at 'Afīfī and Hasan Nasr Allāh's about the video's producers actually serving 'Zionism' shows how insidious this rumour could be. Similarly, *al-Da'wa al-Salafiyya* asserted in its statement that 'some idiots among the Copts of the diaspora acted, and behind them one of the American Churches, and behind all of them, the Jews',[119] implying the ease with which Christians could be 'seduced'. Sebastian Elsässer highlights this issue:

> [A]nother great concern of national unity narratives is to prove the patriotic loyalty of the Copts. This theme pops up whenever the presence of foreign Christians creates an element of 'seduction' for the Copts, inducing them to side with their co-religionists rather than with their compatriots.[120]

Yet, as Gudrun Krämer notes, in Islamic anti-Semitic writings featuring the Qur'anic Jews, the latter 'are not always singled out, but treated as part of a wider group of non-Muslims'.[121] The Christians' risk of being excluded from the social fabric persisted.

Egypt, Jordan and Lebanon have had different experiences dealing with their respective Jewish communities and Israel. While Jewish life in Egypt came to a brutal end in the 1950s and 1960s due to the mounting tensions and wars with Israel, the Jewish population of Lebanon initially increased during the 1940s but then gradually vanished due to increased regional tensions and the wars of 1958 and 1975–90.[122] There had never been a significant Jewish population in Jordan. By now, entire generations have grown up without a Jewish presence in these countries. Although Jewish community life has vanished, Judaism as a religion continues to be recognized, together with Islam and Christianity. Arab nationalism and Nasserism saw themselves as a vanguard against colonialism and its alleged extension, Zionism, in the form of the state of Israel.[123]

After the war of 1956 and the humiliating defeat of 1967, under President Anwar al-Sadat Egypt gradually chose the path of peace, culminating in the Camp David Accords of 1979–80. Relations between Jordan and Israel had been equally hostile, with wars in 1948 and 1967, and the subsequent Israeli occupation of Jerusalem and the West Bank, which had been annexed by Jordan after the 1948 war. Jordan continues to run religious matters there, even though it relinquished its claims over the West Bank in 1988.[124] A key factor here is the high proportion of Palestinian Jordanians. The situation in Lebanon, by contrast, is different, because its territory was occupied by Israel from the late 1970s onwards, extending as far as Beirut in 1982 and remaining in the south until 2000.

This historic background was evident in some reactions against 'The Innocence of Muslims'. The Orthodox Society in Jordan, which comprises East Bank and Palestinian Christian members,[125] spoke of a 'Zionist' plan, connecting the video to the phenomenon of the 'price-tag' in the West Bank and Jerusalem.[126] Yet, in most cases the conflation of Jews/Zionism/Israel and the tropes attributed to it were cases of anti-Semitism, an issue which started with the video's producers themselves. As mentioned earlier, Niqūlā Bāsilī Niqūlā initially presented himself as an Israeli real estate agent living in California, who had received five million dollars from 'Jewish donors' to produce a film on Islam, describing Islam as 'a cancer'. Even though the Egyptian media had established the involvement of some Copts living abroad and even though Western media had refuted the speculation concerning 'Sam Bacile', the idea of a Jewish/Zionist/Israeli conspiracy persisted. During a meeting between Benedict XVI and the Lebanese Islamic religious leaders, Mufti Rashīd Qabbānī spoke of a man with 'Zionist and American funding, of Jewish origin who actually has a Coptic name', 'Basilī', who 'gathered five million dollars from the Jewish lobby'.[127] But he put the actual blame on the 'Jewish lobby' which 'believes neither in Christianity nor in Islam at all'.

Despite the risks that the claim of an Israeli/Jewish/Zionist conspiracy entailed – the idea of Christians being seduced – the benefits of this conspiracy abounded for both Muslims and Christians. Muslims engaged in polemics without antagonising Christians, and Christians could fashion themselves first and foremost as victims. As a result, Muslims and Christians *together* emerged as the *real* victims of this potential violence.

Conclusion

As the preceding pages have discussed these various actors' take on violence, the concept of ambiguity has proven useful in this context. Christian actors in the region feared *and* criticised Muslims, while, *at the same time*, pursuing their personal interests. These were genuine condemnations, but there was also an interest in increasing the video's relevance, something that could, however, put a further strain on Christian–Muslim relations. As the dynamic of the controversy unfolded, these actors increasingly channelled the potential for violence and turned it into an arena for more general discussions about inter-communal relations. The goal of this whole undertaking will be explored in the subsequent chapters. For the time being, we have achieved a clearer sense of Muslim and Christian agency. Still, what made these actors 'Muslim' or 'Christian'?

3

THE STAKES OF BEING CHRISTIAN OR MUSLIM: THE OTHER KEY ACTORS OF CHRISTIAN–MUSLIM RELATIONS

Introduction

So far, I have referred to reactions to 'The Innocence of Muslims' as either 'Christian' or 'Muslim' without providing a critical assessment of why these reactions were classified as such. Was it merely the religious affiliation of their authors or their institutional source? In the former case, were actors 'Christians' because they self-identified as 'Christians' and spoke in the name of fellow Christians, or because Muslim actors viewed them as Christians? Or were 'Christian' reactions defined by their content? Quite often, however, as discussed above, 'Muslim' and 'Christian' reactions were similar. Who claimed to speak as 'Christian' or 'Muslim', for Christianity or Islam, and why? Who was able to mobilise based on these claims, and who failed to do so? What was the advantage for some Christians to speak as Christian and for Christians, while others refused to do so?

'The Innocence of Muslims' attracted condemnation and mobilisations of a diverse set of actors. So far, we have encountered the Muslim Brotherhood, *al-Daʿwa al-Salafiyya*, the Nur Party and *al-Gamāʿa al-Islāmiyya* in Egypt; the Hezbollah in Lebanon; and the professional associations, the Muslim Brotherhood, the IAF and a number of Churches in Jordan. There were also actors of official Islam (al-Azhar, the muftis, the minister of Endowments in Jordan) and Christian associations such as the Orthodox Society in Jordan.

This chapter is concerned with introducing other key actors in the question of Christian–Muslim relations: official Islam and the Christian laity. In doing so, it will shed light on the position that these actors carved out for themselves and from which they negotiated inter-communal relations. Together with Islamist and Salafi movements and the Churches, official Islam and Christian laity contributed to the renegotiation of Christian–Muslim relations after the Arab Spring, raising questions about the place and role of confessional identities, the authority of institutionalised religious leadership and the very existence of Christians in the Middle East. Through their positioning as Christian/Muslim actors (or not), with claims of representation (or not), these actors condemned 'The Innocence of Muslims'. But beyond that, they also negotiated their political and communal future in the region.

Therefore, Chapter Three will look more closely at the issue of agency. Chapter One has highlighted how the discourse of Islamist and Salafi figures was constrained by the democratic context, while Chapter Two introduced the idea of Christian agency as ambiguous; hence, the present chapter will explore Christian agency through the choice of whether to put forward a Christian identity or not, noting that there were more issues to officially claiming Islamic leadership.

This chapter will first establish the legal and political foundations of these identities, then explore official Islam, the Christian laity and the Churches and, finally, inquire into the role of each community in framing the other as Christian or Muslim.

The Legal and Political Foundations of Being Christian or Muslim in Egypt, Jordan and Lebanon

The stakes of being Christian or Muslim in Egypt, Jordan and Lebanon are different. Besides the demographics, there is also the legal framework, which will be explored here. An important issue of concern for the Christians in the region is that their numbers have been proportionally decreasing, even though their absolute numbers have actually increased.[1] At the time of the controversy, they represented approximately 7 to 10 percent of the population of Egypt (6–8 million), 5.5 percent in Jordan (350,000), and 36 percent in Lebanon (1 million).[2] However, these estimates vary: 5.5 percent of the population in Jordan was Christian according to Bernard Heyberger;[3] 4 percent according to Géraldine Chatelard;[4] and only 3 percent according to Latin Bishop Mārūn Lahhām of Amman and ʿĀmir al-Hāfī, the vice-director of the Royal Institute for Inter-Faith Studies.[5] In the case of Egypt, the numbers are a matter of controversy. While the Coptic Orthodox Church claims 15 to 20 percent, the state put the number at less than 6 percent in 1996.[6] In Lebanon, the numbers are estimates based on the last census of 1932.

In addition to the Christian–Muslim divide, there are further demographic divides which impact inter-communal relations. In Egypt, up until the 1960s, there used to be significant Syro-Lebanese, Jewish and European populations who played a key economic role (see further below). In Jordan, the Transjordanian or East Bank versus Palestinian divide has dominated Jordanian politics since 1948, when, as a result of the annexation of the West Bank by Transjordan, its population grew by nearly 300 percent, from 375,000 to one million persons[7] (and thus became 'Jordan'). The war in 1967 led to the flight of another 300,000 Palestinians to Jordan.[8] The Gulf War in 1991 and the expulsion of Palestinians from Kuwait resulted in the return to or settlement of 250,000 Palestinians in Jordan.[9] It is noteworthy that the Palestinian population in Jordan also includes Christian Palestinians. In Lebanon, while there is significant diversity on the Christian side, there is a significant divide on the Muslim side, too, as the Shiʿi Muslim population now forms the largest group, followed by the Sunni, Druze and Alawi. As of 2012, there were approximately 260,000 to 280,000 Palestinian refugees.[10] In addition, in April 2012 Lebanon officially numbered 18,000 Syrian refugees, a number that rose to 356,000 in April 2013, reaching 1 million in April 2014.[11] The former Maronite Bishop of Baalbek and Dayr al-Ahmar, Samʿān ʿAtāʾ Allāh, expressed his concerns regarding the presence of these Syrian refugees in Lebanon: 'We have two million Syrians in the country as refugees. [. . .] Many will return to their homeland when the war is over. But many refugees will remain and apply for Lebanese citizenship in ten years. [. . .] What will become of us Christians then?'[12]

Lebanon thus provides the best illustration of the political wars waged over demographics that lie at the heart of Christian concerns. As early as 1924, Christian refugees from Ottoman Anatolia such as Armenians and Syriac Christians were granted Lebanese citizenship.[13] Likewise, Christian Palestinians who fled to Lebanon in 1948 and 1967 were granted easier access to citizenship.[14] Maya Mikdashi concludes that the issue of Palestinian (and

Kurdish) refugees in Lebanon is actually a problem of '*poor Sunni Moslem* Palestinian refugees [italics in original]'.[15] The confessional system guarantees the representation of the dominant communities; the president is a Maronite, the prime minister a Sunni Muslim, the speaker of the parliament a Shi'i Muslim and the vice speaker of parliament a Greek Orthodox Christian. However, after the Civil War, the allocation of seats (six Christians to five Muslims) was changed to yield an equal split between Christians and Muslims.[16] By contrast, in Jordan, the influx and naturalisation of Palestinians has not affected the strong representation of Christians in parliament. A quota system guarantees that Christians constitute 9 percent of the parliament and 6 percent of the senate, and every government usually includes one of two Christian ministers.[17] The Hashimites have relied on Christians since the establishment of Transjordan, with Emir 'Abd Allāh nominating three Christians to the first consultative council.[18] This meant that the mostly urban Palestinian Jordanians were under-represented when compared to the rural areas, mostly inhabited by East Bank Jordanians, and this constituted one of the grievances voiced during the Arab Spring concerning the electoral law.[19] By contrast, Egypt did not introduce a quota system (until 2014), even though there were debates in 1923 and then again in 2012.[20] In the second half of the twentieth century, however, it grew increasingly difficult for Copts to get elected, and this was compensated for by the nomination of Christians by the respective president.[21]

In addition to the translation (or absence of translation) of political representation, some of these countries still apply separation in matters of personal status. The regime established by the Free Officers in Egypt abolished community courts in 1955,[22] with Christians still being subject to canon law in civil courts for matters of personal status. Still, Saba Mahmood notes the 'exaggerated importance accorded to family law as the exemplary site for the preservation and reproduction of religious identity'.[23] In Jordan, in 1938, Christian ecclesiastical courts were recognized alongside Islamic courts for personal matters.[24]

The level of differentiation between Christians and Muslims is thus least institutionalised in Egypt, where there are no quotas or separate community courts (but canon law is applied in civil courts).[25] By contrast, in Jordan and Lebanon there is a high degree of differentiation, and Christians occupy a more prominent role. However, in the context of 'The Innocence of

Muslims', Coptic Orthodox Christians, especially the Coptic Orthodox youth and the Coptic Orthodox Church were more likely to differentiate between their individual groups than Christians in Jordan, where claims of identity were determined by the situation. It is noteworthy, however, that in their reactions to 'The Innocence of Muslims', Christian Jordanians claimed to speak *as Christians*.

Another Key Player: Official Islam

When it comes to modern discussions on Islam, actors of official Islam – that is, actors recognized by the state – do not feature prominently. Scholarly attention largely focuses on figures of Islamism and Salafism and the myriad of non-institutional movements that strive to establish some 'Islamic order' (see Chapter One). But the representation of official Islam – al-Azhar, the Sunni muftis, the Higher Islamic Shi'i Council in Lebanon – played an important role in the controversy over 'The Innocence of Muslims'. Like Islamists, they claimed to speak for Islam, specifically embodying a 'moderate' form of Islam; as a result, they presented themselves as being more fit to interact with Christians. Yet, the Arab Spring had challenged the position of official Islam in the region. It produced another Islamic approach to local Christians and thus significantly contributed to debates in the post-Arab Spring political landscape.

Islamism and Salafism are children of the late nineteenth and twentieth centuries, and so is official Islam – with the noticeable exception of al-Azhar which was established in the tenth century. The actors of official Islam discussed here – Shaykh al-Azhar Ahmad al-Tayyib, the Egyptian Mufti 'Alī Gum'a, the Lebanese Mufti Rashīd Qabbānī, 'Abd al-Amīr Qabalān, the vice-president of the Lebanese Higher Islamic Shi'i Council, and the Hashimite monarchy in Jordan – achieved their present form over the course of the twentieth century. They are characterised by a clericalisation of Islam in the context of the modern state formation, political encroachment and competition with non-institutional Islamic actors (Salafism, Islamism).

Al-Azhar was established in the tenth century by the Fatimid dynasty, and its role grew significantly in opposition to the British occupation starting in 1882, but Gamal Abdel Nasser basically nationalised the institution and brought it under the state's tight control.[26] There had been some tensions in the past between the shaykh al-Azhar and the mufti, whose office was established in 1895 and who since has been linked to the Ministry of Justice,[27] over their competences, with the shaykh al-Azhar eventually accepting the plurality of institutions issuing legal opinions (*fatwā*, plural *fatāwā*).[28] In Lebanon, *Dār al-fatwā* was established in 1922 under the French Mandate, and the position of mufti was created in 1932.[29] The mufti names the imams, preachers, teachers, muezzins and the provincial mufti, and he manages the Islamic endowments.[30] Like official Islam in Egypt, *Dār al-fatwā* has faced repeated political encroachment. After the Lebanese Civil War, the Sunni political leadership in the form of the Future Movement tried to increase its political hold on this religious institution. Following a reform initiated by Rafīq al-Harīrī in 1996, the electoral base was reduced,[31] to such an extent that the institution now lacks any popular legitimacy. Under the premiership of Fouad Siniora (2005–8), a new law was proposed to modify the 1955 law, redefining the position of the mufti so that he is no longer the 'religious leader of all Muslim sects', but the 'religious leader of Sunni Muslims'.[32] In 2012, the Lebanese mufti Rashīd Qabbānī, who allegedly lacked charisma[33] and authority,[34] faced pressure from both politicians and Sunni clerics.

In the case of Jordan, official Islam stands in the shadow of the Hashimite monarchy which enjoys a high level of Islamic authority; Jordan has been described as promoting 'conservative secularism'.[35] Due to its affiliation with the Prophet Muhammad, the Hashimites protected Mecca and Medina until their expulsion by ʿAbd al-ʿAzīz Āl Saʿūd in 1924. The former crown prince, Prince Hassan bin Talal, promoted the concept of '*wasatiyya*', or 'moderation',[36] which materialised alongside inter-religious and inner-Islamic initiatives. Similarly, his nephew, King Abdullah II, has promoted more initiatives with an international echo, particularly the 'Amman Message' and 'A Common Word', mentioned above. The 'Amman Message' highlights the monarchy's claim to Islamic legitimacy, emanating from the 'inherited spiritual and historical responsibility carried by the Hashemite monarchy, honored as direct descendants of the Prophet, the Messenger of God – peace and blessings upon him – who carried the message'.[37] In October 2007, the Al Bayt Institute for Islamic Thought, founded in 1981 by Prince Hassan bin Talal, released another programmatic document, titled 'A Common Word Between Us and You'. It was signed by 138 Sunni and Shiʿi Muslim scholars and leaders from all over the world.[38] The document was formulated in response to Benedict XVI's speech in Regensburg in 2006 and constituted a call to Christian leaders for mutual understanding.[39] In particular, 'A Common Word' established shared values in both the scriptures of Islam and Christianity for the love of God and one's neighbour.[40] Despite the importance of institutionalisation, the actual authority of the representatives of official Islam lies in their personal charisma. As Peter Makari notes, the shaykh al-Azhar exerts an influence that is 'derived from his personal reputation as a pious leader or "knower" of Islam'.[41]

In the context of the Arab Spring, all these actors of official Islam were challenged by the rise to greater prominence of the non-institutional actors of Islamism and Salafism. As Zoltan Pall notes in the case of Lebanon, 'many people started to see Salafis as a potential alternative to their Sunni Muslim leaders'.[42] Salafis used this renewed interest, 'employ[ing] their economic abilities, social ties, and mastery of religious knowledge and practices to gain more influence in society'.[43] Al-Azhar, or at least some azhari scholars, has been particularly critical of Salafism, viewing it as 'dangerous to both the individual and society', and in 2008 published a volume of fatāwa to counter Salafism.[44] Similarly, the relationship between al-Azhar and the Muslim Brotherhood has been ambivalent. On the one hand, the Muslim Brotherhood can be seen as competing with Al-Azhar, as the organisation has promoted a revival of Islamic religious practice since its establishment, thus questioning the monopoly of Al-Azhar over religion. However, on the other hand, the Muslim Brotherhood counts no high-ranking 'ulamā' of Al-Azhar among its members, except for dissident azharis such as Yūsuf al-Qaradāwī.[45] Following the Revolution of 25 January 2011, al-Azhar has remained privately concerned about the strength of the Muslim Brotherhood and the Salafis.[46] The new constitution – forcefully implemented by Muhammad Mursī at the end of 2012 – amplified al-Azhar's role because it enshrined the institution's role in defining the conformity of new laws with sharī'a law. This function had previously been carried out by the Constitutional Court.[47] Later, however, tensions developed between Muhammad Mursī and Al-Azhar, and the Muslim Brotherhood was accused of trying to infiltrate all state institutions, including Al-Azhar.[48] In Lebanon, *Dār al-fatwā* lost much of its leverage and power after the Civil War, as well as its 'ability to provide for the religious needs of [its] communit[y]'.[49] From below, non-institutional elements have felt compelled to take over the defence of Sunni Orthodox Islam. Māhir Hammūd, a rather pro-Hezbollah Sunni Islamist,[50] was among a group of 'ulamā' accusing the mufti of corruption: 'Does not the mufti see in religion anything but the money and the wealth he robs from the *Dār al-fatwā* with the backing of Siniora, al-Harīrī and their likes?'[51]

For all these actors of official Islam, 'The Innocence of Muslims' presented an opportunity to strengthen their own positions in contrast to Islamist forces. In particular, the image that the Egyptian Mufti 'Alī Gum'a presented towards foreign media was that of the reasoned and moderate voice of Islam. He published a statement in English in the *Washington Post* on 18 September 2012, in which he addressed a Western audience, amply emphasising the need for official Islamic institutions:

> The world is sorely in need of such lessons which represent the authentic teachings of the Koran and the prophet of Islam. It is important to separate these noble messages from those that are bandied about by those who have no competencies in religious interpretation, Koranic hermeneutics or the history of Islamic thought.[52]

'Alī Gum'a expressed his esteem for Christianity, especially 'Abraham, Moses and Jesus': 'They are revered teachers who taught us the very nature of reality, the purpose of our existence, and how to connect with God Himself'.[53] Like other figures of official Islam, he insisted on Islam's compatibility with human rights and democracy, as values contributed by the Prophet Muhammad himself: 'how he founded a state based on the rule of law, justice and equality', 'how he spread Islam in the rest of the world with wisdom', 'how this religion preserved the rights of women', and 'how Islam reversed the big and was merciful with the small'.[54] In short, sharī'a is said to equate human rights, and democracy is defined as 'tending towards equality', which, according to the mufti, is backed by the Qur'an. One can find similar phrasing in the statement of the spokesman of the Jordanian government and the Minister of Islamic Endowments, Islamic Affairs and Sacred Places, 'Abd al-Salām al-'Abādī, quoted in Chapter One: 'a religion of mercy, humanity, *tolerance, moderation, and balance* [my emphasis], a religion of justice and peace, a religion that has condemned the contemporary meaning of terrorism'.[55] Despite Mufti 'Alī Gum'a reaching out to a Western audience, the West was the actual focus of criticism by official Islam. The shaykh al-Azhar offered his reflections on the West's alleged uneasiness with Islam: '[w]hat we see today, the hatred against Islam and its civilisation is not a child of the moment'.[56] Rather, according to al-Tayyib, this hatred is part of the 'legacy of European collective consciousness since the Middle Ages' and related to the very nature of the West, which does not 'accept the belonging to a religion (*tadayyun*)'. To illustrate this, he put forward the examples of the Crusades and the fate of the Jews and Muslims in Andalusia.

When it comes to their attitudes toward Christians in the context of 'The Innocence of Muslims', actors of official Islam took a stance radically different from that of the Islamist and Salafi movements. Not only did they not enter polemics, unlike the Nur Party, but they also refrained from making local Christians the focus of their reactions. As mentioned in Chapter One, ʿAlī Gumʿa referred to local Christians only after having been asked by *al-Ahrām* about his 'satisfaction' with their reactions, to which he responded by insisting on national unity. In general, actors of official Islam only mentioned local Christians when warning against a greater danger posed by the video. For instance, while Shaykh al-Azhar Ahmad al-Tayyib seemed to concede the involvement of 'Copts in the diaspora', he also asserted that 'such acts' did not express the view of 'Egyptian Christians who have explained their respect for all religious figures more than once', insisting that such actions only fanned the flames of 'the fire for *fitna* between the sons of the united nation'.[57] On 17 September 2012, *al-Ahrām* quoted Ahmad al-Tayyib praising the position of the 'Egyptian Churches against the offending film'.[58] Similarly, the Lebanese Mufti Rashīd Qabbānī warned against the risks of *fitna*. In his letter to the Lebanese people and the Muslims published on 13 September 2012, he claimed that 'The Innocence of Muslims' aimed to 'plant strife between Muslims and Christians in the world'.[59] He mused that for the United States, 'the most powerful country in the world', which 'tries to extend its influence everywhere in the world, it is not possible that they do not know or are not aware' of it. Qabbānī thus demanded a national Lebanese response: 'We repeat our call to Muslim and Christian Lebanese to be united (*al-sawt al-wāhid*) in the refusal of offense [. . .] so that Lebanon remains [a] message and [a] model of coexistence between all religions'. On 21 September 2012, Rashīd Qabbānī invited the *shuyūkh* and imams to Dār al-fatwā and claimed again that 'Christians and Muslims in Lebanon are strongly united (*yad wāhida*)'.[60] In Jordan, no explicit references to local

Christians or Christians in general were made by any representatives from the government, the Ministry of Islamic Endowments, the *Dā'irat al-iftā'*, the Upper and Lower House, or the municipal council of Greater Tafileh. The spokesman asserted the government's respect for all 'revealed religions', as did the *Dā'irat al-iftā'* that once again called attention to the inherent tolerance of Islam, which compels Muslims to respect all prophets, messengers and the other revealed religion, quoting Qur'an 2:285.[61]

The claim of official Islam to leadership and authority rested on an elaborated conviction of their own authority, according to which Christians were quite instrumental, and which set them apart from Islamist and Salafi movements. Their authority varied, and none of these actors tried to mobilise their followers. Nevertheless, they constituted an important counter-part in Christian–Muslim relations.

The Forgotten Christian Laity

When discussing Christians in the context of this controversy, terms such as 'Coptic Orthodox', 'Latin', 'Protestant', 'Maronite' have appeared, illustrating the extraordinary diversity of Middle Eastern Christianity. Within the Christian population, the Coptic Orthodox Church represents the largest group in Egypt (roughly 95 percent), followed by the Coptic Catholic Church and the Protestant Churches. In Jordan, the Greek Orthodox used to constitute the dominant group but, due to conversion efforts in the nineteenth century, Christian Jordanians are now split between Greek Orthodox, Latin and Greek Catholic Melkite Christians.[62] In Lebanon, Maronites are the main Christian group, followed by Greek Orthodox and Greek Catholic Melkites. Of all these Churches, the Coptic Orthodox and the Maronite Churches have historically made strong claims to being national Churches.[63]

Speaking of Middle Eastern Christianity thus seems to be a conversation about Churches. But 'The Innocence of Muslims' highlighted the importance of lay Christianity[64] in embodying, representing and speaking for Middle Eastern Christians. The controversy, in fact, illuminated the tensions between the Churches and Christian lay figures in this regard. The issue was most virulent in the case of the Coptic Orthodox community, where the Arab Spring also took the shape of an inter-Coptic revolution rooted in growing discontent with the political role of the Church. Moreover, the controversy in September

2012 and the way in which Coptic Orthodox and Jordanian Greek Orthodox figures in particular positioned themselves are the product of varying historical circumstances.

As Maurits H. van den Boorgert notes, '[t]hroughout the Ottoman [Empire] non-Muslim communities tended to have both an ecclesiastical and a lay leadership at the same time. The lay leaders, who were generally elected by the community, were responsible for administrative and financial matters. All arrangements with regard to taxes were thus made by the lay elites'.[65] In this regard, Heather Sharkey highlights the impact of the Ottoman state in empowering certain members of the Christian communities: 'From the perspective of the Ottoman state, Christian and Jewish leaders who really mattered included laymen who helped the state to generate revenue. These lay leaders included merchants, financial advisors, tax collectors, and moneylenders'.[66] In addition, the nineteenth century was a time of major shifts within the Christian communities, with 'the rise of rural notables within the millet, the birth of industrial and commercial elites in the cities, and finally the appareance of a lay intelligentsia'.[67]

A crucial aspect of the laity's leverage has thus been its economic role, which, in the case of the Coptic Orthodox, diminished over the second half of the twentieth century, while in the case of Jordan it remained unchanged or even increased. Over the course of the nineteenth century, a Coptic landowning class emerged. In 1914, the Coptic elite 'owned one-fifth of all agricultural land in the country as well as buildings and monetary assets'.[68] In Ottoman Transjordan, as part of a growing class of merchants, Christians started to acquire land before succeeding in other economic fields. The Greek Orthodox Abū Jābir family, a driving force in the Orthodox Society that issued a statement against 'The Innocence of Muslims', was part of these successful Christian Transjordanian tribes who acquired large portions of land.[69] These new Christian elites wanted to translate their wealth into greater political and communal influence. With the help of the Ottoman and the Egyptian khedival states, the Christian communities were reorganised to increase lay oversight over Church finances and to end the clergy's corruption.[70]

Thus, in the nineteenth century, impulses for reform in the Coptic Orthodox Church came from lay efforts. In 1874, a Coptic Lay Council (*al-majlis al-millī*) was established to ensure lay control over Christian endowments: it was composed of twelve lay members and twelve deputies elected by general suffrage.⁷¹ A group of reformists emerged from among this landed Coptic elite,⁷² and in 1907 the Coptic Reform Association was founded for defending Coptic rights and access to education.⁷³ In the 1950s, President Gamal Abdel Nasser destroyed the landowning class, including its Coptic members, through his economic and agrarian reforms. By contrast, in Jordan the laity continued to thrive. The Latin Bishop of Amman, Mārūn Lahhām, who condemned 'The Innocence of Muslims', summed up this situation: 'We are 3 percent, but 35 percent of the economy in Jordan is in the hands of the Christians. So, there is a sense of "ok, we are 3 percent, but our presence is much more [strong]". And this sense of well-being does not exist in Egypt'.⁷⁴ Bāssim Farrāj, secretary general of the Orthodox Society, noted the Jordanian Christians' presence in 'banks, the car dealerships, the air-conditioning, business-trading, industry, services'.⁷⁵

This significant economic leverage has been translated on several levels in Middle Eastern Christianity: identity, intra-Christian relations and Christian–Muslim relations. First, in the case of the Jordanian Greek Orthodox, their dominant role has been somewhat of a necessity due to the 'Orthodox Issue' (*al-qadya al-urthūdhuksiyya*), a conflict within the Greek Orthodox Patriarchate of Jerusalem that has been raging since the nineteenth century between a then (as of 2012) largely ethnic Greek Church leadership and an Arab low-ranking clergy and laity concerning decision-making in the Church, alleged corruption, estrangement between the clergy and the laity, and a perceived lack of pastoral care.⁷⁶ In the early 2010s, there were also conflicting reports about who ran the services provided by the Church – the kindergartens, the schools, the church buildings and renovations – with the laity claiming that they largely funded it.⁷⁷ In reaction to this conflict, the Greek Orthodox laity has increasingly stressed its Arab identity, so much so that it has come to reject the label *rūm*, usually used in Arabic to designate the Greek Orthodox.⁷⁸ Second, the economic leverage has had an impact on intra-Christian relations – for example, in Jordan where, faced with many cross-denominational marriages, the laity managed to impose a unification of the date of Christmas and Easter festivities; Christmas according to the Gregorian calendar and Easter according to the Julian calendar.⁷⁹ Third, this power has had an impact on Christian–Muslim relations, as Greek Orthodox Jordanians in particular have developed an openness towards Muslims. For instance, the Orthodox Club, like most Orthodox associations, is open to all communities:[80] 'Unable to take full control of the Greek Orthodox ecclesiastical system, the Arab Orthodox laity engaged in the autonomous development of the Jordanian Greek Orthodox community, opening its communal spaces to the rest of the Jordanian population at large in order to build up a close political and economic relationship with the regime'.[81]

In Egypt, however, the laity lost this leverage and ability to define the community's identity and boundaries. However, it did not entirely cease to play a role. Inside the Coptic Orthodox Church, attempts at renewals started in the mid-nineteenth century and reached their climax under the patriarchate of Shinūda III (1923–2012, in office 1971–2012), who institutionalised the Sunday School Movement.[82] This renewal marked a tradition that was cleansed of its 'foreign' – Latin, Greek, Islamic – influences.[83] It aimed to re-Christianise the Christians, much like Islamism re-Islamised Muslims, by establishing the Church as the only moral, historical and pedagogic framework.[84] The reform encompassed a reorganisation and centralisation of the dioceses and a revival of monasticism.[85] Before the accession of Shinūda III, there were twenty-three Coptic Orthodox bishops, while by the late 1990s there were eighty-three.[86] The newly established Bishopric for Youth promoted the creation of Coptic student associations (*usar*).[87] All these measures aimed to fully assimilate the Coptic community and Coptic youth into the Church,[88] but, according to Laure Guirguis, Shinūda III also contributed to the creation of a sense of minority.[89] As a result, a type of laity emerged, which Angie Heo defines as a 'new generation of youth who were raised, educated, and liberalized from within the Coptic Church itself – as priests, deacons, and lay servants'.[90]

No similar developments took place in Lebanon and Jordan; this would not have been possible. Unlike the Coptic Orthodox Church in Egypt, the Churches in Lebanon and Jordan face a higher level of Church competition. Bishops are the highest-ranking level of clergy in Jordan, whereas the see of the Latin and Greek Orthodox Patriarchates are located in Jerusalem and that of the Greek Catholic Melkite Church is in Damascus. Nevertheless, some Churches have claimed political leadership, in particular the Maronite Church. Sami Baroudi and Paul Tabar note that the actual political role of the Maronite Church is impacted by '(1) the political and social standing of the church within the Maronite community; (2) the church's relations with lay Christian and non-Christian leaders; and (3) the Maronite community's placement within the overall confessional power balance'.[91] A defining aspect, however, is the person in charge. Patriarch Shinūda III embodied this political religious leadership, which resulted in a growing estrangement from the Coptic youth following the Arab Spring. By contrast, the patriarchal caretaker Bākhūmyūs started to reframe the political position of the Church but was hindered in his efforts.

The Churches Upset

The specifically political role of the Church as a representative of its community and at the expense of the laity is the result of several factors. The personality of the patriarch is a key element. But the state's attitude is equally, if not more, important. The level of institutionalisation of religious difference discussed at the beginning of this chapter also plays a role. The laity's willingness to accept a political role for the Church and the attitude of the general Muslim population are other key factors illuminated by the controversy. This issue was particularly salient in the case of the Coptic Orthodox Church.

The level of institutionalisation of Christian representation has an impact on the Church's ability to act as a representative for Christians. As mentioned at the beginning of this chapter, Christians have a quota system in Lebanon and Jordan. Consequently, Christian MPs may naturally act as political representatives of their communities – without necessarily siding with the Churches, something Mārūn Lahhām highlighted in an interview; these deputies are supposed to be the 'Christian voice', but in a disagreement between the government and the Churches over the ecclesiastical courts, these same Christian deputies sided with the government.[92] In Lebanon, too, this has limited any overly far-reaching political ambitions of the Maronite Patriarch. Nevertheless, Maronite Patriarch Bishāra Butrus al-Rāʿī has tried to promote the see of the patriarchate, Bkerké, as an 'umbrella for all Christian forces'; he stated that 'the [Christian] command is [his]'.[93] By contrast, Egypt has never introduced a quota system (until 2014) and, therefore, no 'natural' Christian lay leadership has emerged.

As the case of the Coptic landowning class illustrates, the state plays a key role in tipping the balance towards the Church or the lay leadership. This can be seen in the destruction of the old elite under Gamal Abdel Nasser, who also abolished the Coptic Lay Council (*al-majlis al-millī*).⁹⁴ The state resolved the long conflict between the Church and lay notables for supremacy in the Coptic community, to the benefit of the Church. This new relationship between Nasser and the Coptic Patriarch, Kyrillos VI, was termed a '*millet*'-partnership; they were united, crucially, by 'their shared aversion to the Coptic lay elite'.⁹⁵ Yet, unlike Gamal Abdel Nasser, the monarchy preferred to deal with the Coptic lay elite.⁹⁶ Angie Heo, however, argues that the Coptic Orthodox Church does not have much of a choice:

> It is the Egyptian state that regulates the Church through a range of disciplinary acts, from denying permits for places of worship to withdrawing security in contexts of sectarian tension. The church-state alliance is far from a reciprocal exchange; it is, rather, a hierarchical relationship that is also deeply marked by repression and marginalization.⁹⁷

And even though the patriarchal caretaker Bishop Bākhūmyūs aspired to reduce the political role of the Church in 2012, the state – in the form of Muhammad Mursī – carried on with this *neo-millet* system. During the presidential elections in June 2012, Bishop Bākhūmyūs announced that the Church would remain neutral towards all candidates and punish any priests who did not do so.⁹⁸ The new political leadership, however, continued in this approach of considering the Church the sole representative of Egyptians who happened to be Christians. For instance, in early September 2012, President Mursī met with Church leaders to reassure the Christians in Egypt through them.⁹⁹ The relevance of the Council of Churches in Jordan is another example of the state's hand in Christian political leadership. It was established in 1999 on the initiative of the four bishops of Amman: the Greek Orthodox Bishop, the Latin Bishop, the Greek Catholic Melkite Bishop and the Armenian Apostolic Bishop.¹⁰⁰ It was recognized by the government as the body which would officially deal with Christian matters.¹⁰¹ As Hannā Kildānī explained, this council did not deal with theological matters but with every-day matters and the government. Yet Jiryis Habāsh, an Evangelical priest, criticised this council as not having any legal basis.¹⁰² The Council of Churches ceased to exist in late 2012 or early 2013.¹⁰³

Alongside the (often Muslim) state, Islamist and Salafi figures were instrumental in increasing the relevance of a certain Church. Of all the Churches in Egypt, this was particularly the case for the Coptic Orthodox Church, thanks to Muslim figures who explicitly called on her to take a stance against the video (albeit with polemical undertones). As mentioned in Chapter One, Wisām 'Abd al-Wārith, a preacher on the channel *al-Hikma*, demanded that the Church issue a clear position towards the film.

Finally, the Christian laity does have a say in recognizing the Church as its political spokesman. The issue grew especially heated in the Coptic Orthodox community, where the Arab Spring contributed to a growing estrangement between the Church leadership and the youth. Following the above-mentioned attack in Nag Hammadi in January 2010 on worshippers leaving Christmas mass, Copts protested for the first time outside the walls of the Church. In November 2010, Coptic protesters and the police clashed in al-Umraniyya, in the governorate of Giza near Cairo, because the local authorities refused to turn a cultural centre into a church; following this refusal, the Copts reportedly stormed the headquarters of the local governorate.[104] In reaction, Patriarch Shinūda III retreated to the monasteries of Wadi al-Natrun to pressure the government into releasing all imprisoned Copts.[105] This event was widely regarded as a turning point: for the first time, it was average citizens instead of high-profile figures who were publicly expressing their discontent, and this outside church walls.[106] The bombing of the Two Saints Church in Alexandria, which killed twenty persons on 1 January 2011 – just before the revolution – provoked a new level of turnout at protests.[107] Despite the patriarch's calls to the contrary, young Copts participated in the protests of the revolution in January 2011. The estrangement escalated further following the Maspero Massacre in October 2011, during which up to forty persons, mainly Coptic protesters, were killed and more than 300 were wounded by the army.[108] Strikingly, the Maspero Massacre is an example of violence against Copts that has been 'silenced', as mentioned by Angie Heo in Chapter Two. Unlike the victims of Alexandria, who became objects of national mourning, the victims of Maspero have remained invisible. Instead, the Holy Synod issued then a statement conforming to the official narrative, according to which the protesters had attacked the security forces:

> And if we insist on our Christian faith [that] does not employ violence in any of its forms, as we do not forget that some foreigners have lurked among

our sons and committed the errors that were connected to them [. . .]. The Holy Synod calls on the Coptic people for a three-day prayer and fast starting tomorrow.[109]

Coptic protestors ignored the call of the Church not to demonstrate on the fortieth day after the massacre.[110]

After January 2011, as attacks on Copts and churches continued, Coptic activism was gradually institutionalised, and a number of Coptic organisations emerged, in particular, the Coalition of Egypt's Copts (*I'tilāf aqbāt Miṣr*),[111] the Maspero Youth Union (*Ittiḥād shabāb Maspero*), the Movement of Copts Without Restrictions (*Harakat aqbāt bilā quyūd*)[112] and the 'Christian Brothers' (*al-Ikhwān al-masīḥiyyūn*) – all of whom reacted to 'The Innocence of Muslims'. The Maspero Youth Union was reportedly founded following the events in the village of Atfih, 80 kilometres from Cairo, where a love affair between a Christian man and a Muslim woman had led to the expulsion of the Christians.[113] According to Mīnā Magdī, general coordinator of the MYU, these expelled Christian inhabitants staged a sit-in in Maspero Square – which became a location of protest, parallel to Tahrir Square, for specifically Christian demands.[114] The sit-in ended on 25 March 2011, and it was then that the Maspero Youth Union was created.[115] The 'Christian Brothers' was established in July 2012 as a reaction to the presidency of Muhammad Mursī.[116] All shared the same goal of reducing the Church's political role and limiting it to religious matters.[117]

During the controversy, the reactions of the Coptic youth associations differed from those of the Church and Christian Jordanians. Some were particularly critical. Although the Coptic organisations displayed a heightened concern for the potential backlash against local Christians, they did express a number of explicit criticisms. Some openly denounced the conflation of the producers of the video with Copts in Egypt. The Movement for Civil Rights for Christians, a youth organisation established in 2011, particularly rejected the 'insults and threats directed towards Christian Egyptians for they did not participate, either directly or indirectly, in the production of this offending film'.[118] Some actors criticised how the whole controversy over this poorly made video actually revealed 'double standards' in Egyptian society. As mentioned in Chapter Two, Copts Without Restrictions asked in its official statement published on

10 September 2012: 'Why are these voices not raised to condemn more extremist positions of institutions and the media in Egypt against the Christians and their sacred items and symbols?'[119] The statement particularly criticised the silence of society, the state and the media when Christians were accused of being 'unbelievers' and when they and their properties were attacked. To back its argument, the organisation employed the discourse of national unity. Unlike the Coptic Orthodox youth activists, Jordanian Christians were more lenient towards Muslims. For the Orthodox Society, 'the showing of the film [which] offends Islam and the Muslim brothers and assaults religious sites and the Islamic creed' as well as 'the feelings of Muslims and Christians'.[120] The expression 'Muslim brothers' is repeated three times in the statement.

Even though there was general discontent with the role of the Church as being too political, some Coptic organisations expressed discomfort with the *need to speak as* Christian. Arguably, one can condemn 'The Innocence of Muslims' as Christians – or actors who happened to be Christians – without having to officially condemn *as Christians*.

Speaking *as* and *for* Christians

I have gradually begun to touch on more significant questions: what were the stakes of speaking *as a Christian*? As I will show, Christians in Jordan chose to speak as Christians, whereas in other contexts they chose not to emphasise this aspect of their identity. In the context of the conflict with the Greek Orthodox Patriarchate of Jerusalem, the fifth Orthodox Congress, which gathered in 1992, stated that 'our national belonging precedes our confessional (*tā'ifī*) belonging'.[121]

This chapter so far seems to have suggested that being Christian or Muslim is a reality that pre-exists an individual. While there exists a political quota system in Lebanon and Jordan, there was none in Egypt. In Lebanon, religious affiliation supersedes any political or ideological stance, as in the case of the SSNP, to be discussed below. However, as the chapter has also suggested, Muslims play a role in defining Christians as Christians. Thanks to the presence of Christian SSNP leaders, the Hezbollah/Amal protests were joint *Christian–Muslim* protests. This illustrates the assertion of George Sabra about Christians:

> [A]ll those who have been baptized in the name of the Triune God, whether they like it or not, whether they believe what their church believes or not,

whether they practice their Christianity or not, are regarded and treated by the larger Islamic majority as 'Christians'.[122]

Géraldine Chatelard, however, puts forward another approach:

> The issue here is not to define who is Christian, but in what kind of interactions it is preferable to identify as Christians, in which cases one is solely considered Christian [. . .] and finally in which cases one can credibly claim other belongings and which ones [. . .]. Being Christian is to identify or be identified as such. This also applies to all and any other types of social identity.[123]

The controversy over 'The Innocence of Muslims' presents us with both instances: 'Christians' defined as Christians and Christians who chose to speak as Christians; being Christian as an imposition and as a choice. This is significant as it manoeuvred the various actors into different positions towards Muslims. However, as I have argued earlier, the controversy was used by all Christian actors as an opportunity to discuss their political future.

The SSNP in Lebanon and the Egyptian politician George Ishāq both illustrate Sabra's claim regarding the defining role of Muslims in assigning a Christian identity. The SSNP is an anti-sectarian party, founded by the Greek Orthodox Antoun Saadeh in 1932, and includes Druze, Shiʿa and Greek Orthodox members.[124] Its secretary general, Asʿad Hardān, holds the Greek Orthodox seat of Hasbaya, while its vice-secretary general, Marwān Fāris, holds the Greek Catholic Melkite seat of Baalbek.[125] In its two condemnations of 'The Innocence of Muslims', the party did not make any Christian reference, instead resorting to an anti-colonial narrative that connects it to how 'the extremism that bloodies our countries with terror, murder, slaughter, and destruction is met with every backing and support by Israel and the colonising forces of the West'.[126] Yet, Marwān Fāris participated in the Hezbollah/Shiʿi protests in Baalbek and Hermel and was used by Hezbollah as the symbolic Christian in its 'Christian–Muslim' front against 'Zionism' (see Chapter Five). Similarly, at the founding conference of *Hizb al-dustūr* in Kafr al-Shaykh, Egypt, on 13 September 2012, the Christian Egyptian politician and activist George Ishāq did not refer to himself as a Christian, nor did he claim to speak in their name when he addressed 'The Innocence of Muslims'.

Instead, in the name of the party, he demanded that the United States punish the producers of the video and stop its dissemination, stating that 'Egypt [was] undamaged in its strong Coptic and Muslim woven fabric'.[127] In March 2011, however, following sectarian clashes in the village of Atfih, in the governorate of Helwan, Ishāq and the Salafi preacher Muhammad Hassān were engaged by the then-ruling SCAF to negotiate a peace settlement in the village.[128]

In the case of Coptic Orthodox youth activism, this assigned identity seemed more significant. They unapologetically insisted on speaking as Copts and Egyptians, but not necessarily *for* fellow Christians. Organisations such as the MYU, Copts Without Restrictions, the Coalition of Egypt's Copts and the Christian Brothers, which have sprung up from the young generation of Coptic activists, were vocal and countered the monopolisation of the Christian voice by the Coptic Orthodox Church. They often held a stance much more critical than the Church (see Chapter Five). However, apparently under pressure from Muslims, a discussion broke out among these organisations over their participation in the protests at the US embassy on 11 September 2012: the Maspero Youth Union and the Coalition of Egypt's Copt participated, while the Christian Brothers refused, asserting that they did not see a need for Copts 'to go out and protest on the streets to dissociate' themselves from something for which they were not responsible in the first place.[129] Especially in Egypt, speaking as Christian entailed the risk of being conflated with the video's producers.

When it comes to Jordan, one may compare the controversy over 'The Innocence of Muslims' with another instance in which Christian Jordanian figures did not mention the Christian element: the murder of Christian Jordanian journalist Nāhid Hattar in 2016. Hattar was a controversial leftist journalist, known for being one of 'the most exclusivist voices in the Transjordanian Christian community', for whom 'the Palestinians' presence in Jordan is a triumph for Zionism'.[130] Prior to his death, he had published on his Facebook page a cartoon depicting an IS fighter in paradise together with a representation of God,[131] something deemed so offensive that it compelled the Jordanian government to prosecute him. Hattar was killed outside the courthouse by an IT engineer from the Ministry of Education,[132] who was then executed in March 2017. The fact that Hattar was a Christian was not mentioned at all in the reactions to his killing. Instead, Latin Bishop Mārūn

Lahhām offered his condolences to 'the united Jordanian family [. . .] and [the] Āl Hattar tribe'.[133] Yet, in the context of 'The Innocence of Muslims', Christian figures and organisations established their Christian belonging as a starting point from which to promote a narrative of national unity with Muslims. MP Ridā Haddād, for instance, illustrated this with his statement on 'we Arabs, Muslims and Christians' whose 'state of brotherly coexistence between Muslims and Christians in this country constitutes a model to be followed'.[134] According to the Orthodox Society, '[t]here is a Zionist plan targeting Christian and Muslim Arabs' and aiming to ignite 'strife between the children of the united Arab community'. Indeed, the context has dramatically changed between 2012 and 2016 with the emergence of the IS and its atrocities.

Yet, why would Christians in Jordan choose to highlight their Christian identity in the context of 'The Innocence of Muslims', especially since there was hardly any reference to them in Jordanian (Muslim) reactions? It is precisely this avowal of a Christian identity which needs to be considered in a context of invisible Christians in Jordanian organisations and a claim of loyalty to the monarchy on the part of the Christian figures and organisations, one that contrasted with the September 2012 protests to express discontent towards the monarchy. As mentioned earlier, there are Christians in the professional associations and the party *Hizb al-du'ā'*. In 2007, the IAF elected Christian 'Azīz Musā'ada to its leading committee.[135] The greater stakes will be explored further in the next chapter.

Conclusion

This chapter has introduced other key players and internal dynamics concerning representation and authority in each community. We have also contrasted the legal and political foundations of Christian identity with the way in which it unfolded during the controversy. Surprisingly, Christian organisations and figures in Jordan chose to highlight their Christian identity alongside their Arabic one. I have chosen not to answer the question why they did so, just yet. For now, suffice it to say that there were major discussions in the Christian communities, particularly in the Coptic Orthodox Church, between the Church leadership and the lay organisations about political representation and the way in which the Churches handled Christian–Muslim relations.

4

SEARCHING FOR PROXIMITY TO THE OTHER: REDEFINING *FITNA* AND *DHIMMA*

Introduction

Instead of causing anti-Christian violence in the region, the outcry over 'The Innocence of Muslims' soon morphed into an event that actually strengthened Christian–Muslim relations. Both Christian and Muslim figures channelled the potential for violence into a positive outcome for inter-communal relations and their own personal interests. Based on the first three chapters, which set the stage, the subsequent chapters will investigate the materiality and the mechanisms of Christian–Muslim relations that unfolded during this brief polemic.

This chapter is concerned with the 'anomalies' of the controversy: strong affirmations towards the other community and (some) joint reactions. I have already mentioned several joint protests, such as those in Egypt and the Hezbollah/Amal protests in Lebanon. In addition, there have been mentioned comments of moderation toward Christians by Islamists. On the Christian side, there were also comments that went beyond mere condemnations of the video and expressed admiration for Islam. The Council of Churches in Jordan, for instance, claimed: 'If Muhammad was for all Arabs, then all Arabs are for Muhammad'.[1] Instead of considering these comments shallow and signs of Christians' submission to Islam, I argue that such comments were rational choices made to strengthen their positions. Some Christian Jordanians displayed an ambiguous use of the term *dhimma* as a means to pressure

Muslims and the state for political equality. This seems counter-intuitive in the case of some Islamist movements such as the Nur Party, which was known for its polemical stance. However, even Islamists *needed* Christians if they wanted to realise their political ambitions. Crucially, neither community needed the other as individuals or actors, but rather as symbols of their communities, as passive Christians or ideal, tolerant Muslims. This chapter will explore the various, often surprising dimensions of these searches for proximity to the other community that redefined traditional Islamic terms such as *dhimma* and *fitna*. The controversy over 'The Innocence of Muslims' offered particular salience, as theological, political and national elements came together in a quest for the advancement of personal ambitions.

There is a growing body of literature on Muslim attitudes towards Christians, and Egypt has attracted the most attention,[2] followed to a far lesser extent by Lebanon.[3] To my knowledge, there exist no studies on Islamist attitudes towards local Christians in Jordan. Christian attitudes towards Muslims are generally discussed as part of studies on Christian communities.

This chapter will start by looking at the classical attitudes of each community towards the other, which sharply contrasts with the moderate stances expressed during the controversy, first by Islamists and then by Christians. Finally, I will explore whether there was a need for any institutionalisation of this proximity.

Classical Islamic and Christian Attitudes: Polemics

Chapter Three made no reference to classical Islam in its dealings with Christians, simply because it did not help explain the current situation. Saba Mahmood argues:

> While Islamic concepts and practices are crucial to the production of this inequality, I argue that the modern state and its political rationality have played a far more decisive role in transforming preexisting religious differences, producing new forms of communal polarization, and making religion more rather than less salient to minority and majority identities alike.[4]

Classical Islam, however, is crucial when it comes to modern attitudes towards the other, as it continues to shape inter-communal relations.

The foundations for the coexistence of persons who happened to be Christians and persons who happened to be Muslims were established by Islam early on and are associated with terms such as *dhimma, dhimmī, jizya* and, later on, *millet*. This essentialised approach, however, needs to be put in its historical and historiographic context.

The Christians' presence in Islamic society was a legal question resolved on the basis of revealed texts. The Qur'an mentions Christians and their practices – at least the ones it knew – fifty-four times, referring to them as '*naṣārā*'.[5] As a 'revealed message', Christianity is regarded as the result of Jesus Christ's received revelation in the form of a book, the Gospel. However, due to the dogmas of Incarnation and the Trinity, Christians are said to have turned away from the original Abrahamic religion that Islam claims to restore.[6] The question of whether this diversion makes Christians a community of believers historically preceding Islam, or polytheists – nay unbelievers – is still a matter of debate in Islam, even in September 2012. Regarding social interactions with Christians, on the one hand, Islam envisions the possibilities of good neighbours, even friendship; yet, on the other hand, Muslims are warned against trusting Christians,[7] the rationale being that it is Christians' attitude towards Muslims which determines the latter's attitude. This is the principle of reactivity. Gudrun Krämer observes: 'It is the non-Muslims' behaviour towards Muslims that determines their status and treatment'.[8] The ball was in the Christians' court, and a misplay could be catastrophic.

As Arab tribes conquered the Near East and North Africa, conversions to Islam were not initially a priority, and the basis of the new government was formed by *ad hoc* treaties between the tribes and local notables.[9] The Arab tribes came to rule over populations estranged from their previous rulers, specifically miaphysites (Copts and Syriacs) in the Byzantine Empire and members of the Church of the East ('Nestorians') in the Persian Sasanian Empire,[10] in addition to Chalcedonians (also called 'Melkites', or later Greek Orthodox) in the Byzantine Empire. While these conquests and the ensuing peace settlements created a framework for coexistence, the legal and theoretical foundation was only established from the ninth century onwards, under the Abbasid Caliphate. There is no treaty that exclusively deals with the question of *dhimma*, and the issue of taxation specifically affecting non-Muslims was first outlined in the *Handbook on Land Property Taxation* by Abū Yūsuf (d. 798).[11] Jurists of the twelve century retrospectively credited the Covenant of 'Umar, said to define the terms of the *dhimma* contract, which the second Caliph 'Umar (r. 634–44) was to have concluded with the population of Syria, guaranteeing the protection of the life, property and religious practices of non-Muslims in exchange for *jizya*.[12] The Covenant as outlined in the ninth century also included a number of discriminatory measures that would later constitute the core of the idea of 'dhimmitude': non-Muslims were forbidden to carry weapons, ride a horse and build new churches and monasteries.[13] The oldest complete version of this covenant was recorded by a jurist in Andalusia, Abū Bakr Muḥammad al-Turṭūshī (1059–1126).[14] In reality, the implementation of these measures largely depended on the Islamic ruler and the geographic location, cities being more easily subjected to such measures than mountainous regions such as Mount Lebanon.

'The Innocence of Muslims' very much reflects medieval Christian polemics, blended with a modern touch – that is, the influence of Fr Zakaryā Butrus, born in Egypt in 1934, often described as a 'Coptic televangelist' famous for his spirituality and style.[15] In the 1970s, he openly challenged the Islamist movement in Egypt, calling on Muslims to convert to Christianity, and therefore was sent to Australia.[16] But Patriarch Shinūda III also resented Butrus' charisma and popularity.[17] When his name started to appear in connection with the video, however, Zakaryā Butrus published a statement denying any involvement, 'in any shape or form in the creation, production or finances'.[18] However, he remarked that '[n]o one appreciates such provocative scenes, they are offensive and unnecessary, yet the real problem is that they are consistent with the story of Mohamed as revealed in the authoritative Islamic literature'. Nevertheless, Christian polemicists of early medieval Islam and Fr Zakaryā Butrus, who drew on them, formulated three key areas of criticism of Islam: the foundations of Muhammad's revelation, the violence with which Islam is said to have spread, and the sexuality of Muhammad and his companions – tropes that are all discussed in the video.[19] The polemicists and the video questioned the veracity of Muhammad's revelation in several particulars. In one scene, the video depicts the first time Muhammad has a revelation by putting the character between the legs of his wife, Khadīja, who asks him: 'Do you still see [it]?' Butrus mentioned this so-called 'test by Khadīja' several times, listing all the Islamic biographies in which it occurs, concluding: 'The numerous references to this story confirm its veracity'.[20] In another instance, the video challenges the Islamic view of the Qur'an, showing a priest dressed as a Coptic Orthodox monk, saying: 'I will help you, Khadīja. I will make you a book for him. It will be a mix between some versions of the Torah and some versions of the New Testament, and [I] will mix them into false verses'. This Coptic priest represents the monk Bahīrā whose story has been recounted in Syriac, Christian Arabic and Armenian,[21] as proof that Muhammad had been in contact with 'heretic' Christianity, especially with 'Nestorians' (members of the Church of the East) and Arians,[22] thus questioning the existence of Islam as a religion separate from Christianity.

Discrediting Muhammad through his wife Khadīja is closely connected to charges of the prophet's alleged sexual perversion, ranging from paedophilia to homosexuality (perceived in this context as depravity) and uncontrolled lust (in sharp contrast to Western secular criticism of Islam). John of Damascus (675–749) claimed that the revelation actually served Muhammad's sexual appetite.[23] Similarly, the thirteenth-century Coptic chronicle *The Martyrdom of John Phanijōit* tells the story of a Copt converting to Islam in order to satisfy his sexual desires: his return to Christianity and martyrdom is depicted as a 'moral purification'.[24] 'The Innocence of Muslims' claims that Muhammad abolished adoption so that he could have sex with a woman. That charge was also alluded to by Zakaryā Butrus concerning the story of Zaynab, the daughter-in-law of Muhammad's adopted son.[25] And the video likewise brings up the case of 'Ā'isha, who was married to Muhammad at the age of nine.

Besides these two topics, the video repeats charges of violence levelled against Muhammad, drawing upon Zakaryā Butrus' views. In the video, Muhammad appears as a ruthless warrior who exhorts his followers: 'Killing the men, capturing the women, we shall loot the goods, the cats, any animals and anything else we find. [. . .] May you use whom you wish of the children. The rest shall be sold as slaves to buy more horses and swords'. The torture of an old woman who denounces him for his violence and is attached to two camels and quartered is particularly cruel and constitutes a story that Zakaryā Butrus mentions in an episode titled 'Muhammad confronted by the Great Principles of Ethics and the Murder of his Enemies'.[26] In addition to charges of arbitrary violence, the video aims to represent cases of systematic violence against those opposing Muhammad's prophecy: specifically,

Muhammad grows increasingly uncompromising towards non-Muslims or reticent Muslims. In an early scene, he says: '[I]t is not enough to believe in one God. You must say "God and Muhammad his Messenger". Now, go, read the Qur'an. Move to Palestine or pay the extortion'. Later on, this turns into 'pay the extortion or die'. The distinction between unbelievers and Christians and Jews belonging to the *ahl al-kitāb* disappears; instead, the video ends with Muhammad stating: 'Every non-Muslim is an infidel!' In one instance, a captured Jewish man is executed in front of his wife. In one of his episodes, Zakaryā Butrus lists the reported cruelties of Muhammad towards his enemies, including women and children.[27]

The legal and social position of Christians changed dramatically in the nineteenth century. However, prior to that, even though the Ottoman state was committed to respecting the provisions of the *dhimma*, its officials used derogatory language towards Christians.[28] What changed in the nineteenth century was that not only the legal subordination of Christians ceased but also that the emergent modern state of the Ottomans and the Khedives in Egypt were committed to displaying respect towards non-Muslims. The 1856 edict *Hatt-i Hümayun*, which established equality, forbade the use of derogatory language.[29] This was closely linked to the desire for these rulers to appear 'modern'. The Albanian commander of the Ottoman army, Muhammad 'Alī (1769–1849, in office 1805–49), established a highly centralised administration that was headed by a Turco-Circassian elite,[30] and he implemented control over the whole of Egypt, including agricultural production and manufacturing industry, as well as internal and external commerce.[31] His state required immense human resources and included the Copts, who were better trained in accountancy and land surveying.[32] At the end of the nineteenth century, Copts numbered 45 percent of the civil servants in the ministries of finance, interior and the railways.[33] Muhammad 'Alī also sought to attract Armenians, in addition to Christian Syro-Lebanese and Europeans who settled in Egypt, drawn by the country's many opportunities.[34] As a result, Muhammad 'Alī also searched for a certain proximity to Copts, affirming that 'I do not wish there to be any difference between my subjects based on difference of religion, the only difference is the way they pray in their temples'.[35]

Yet, especially in the Arab Ottoman provinces, parts of the Muslim populace did not follow this moderation, resenting the loss of their legal supremacy and the economic and social prosperity of Christians, who sometimes displayed this wealth, while Muslims payed a high toll for their conscription, especially in eastern Anatolia.[36] At the same time, the region witnessed growing European cultural, economic and political encroachment, coupled with the territorial losses of the Ottoman Empire, a weakening state and the influx of Muslim refugees from the Balkans, the Caucasus, the Crimea (approximately five million people between 1854 and 1908) and the emergence of an Islamic discourse which embraced modern technologies while promoting the return to a 'pure' version of Islam.[37]

The Moderation of Islamist Attitudes towards Christians

From here on, this chapter will take an entirely different direction and explore the search for proximity to the other community. Besides the polemics that quickly emerged in the context of the controversy surrounding 'The Innocence of Muslims', there were also many moderate comments by Islamists and Salafis, which were especially surprising in the case of *al-Gamā'a al-Islāmiyya*, given its history of violence against Copts. While the previous chapters have discussed the attitude of Hezbollah, the Nur Party and official Islam towards Christians, this section is concerned with lesser-known figures, such as the Egyptian *al-Gamā'a al-Islāmiyya* and the Lebanese Salafi preacher Ahmad al-Asīr. Unlike the Nur Party, they navigated the controversy with much more ease and, instead of condemning the video by antagonising local Christians, they integrated the latter into their responses in a way that reinforced their claims to political leadership. Their case can be considered a typical example of 'Islamist groups behav[ing] in ways that were sometimes surprising and unprecedented given the established literature on Islamist political participation',[38] which has often been explained by the 'inclusion-moderation hypothesis', according to which 'political actors will become more moderate if they are allowed to participate in legitimate competitive political processes, such as democratic elections, a free civil society, legal protests and demonstrations, and so on'.[39] In this and the following section, I suggest a different explanation for this surprising moderation. The present section argues that the cases of *al-Gamā'a al-Islāmiyya* and Ahmad al-Asīr, who follow in the steps of Hezbollah and the Muslim Brotherhood in Egypt and Jordan, show the power of political constraints to which these figures are, in fact, subject, if they aspire to national leadership or at least some national relevance. Consequently, Christians are useful political tools, an aspect to which the scientific literature has paid little attention.

There has been growing scientific engagement with the shift towards moderation in Islamist discourses, explored as 'the ways in which the concepts of religious tolerance, pluralism, and citizenship, and the relationship between religion and state are articulated and understood within the Egyptian Islamist framework'.[40] For the period prior to 2011, most of these studies highlight the theoretical and idealised discussions of Christians in Egyptian Islamist discourses.[41] Even in those cases where Islamist actors had already entered the political game, their discussions remained abstract.[42] As for Lebanon and Jordan, there is a lack of more recent and comprehensive studies.[43] Christians, however, are not only envisioned as part of an ideal Islamic order, but, one after another, all these non-institutional Islamist actors discovered local Christians as useful political tools, irrespective of the latter's actual demographic and political size.

Islamist actors with longer political experience already knew the benefits of using local Christians without compromising (parts of) their ideological stance. Jillian Schwedler explains this phenomenon as part of the liberalisation that occurred across the Middle East in the 1990s, which 'have all led to expanded instances of cooperation between Islamists and their historic ideological rivals, notably communists, socialists, and liberals'.[44] As discussed in Chapter One, Hezbollah has perfected its stance, all the while remaining a politicised Twelver Shi'i movement. Setting aside the grievances of the Lebanese Civil War, it has struck political alliances with Christian parties, such as the FPM of Michel Aoun, the Marada Movement, or the SSNP, and, together, as part of the March 8 Alliance, Hezbollah has won parliamentary elections. Hezbollah has also heavily invested in the symbolic dimension of this search for proximity. The alliance with the FPM was sealed with a 'Document of Mutual Understanding' (*wathīqat al-tafāhum*) that was solemnly made public in a room of the Church Mar Mikhail in Haret Hreik, a formerly mixed neighbourhood in Beirut, but now under Hezbollah's control.[45] During Benedict XVI's visit to Lebanon in September 2012, Hezbollah sent scouts to welcome him on his road through south Beirut from the airport.[46] Christians are also part of these Islamists' anti-colonial rhetoric, as Hasan Nasr Allāh's claim regarding 'The

Innocence of Muslims' has shown. Similarly, in Jordan, the Muslim Brotherhood, which has been co-opted by the monarchy, has cultivated a similarly pragmatic approach. The Jordanian Muslim Brotherhood and its political arm, the IAF, which elected the Christian 'Azīz Musā'ada into its leading committee in 2007, have viewed their relationship with Christians within an Islamic framework. Ziyād Abū Ghanīma, the spokesman of the Muslim Brotherhood, stated: 'Islam is very clear on the relations between Muslims and non-Muslims. We believe in Jesus Christ and Moses. We believe that Christians and Jews are the people of the Book (*ahl al-kitab*) and we are ordered by God to behave very kindly to them'.⁴⁷

Marion Boulby argues that the Muslim Brotherhood in Jordan envisions Muslim–Christian cooperation primarily in the framework of 'exposing Zionist ambitions'.⁴⁸ In addition, for the IAF leader Abū Fāris Islam 'legitimises such friendly relations with non-Muslims based on their behaviour [referring to] 60:8'.⁴⁹ However, Joas Wagemakers noted in an email to the author that the issue of Christian Jordanians is very sensitive, because they are seen as under the protection of the monarchy; hence, the Islamist movement refrains from discussing this issue.⁵⁰ In Egypt, prior to the Arab Spring, the Muslim Brotherhood had already entered the political game and interacted with leftist and secular politicians, some of them Copts, like former MP Gamāl As'ad.

The novelty with the Arab Spring was that, in Egypt, groups with an uncompromising stance towards Christians such as *al-Gamā'a al-Islāmiyya* or the Salafi movement entered the new political arena and also searched for proximity to local Christians. In March 2011, after his release from prison, 'Abbūd al-Zumur, a leader of *al-Gamā'a al-Islāmiyya*, wished for a party that would be 'open to all Egyptians, Muslims and Copts'.⁵¹ 'Imād 'Abd al-Ghaffūr, the secretary general of the Nur Party, expressed his disappointment over the lack of Christians in his party.⁵² Even though political parties were required to include Christians, the FJP and the Nur Party exaggerated the number of Christians in their ranks. The Nur Party claimed to have fifty Copts as members,⁵³ even though there were actually only five, according to Mariz Tadros.⁵⁴

The cases of Egypt and Jordan thus show that Christians do have some leverage, despite their demographic minority. Accommodating Christians was necessary to prove political credentials and statesmanship. The stance of the Nur party as opposed to *al-Gamā'a al-Islāmiyya* during the controversy in September 2012 illustrates this. The perils of not taking Christians into account or, worse, antagonising them was evident in the Nur Party's initial stance that jeopardised its political position. As mentioned earlier, Spokesman Hammād challenged the Copts's loyalty so forcefully, coupled with inflammatory comments by other Salafi figures, that the media spokesman of the Nur Party, Nādir Bakkār, had to weigh in, rejecting any allegation that Salafis had agitated against Copts. This might suggest, according to Richard Gauvain, 'that many Salafis have fallen back on well-established and deeply rooted sentiments of animosity in order to maintain the boundary lines between Muslims and Christians'.[55] But if we look at the attitude of *al-Gamāʿa al-Islāmiyya* throughout the controversy, the movement clearly made the *choice* to incorporate Christians and to use the controversy as an opportunity to improve its relations with Christians.

The formerly violent Egyptian group *al-Gamāʿa al-Islāmiyya* succeeded in enrolling local Christians in its condemnations and thus appeared as both an Islamic leader and serious Egyptian political contender, a most surprising development considering that *al-Gamāʿa al-Islāmiyya* attacked Copts in Upper Egypt in the 1970s and 1990s and called on Muslims to shun them socially and economically.[56] Unlike the Islamic tradition, it considered the *dhimma* contract temporary and bound to the Christians' attitude.[57] During the controversy in 2012, following Abū Islām's burning of a Bible copy, *al-Gamāʿa al-Islāmiyya* sent a notification to the general prosecutor.[58] Safwat ʿAbd al-Ghanī of the Building and Development Party described the producers of the video as working for 'suspicious sides, which neither express [the views] of Copts in Egypt nor Christianity nor Copts in the diaspora'.[59] The party also co-organised a conference that brought together two leading members of the party and the movement, Safwat ʿAbd al-Ghanī and ʿAbbūd al-Zumur, as well as the priest of the Episcopal Church in Giza.[60] During this conference titled 'Muslims and Copts … Together Against the Offending of the Prophet of Islam, Muhammad (PBUH)', ʿAbbūd al-Zumur conceded that 'a small group of expatriate Copts' was responsible for this video,[61] but he mainly viewed it as a 'result of Western culture' cultivating hatred of Islam.[62]

Even on the lower levels of the Islamist movements, searching for and expressing proximity to local Christians is paramount to building communal and national leadership. The 'alter ego' of Hasan Nasr Allāh during the controversy, the Salafi preacher from Sidon, Aḥmad al-Asīr, also engaged in these practices. A hitherto little-known Salafi preacher, he used the controversy surrounding the video as an opportunity to claim the leadership of the Islamic and specifically Sunni community for himself, in the wake of the power vacuum left by the exile of former Prime Minister Saʿd al-Ḥarīrī. He had recently risen to national prominence as an outspoken opponent of Hezbollah. This opposition dated back to the 'mini Civil War' of 2008,[63] until which al-Asīr had consistently avoided political issues.[64] During the clashes of 7 May 2008, however, faced with mounting reports of 'the persecution of the Sunni community at the hands of the resistance [that is, Hezbollah]',[65] al-Asīr started directing verbal attacks against Hezbollah and the 'hegemonic project of the party of resistance'.[66]

Countering 'The Innocence of Muslims' was therefore another opportunity for him to vilify Ḥasan Naṣr Allāh, claiming that he, al-Asīr, had been the first preacher to call for protests in Lebanon, but that he had postponed them because of the pope's visit.[67] Al-Asīr organised a sit-in on Friday, 21 September 2012, from 3pm to 8pm in downtown Beirut, in Martyrs Square. The choice of this location, next to the Muḥammad al-Amīn Mosque, where the late Prime Minister Rafīq al-Ḥarīrī is buried, was no accident: al-Asīr was laying claim to al-Ḥarīrī's heritage of the leadership of the Sunni community. Yet, many participants of this sit-in were, in fact, Syrians and Palestinians, the latter from the Ayn al-Helweh refugee camp in Sidon.[68] The desire was to demonstrate that '[w]e Sunnis are also here'.[69] To back his ambition for leadership, al-Asīr competed with Ḥasan Naṣr Allāh on the level of mobilisation, optics and rhetoric and the recruiting of Christians. Like Naṣr Allāh, the Salafi preacher switched between Modern Standard Arabic and Colloquial Arabic to display his connectedness with the people of Lebanon and tried to work up his audience, which responded with a few cries of 'Umar, Umar' and 'Lā ilāha illā Llāhu'.[70] Unlike the Muslim Brotherhood and the Nur Party in Egypt, but like Hezbollah, the Salafi preacher navigated the requirements of public debates more easily, defending Islam without having to antagonise Christianism, trying instead to integrate them into his response – albeit on a smaller scale than Hezbollah. Al-Asīr's 'Christian credential' was a representative of the 'Free Christians',[71] who claimed: '[W]e as Christian and Muslim Lebanese of different social and political affiliations [condemn] the offensive film "The Innocence of Muslims"'.⁷² Al-Asīr also expressed public praise for President Michel Sleiman and the Maronite patriarch, mistaken here as the leader of all Christian communities: 'At their head, Christians in Lebanon and, at their top, the respected president of the Republic, because he was the first to condemn [the video], and, at their head, the leader of the Christian Church in Lebanon, Patriarch al-Rā'ī'.⁷³

This search for proximity was part of a larger desire by al-Asīr to build his national leadership. In early September 2012, Samīr Geagea's visit to al-Asīr provoked protests in Sidon because of crimes committed in that city by the Lebanese Forces during the Civil War.⁷⁴ During a visit to the northern governorate of Akkar in December 2012, he met with leading figures of the region, among them Christian leaders, where he stated: 'We want to emphasise coexistence. We have to extend our hand, especially to Christians. The Christians are the closest to us. We have coexisted with them for 1,400 years'.⁷⁵ Yet, the polarisation with Hezbollah reached such a level that in November 2012 al-Asīr was expected to announce the creation of a militia.⁷⁶ His followers regularly clashed with the Lebanese army and killed soldiers.⁷⁷ Al-Asīr also became involved in the war in Syria and was finally arrested in August 2015.⁷⁸

As discussed in Chapter One, Hezbollah under Hasan Nasr Allāh was most effective in searching for proximity to Christians to promote its interests, and it managed to mobilise high-ranking political figures and clerics. But this raised the question of the status of Christians in all these undertakings, as well as for al-Asīr and *al-Gamā'a al-Islāmiyya*. In fact, all too often, Christians were reduced to the status of passive bystanders. Apart from Bishop Sam'ān 'Atā' Allāh in Baalbek, there are no reports of Fr Antoine Daw, the secretary general of the Maronite Bishopric Committee for Christian–Muslim Dialogue, or SSNP's secretary general, As'ad Hardān, having delivered speeches at the Hezbollah/Amal protests. In these contexts, 'Christian' figures, whether clerical or lay, were needed as distinctively 'Christian' and mere 'window-dressing' to demonstrate these Muslim actors' ability to participate in a peaceful and inclusive democratic process. These 'token Christians', however, managed to contribute to the long-term, highly ritualised process of reciprocity and solidarity of Christian–Muslim relations, which does not necessarily mean that both elements must be equally vocal and active. Being reduced to symbolic objects is often sufficient. All of the above are examples of how Muslim figures in the Middle East have used local Christians as political assets.

The passive status of Christians extended to Islamist positions that curtail their purported moderation. Quite often, Islamist figures resorted to Christian actors to sanction their own ideological aspirations. In Egypt, local Copts were particularly useful when it came to backing Islamist and Salafi calls for implementing the 'sharīʿa' (its specific contours will be specified in Chapter Six). In 2011, a leader of *al-Daʿwa al-Salafiyya* published an article titled 'When the Nazarenes Look at the Implementation of Sharia with the Eyes of Reason', in which he quoted the comments that Patriarch Shinūda III had made to the newspaper *al-Ahrām* in 1985, saying: 'The Copts under the rule of Islamic Sharia would be happier and much safer'.[79] During the Arab Spring, even smaller Salafi groups discovered the benefit of using Copts. When the Salafi Front founded a political party, the People's Party (*Hizb al-shaʿb*), in October 2012, it did so with the blessing of a Coptic organisation that called for the establishment of sharīʿa law over all Egyptians, including Christians.[80] This organisation, called 'Copts 38', emerged from the controversy over divorce law within the Coptic Orthodox Church, access to which had been severely restricted under Shinūda III.[81]

In this section, I have tried to shed light on a little-known phenomenon: the Islamists' search for proximity to Christians. This was partly due to the requirement to be part of the political game which induced a certain level of moderation. There were caveats to this. For one, Christians – or rather, figures who happened to be Christians – were often reduced to the status of passive bystanders. On the other hand, the latter were often used as symbols to back the ideology and ambition of Islamist figures. But the 'inclusion–moderation' hypothesis does not provide a sufficiently satisfactory explanation for the moderation of these various figures. Also, it does not explain why the Nur Party and *al-Gamāʿa al-Islāmiyya* took such divergent stances during the controversy, despite their overall efforts at moderation.

The Fear of *Fitna*

Chapter Two has investigated the actors' take on violence, arguing for the need to look at where they located violence – that is, the potential violence and thus the far greater danger that the video could have caused. Similarly, one may now wonder as to what the moderation and search for proximity to Christians was the antidote to. Again, Hasan Nasr Allāh's claim was paradigmatic: he asserted that the video aimed to produce 'strife between Muslims and Christians', propelling them into a 'a bloody religious, sectarian conflict'.[82] Nasr Allāh uses the term *fitna* for strife, a term recurrently used in both Christian and Muslim reactions. In Chapter Three, we have seen the Lebanese Mufti Rashīd Qabbānī warning in a letter to Muslims against the risks of *fitna*, the video aiming to 'plant strife between Muslims and Christians in the world'. Similarly, on 27 September 2012, Shaykh al-Azhar Ahmad al-Tayyib warned against the 'existence of some forces in the service of worldwide Zionism that lure Egypt as well as the Arabic and Islamic *umma* into division'.[83] This section thus explores the fear of *fitna* as the most powerful tool for moderating Islamist attitudes towards Christians – or not, depending on what and whom Islamists and Salafis considered the cause of *fitna*.

Fitna means not only sedition or strife, but also temptation. In an early Islamic context, it designated anything that could lure the newly converted Muslims away from Islam.[84] It also designates the two early civil wars that split the once united Islamic community into irreconcilable fractions. Over time, however, *fitna* experienced two significant semantic alterations that made it susceptible to wider usage. First, Heather Sharkey notes that, '[h]istorically, Muslim thinkers had identified the prevention of *fitna*, or public disorder, as one of the main responsibilities of an Islamic state'.[85] This partly explained why the Ottoman state reacted so vehemently to the massacre of Christians in Damascus in 1860: 'On one day in August 1860 alone, Ottoman authorities executed 167 men as their families and other members of the public looked on; they then suspended the corpses of 57 of them in bazaars and streets, and on gate-posts, as grisly memorials of the punishment'.[86] She contrasts this attitude with the Ottoman state's reaction to the massacres targeting Armenians and other Christian communities in Anatolia in the 1890s – that is, *nothing*:

> By allowing attacks to drag on for years, authorities broke from three ideals of Ottoman statecraft. Two had deep roots in Islamic history: first, the notion of protecting non-Muslim subjects and, second, the idea of maintaining public order whenever possible to avoid strife, or *fitna*. The third was the newer Tanzimat notion of treating non-Muslims and Muslims equitably in relation to the state.[87]

Thus, the well-being of Christians is connected to the avoidance of *fitna*. Gudrun Krämer sums this up masterfully:

> The memory of the 1919 Revolution [against the Birtish occupaption] and the collaboration between Muslims, Copts and other minorities inside the Wafd party helped strengthen this vision [. . .] [T]he sacred principle defended by both the rulers and the scholars of the classical period – that of avoiding any disorder and dissent (*fitna*) to preserve the unity of the community – becomes a prime priority. Since 1919, and again since the 1970s, it is *fitna tā'ifiyya*, the sectarian violence ripping the national body apart that needs to be avoided and fought at all costs. It is, however, no longer the Muslim community that needs to be defended but the inter-denominational, national unity.[88]

The fear of *fitna* in its connotation of sedition or chaos pervades Islamic and Salafi thinking, as the literature has only hinted at so far. It has compelled the Jordanian Muslim Brotherhood to make compromises with the monarchy, despite the latter contradicting its core ideological values 'because the alternative was bound to be much worse'.[89] The fear of *fitna* is particularly pervasive in Salafi thinking, something that has long explained its apolitical stance and initial rejection of the Arab Spring, as 'they are not in favour of any revolts since they generally believe that the result (chaos) will be worse than the problem (dictatorship)'.[90] The other way around, Zoltan Pall shows that the Salafis' success in Lebanon during that time resulted from their having heavily invested 'in resolving social disagreements and conflict'.[91] One of the most surprising transformations after the Arab Spring was that of the Salafi preacher Muhammad Hassān from a polemicist against Christians into a figure actively involved in promoting Christian–Muslim coexistence.[92] As we have seen in Chapter Three, in March 2011, he and George Ishāq were enlisted by the SCAF to restore peace in Atfih in the governorate of Helwan. He apparently convinced local Muslims to restore the church.[93] Following the Maspero Massacre in October 2011, Hassān claimed at a conference of the Nur Party gathering of 3,000 Salafis that 'Egypt is the country of Muslims and Copts and not the property of Muslims alone, and we must learn that, if *fitna* burns, it will burn Muslims and Copts together. We are in one boat'.[94] Similarly, the Islamic Jihad convened a conference together with the Coptic Orthodox Church in Beni Suef, in June 2012, in the wake of Muhammad

Mursī's election, during which one of its leaders called on Muslims: 'The crisis of any minority is the crisis of the majority. The Muslims have the duty to reassure Copts, and Islamic preaching needs to change to reassure the Copts after the revolution that their rights will be preserved'.⁹⁵

One may thus argue that a number of Salafi and Islamist figures adopted the understanding of *fitna* as *fitna tā'ifiyya* and therefore included Copts as part of the community to be preserved. *Al-Gamā'a al-Islāmiyya* was one such actor and firmly held on to the idea that the Copts' sense of security was paramount to Egypt's stability and, thus, the greater project it strove to achieve. This greater project was probably a wider implementation of the sharī'a, as Muhammad Hassān was member of a Council that aimed to 'put pressure on existing political factions so that Shari'a law be implemented to the fullest extent in Egypt'.⁹⁶ Despite the Nur Party's mounting opposition to President Mursī after December 2012, *al-Gamā'a al-Islāmiyya* firmly held on to the latter and, by doing so, maintained a position of moderation towards the Copts. In January 2013, together with an organisation called Coalition of the Copts' Youth, it launched an initiative to tackle sectarian strife, arguing that 'the majority of incidents and conflicts that occur between Muslims and Christians in Egypt are individual [cases] and are not related to religion considering that all revealed religions and laws call for virtue, the renunciation of violence and tolerance'.⁹⁷ By contrast, it seems that *al-Da'wa al-Salafiyya* and some figures of the Nur Party did not endorse this alteration of *fitna*, as evidenced by Yusrī Hammād's initial response to the video. In 2010 *al-Da'wa al-Salafiyya* produced a fatwa reminding its followers that '*fitna* is keeping people away from religion and [does not mean] the difference between Muslims and infidels (*al-kuffār*)'.⁹⁸ In an article published in December 2011, titled 'Muslims and Nazarenes and the Third Option', a figure of *al-Da'wa al-Salafiyya*, 'Abd al-Mun'im al-Shahhāt, writes: '[T]he media calls to what it names "national unity" which transgresses the interest of the nation (*al-watan*), peaceful coexistence and good interactions so that it sometimes comprises the dissolution of the creed! [. . .] Then all are hit at the first disagreement between a Muslim and a Nazarene so that the matter turns into what they call "sectarian strife"'.⁹⁹

As a result, expanding the meaning of *fitna* to include the well-being of Christians as a critical aspect of political and social stability entails a type of compromise that sets this issue at the heart of a larger project for which these various actors strove. This section may thus well illustrate Jillian Schwedler's case for the idea of 'Islamistness', 'which invokes degrees of association or attachment across multiple fields rather than a binary distinction between what is and is not Islamist'.[100]

A Christian Expansion of the Term *Dhimma*

The passive and silent status to which Christians have often been reduced whenever Islamists sought proximity to them may suggest that Christians' expressions of affirmation towards Islam and Muslims during the controversy were mere signs of fear and submission. Fear did play a role. But, as elaborated in Chapter Two, Christian fear was more complex and did not exclude other motivations. Comments such as '[i]f Muhammad was for all Arabs, then all Arabs are for Muhammad'[101] by the Council of Churches in Jordan were highly ambiguous. These were expressions of proximity to Muslims and Islam, but at the same time they were means to pressure them. Just like Muslims, and Islamists in particular, Christians also pursued personal interests and political ambitions and, in doing so, framed an ideal Muslim that suggests an ambiguous use of *dhimma* in the Christian Jordanian case.

Positive comments about Islam and Muslims illustrate one of the two fundamental attitudes of Middle Eastern Christians that George Sabra outlined:

> The fundamental attitude or spirit of the first type is best captured in the phrase: 'Avoid estrangement from Muslims at all costs'. This involves and results in a Christian position of openness to the larger Islamic context, motivated by the desire for acceptance and equality, and aiming at finding common grounds for coexistence and cooperation.[102]

Elements of this attitude are apparent in many of the reactions to 'The Innocence of Muslims'. In Lebanon, for instance, one can find proximity to Muslims expressed within a non-religious, anti-colonial and anti-western narrative, as well as with strong religious references. The SSNP provides an example of such a proximity to Muslims without religious references. The party's secretary general, the Greek Orthodox MP As'ad Hardān, described the video as 'the offence against the Messenger of God, Muhammad', 'this condemning offence of the Messenger Muhammad',[103] who is not mentioned as being relevant to the Muslims, but as *the* messenger of God. At the same time, the video was placed in the context of broader violence and extremism; 'extremism in its different forms and levels, and from various sources', 'hatred, violence, murder and occupation'. This enabled the SSNP to denounce its eternal enemy – that is, 'Zionism', since the video was produced by 'the forces of extremism', by 'the racist, settling Zionist enemy' which causes 'terror, murder, slaughter, destruction in our countries'. The statement insisted on this thesis: 'It is clear that the extremism that bloodies our countries with terror, murder, slaughter and destruction is met with every backing and support by Israel and the colonising forces of the West' in order to 'create the violent environment between the people, infected by ethnic, sectarian, and confessional evil as a condition for the success of the plan to fragment the region and divide it into ghettos'.

In Lebanon, there were also instances of a Christian anti-colonial and anti-western narrative promoted by clerics, foremost among them the Greek Orthodox Metropolitan George Khodr, who discussed 'The Innocence of Muslims' in his weekly column in *al-Nahār*: 'Why this attack by the West on Islam?' and 'What is there in the mentality of the producers of cinema films or press articles that [leads them] to attack Islam?' He concluded: 'There is a desire to beat Islam, with mockery and revenge'.[104] Similarly, in Jordan the reactions featured this same anti-colonial and anti-western narrative, coupled with a strong insistence on being Christian and Arab.

George Sabra explains this type of Middle Eastern Christian attitude: 'The qualification "Arab" is meant to underline the self-understanding [. . .] as bound to Arab identity and history, including Islamic civilization'.[105] Despite the saying that Arabic cannot be Christianised,[106] the connection between Christians and Arabic or Arabness has a more complex history. First of all, it has a geographic and a denominational dimension. On the one hand, depending on their geographic location, Middle Eastern Christians came to adopt and use Arabic at various stages. While the Chalcedonians ('Melkites' or Greek Orthodox) of Palestine had adopted Arabic by the tenth century and produced religious texts in this language,[107] the Copts experienced a renaissance in the thirteenth century, and Arabic helped them join a 'more thorough dialogue with the larger Arabic-speaking world'.[108] By contrast, the Maronites were geographically remote and adopted Arabic in the seventeenth century. In the case of the 'uniate' Churches, Arabic came to fulfil the role of a *lingua franca* for intra-Catholic communication between the Melkites, the Maronites, the Armenian Catholics and the Syriac Catholics.[109] This aspect of being a *lingua franca* was also evident in the case of the Syriac Orthodox who resettled in Syria, Lebanon, Iraq and Palestine after their displacement, as a result of massacres during the First World War in southeastern Anatolia. They used to speak Kurdish, Neo-Aramaic, Ottoman Turkish, Armenian, or Arabic,[110] but after their displacement there was a need for a single language: Arabic.[111]

By then, in the 1920s, however, Arabic also began to have larger political and cultural implications relating to Muslims. At first, however, a closer bond with Arabic emerged from an intra-Christian context and not in an attempt to accommodate Muslims. With the strengthening of the *millet* system under the Greek Orthodox Patriarchate of Constantinople, the Greek Orthodox of Greater Syria and Palestine increasingly resented the growing encroachment of the Patriarchate in Constantinople, all the more as the high-ranking clergy of the Church was filled with ethnic Greeks (resulting in the 'Orthodox Issue' in Palestine and Jordan; see Chapter Three).[112] Furthermore, in the context of the Ottoman reforms and the gradual emergence of a new political contract, '[t]he 1839 edict seemed to address a new kind of Ottoman: someone who would belong to the empire not through coercion or religious allegiance, but through membership, choice, and participation'.[113] But with the massacres of Christians in Aleppo in 1850 as well as on Mount Lebanon and in Damascus in 1860, some of these promises were shattered, and Christian figures started looking for a common ground with Muslims based on a national idea. Deeply affected by the sectarian violence, the Christian Syrian-Lebanese Nāsīf al-Yāzijī (1800–71) and Butrus al-Bustānī (1819–83) began to envision a shared national Arab identity. After World War I and the establishment of the modern states of Syria, Lebanon, Palestine, Iraq and Transjordan, Arabic came to play a more critical role. Until then, 'an Arab [was] a person whose ancestry was in the Arabian Peninsula and parts of the Fertile Crescent. Someone from Jeddah was an Arab, a Cairene was not'.[114] And Arab nationalism was ambiguous at first, as 'both ethnic and based upon a big language'.[115] For the Christian theorists of Arab nationalism, this entailed reducing the distance from Muslims as much as possible and sidelining Christian religious elements. Michel Aflaq (1910–89), the co-founder of the Baʻth party, established in 1947, was an outspoken advocate of this approach, claiming the following:

> The Arab Christians should recognize that Islam forms for them a national culture in which they must immerse themselves so that they may understand it and love it, and so that they may preserve Islam as they preserve the priceless element of their Arabism.[116]

Nowadays, Islam still is seen as encompassing cultural features. The former director of the Royal Institute for Inter-Faith Studies in Jordan, Kāmil Jābir, explains this as follows: 'I am a Christian by faith and I am a Muslim by culture and identity'.[117]

But, as the controversy over 'The Innocence of Muslims' illustrates, this search for proximity to Muslims through Arabism was a choice to carve out a position of strength that did not silence their Christianity. 'We Arab Christians [. . .]', wrote George Khodr.[118] '[W]e as Arab Christians and as Arabs [. . .]', said Fr Nāyif Istifān during one of the conferences in Akkar.[119] Regarding this positioning, the late Greek Orthodox Patriarch Ignatius IV Hazīm wrote that 'the Antiochian Church [. . .] upholds Arab Orthodoxy and Arab Christianity by its own choice'.[120] This idea of choice is also evident in the way in which Arab Christian figures have framed their closeness to Islam and Muslims. In his condemnation of 'The Innocence of Muslims', Metropolitan George Khodr wrote: 'We the Arab Christians, since the conquest, we have decided to live with Muslims in peace and social unity with total liberty for all'. This comment starkly contradicts the persecution discourse conveyed by the video. Yet, in an article titled 'Called by Destiny, not by Chance', the Latin Bishop Mārūn Lahhām explains the need to constantly insist on Arab identity by the fact that Christians in Jordan are too easily associated with the West and, as Christians born in a Muslim country, they experience a 'minority mentality'.[121] However, the emphasis on this Arab identity is not merely circumstantial to Muslims. In a statement issued in June 2014, a group of reform-minded Greek Orthodox clerics in Jordan declared: 'We categorically reject the insinuations of Patriarch Theophilos that we are Greek remnants in our countries. No, we are genuine Arabs, Jordanians, and Palestinians'.[122]

This search for proximity to Muslims seems to entail an assimilation with Islamic language, a clear sign of submission. Yet, this rhetoric move on the part of some Christian figures was actually a means to put pressure on fellow Muslims. In addition to the strong identification with Arabness, the reactions conveyed a very ambiguous understanding of the *dhimma*, which is the strongest means of pressure. Even though the *dhimma* was abolished in 1856 with the *Hatt-i Hümayun*, which established equality between Christians, Muslims and Jews in the Ottoman Empire, it lives on in collective memory. The late Lebanese president (and Maronite Christian) Bachir Gemayel, who was killed in 1982, expressed his desire for 'a real country for Christians where we can hold our heads high, without anyone telling us [. . .] "walk on the left side"'.[123] But the Jordanian case takes the idea of *dhimma*, protection, in a different direction. The Council of Evangelical Churches in Jordan, for instance, claimed: 'We in Jordan, Christians and Muslims, we stand side by side, with a united view, and we will not accept the shattering of our unity, as one Jordanian people that lives in a country beloved in our hearts *under its wise Hashimite leadership*, led by His Majesty King Abdullah II [my emphasis]'.[124] This was in reference to the spirit of 'A Common Word'. Similarly, the Council of Churches drew on the claims of the Hashimite monarchy to embody moderate Islam by referring to the 'Amman Message', the 'Common Word', 'Al Bayt', the Royal Institute for Inter-Faith Studies, and the 'Week of Harmony between Religions', all of which illustrated 'this national effort at openness and co-work': 'We say to our Muslim citizens that we are truly brothers, and God wants us to live together, *united in the faith of the One God and the commandment of the love of God and the love of one's Neighbour* [my emphasis]'.[125] The Council of Churches thus sums up and puts pressure on the monarchy and fellow Muslims to live up to the ideals that Islam allegedly embodies.

As 'A Common Word' called on Christians to focus on shared theological foundations, there have been similar attempts on the Christian side, which stem from reflections of inter-religious dialogue from an Eastern Orthodox perspective, of which Metropolitan George Khodr has been a leading figure. His article 'Christianity in a Pluralistic World: The Economy of the Spirit', published in 1971,[126] presents a theological approach towards Islam that put aside the polemics of the early medieval period expressed, for instance, by John of Damascus (see above). Founding his thought on the Trinity, Khodr argues that the Holy

Spirit offers a means by which Christians can coexist with Muslims, for the Holy Spirit works 'both inside and outside the visible Church': 'The Spirit is present everywhere and fills everything by virtue of an economy distinct from that of the Son'.[127] Khodr's approach is connected to the Orthodox rejection of the Roman Catholic doctrine of *filioque*, the Holy Spirit proceeding from the Father *and the Son*.[128] As a result, from the Eastern Orthodox stance, all of humanity stems from the same source: 'Genesis 1:26–27, humankind is made in the image and likeness of God. This common origin for all persons – regardless of race, gender, time and place or religious orientation'[129] – is conveyed in the comments of George Khodr ('we are one, the *umma* of God') and the Greek Orthodox bishop Bishop Bāsīliyūs Mansūr ('we are the children of God, together on this earth').[130] Bāsīliyūs Mansūr's comment – 'Yes, it is our right to be angry when someone offends *our prophets and our messengers* [emphasis by the author], but we have to be civilised in our behaviour' – suggests a subtle, ambiguous message: both Islamisation and criticism of Islam.

The comments by Bishop Bāsīlyūs Mansūr and Fr Nāyif Istifān during two conferences in the governorate of northern Akkar, Lebanon, illustrate this rhetoric move. Local authorities convened these conferences, one in Bebnine and the other in Halba, attended by figures of the March 14 Alliance, in addition to the two Greek Orthodox clerics. The various comments on unity between Christians and Muslims voiced during these conferences resulted, on the one hand, from the Greek Orthodox dialogue with Islam and, on the other hand, from the specific history of Akkar. Bishop Bāsīliyūs Mansūr's statement – 'our prophets and our messengers' – rests on the idea voiced by George Khodr that Muhammad is also relevant to Christians, as a type of messenger to Christians, at least in its central message of 'submission to God'.[131] Fr Nāyif Istifān, representing Bishop Bāsīlyūs Mansūr at the conference in Halba, even outlined a shared creed: 'Muslims and Christians, we believe in God, His angels, His revelation, and in the resurrection. There is no difference in this between one and the other in any of the ways of the prophets', echoing suras 2:136 and 3:84 (see Chapter Six).[132] On the other hand, Christian–Muslim relations have historically been peaceful in Akkar, which did not suffer displacement and was less affected by violence.[133] It is however one of the poorest regions in Lebanon: its poverty rate at that time was 63.3 percent, whereas the (mainly Christian) districts of Koura, Zghorta, Bsharre and Batroun on Mount Lebanon had a poverty rate of just 24.7 percent.[134] The area is mainly Sunni, but also contains a large number of Maronites and Greek Orthodox, with a significant proportion of Alawis in several districts.[135]

The Christian search for proximity to Muslims occurred in some instances through a shared Arab identity. The key aspect, however, is that this proximity did not entail forsaking or silencing Christian identity and religious difference, even though it took place in an ambiguous, Islamised language. The goal was to include *theological* elements in the condemnation that would constitute the basis for *political* negotiations. As the comments have shown, Arab belonging was always coupled with defining the identity of both Muslims and Christians.

Searching for Proximity to Muslims

In his article 'Two Ways of Being a Christian in the Muslim Context of the Middle-East', George Sabra proposes two different attitudes adopted by Middle Eastern Christians. The first attitude, which he terms 'Arab Christian', seeks proximity through similarity to Muslims, as explored in the previous section – that is, through a shared Arab and Islamic identity. By contrast, the other attitude, . . .

> . . . is best captured in the phrase: 'Save Middle Eastern Christianity at all costs'. This involves and results in a Christian position of affirming the distinctness of Christianity from the larger Islamic context, motivated by the desire to safeguard Christian identity and specificity, and aiming at the establishment (or maintenance) of a free Christian existence.[136]

This attitude, however, has provided many instances of a search for proximity that did not take the road of similarity. Before I close this chapter, it must be mentioned that the second Christian Middle Eastern attitude, that of seeking to maintain a Christian distinction, also resorts to proximity to Muslims for their own benefit. In Egypt, whenever the Virgin Mary appears, the testimony of Muslims is instrumental.[137] Similarly, Emma Aubin-Boltanski notes that the testimony of a Sunni Jordanian boy was instrumental in 'proving' the appearance of the Virgin Mary in the village of Bechouate in the Beqaa Valley, Lebanon, which subsequently became a destination of Christian–Muslim pilgrimage: 'the perfect proof', 'he is detached, disinterested and objective'.[138] Crucially, there are never reports about Muslims converting to Christianity because this would discredit their testimony.[139] Furthermore, in an interview with the author in 2015, the secretary general of the Coptic youth organisation Coalition of Egypt's Copts claimed that the organisation had Muslim members, including an azhari scholar.[140]

This illustrates the large scale of interaction between Christians and Muslims on every level of society and whatever their outlook may be: Salafi, Coptic activists, official Islam and so on.

The Limited Institutionalisation of Proximity

The search for proximity to the other community has led to a certain institutionalisation of Christian–Muslim relations. All in all, there were only two joint Christian–Muslim reactions based on institutionalisation in all three of the countries, as most joint mobilisation did not rest on institutionalised inter-communal relations. In Lebanon, one such action was a regular 'spiritual summit' of representatives of the religious communities. In Egypt, a recently established institution, *Bayt al-ʿāʾila* (House of the Family), issued an official statement condemning the video. But compared to the many other reactions based on individual initiatives, these two reactions were less visible and had a smaller impact. The two institutions were established in response to an acute crisis. They were attempts to deal with the cycle of violence, as described by Élizabeth Picard above, and in this case institutionalise the 'avoidance behaviour coded by highly subtle customs' grounded in ritualised and long-term relations.

The spiritual summit took place in late September 2012 in Bkerké, Lebanon, at the See of the Maronite Patriarchate. It issued a final statement condemning, among other things, 'The Innocence of Muslims'. All communities were represented, except for the Greek Catholic Melkite Church. In recent years, the heads of Churches and Islamic communities have met on a regular basis for 'spiritual summits' to discuss political, economic and social issues. Their discussions are closely connected to the National Committee for Dialogue (*al-Lajna al-wataniyya li-l-ḥiwār*), which was established in 1993, shortly after the end of the Civil War and another war between Israel and Lebanon. The representatives of all religious communities came together in Bkerké on 2 August 1993, which was chosen for the Maronite patriarch's historical role in the independence of Lebanon.[141] But neither the committee nor the spiritual summits ought to be understood as forums for inter-religious dialogue. Hareth Chehab, one of the committee's two general secretaries, regards it as an institution for dealing with everyday matters on a regular basis,[142] as well as for issuing recommendations, which are not necessarily implemented.[143]

The summit and the manner in which the media reported it display a lack of the syncretism that the previous section might have suggested. Lebanese media not only stressed the summit's harmony and agreement, but also hinted at rituals of hospitality and reciprocity. Hareth Chehab recalled that the Maronite Patriarch Bishāra Butrus al-Rāʿī allowed the Muslim representatives and delegations to pray in another room.[144] On 24 September 2012, *al-Nahār* reported that a draft statement was discussed by the representatives in the National Committee and the two secretary-generals, Hareth Chehab and Muhammad Sammak.[145] A sign of the general agreement between Church leaders and Islamic leaders was that only minor changes were made to the drafted statement: the Higher Islamic Shiʿi Council suggested adding a paragraph on the visit of Benedict XVI, thanking him for his visit, while its vice-president ʿAbd al-Amīr Qabalān described 'Lebanon [as] the place of meeting and partnership between all', as opposed to 'Israel [which] is the enemy of all [*sic*]'.[146] Patriarch al-Rāʿī asserted that the 'offence' against Muhammad was an 'offence against Muslims and Christians'.[147] Finally, the summit adopted the following position on the video:

> The film 'The Innocence of Muslims' is offending Islam, its Prophet and its Messenger Muhammad as a lie, a defamation and a dishonesty. [The representatives] have already condemned it individually; they insist that the violation of the sanctity of any religion is a violation of the sanctity of all religions. Likewise, they condemn the violent reactions that resulted in innocent victims and the offences against Christians and the houses of worship in some countries.[148]

The National Committee and the spiritual summit are part of a larger effort undertaken by the religious representatives in Lebanon to improve intercommunal relations. Antoine Daw, who participated in the Hezbollah/Amal protest on Monday 17 September 2012,[149] was then involved in a newly initiated dialogue with Salafi figures in Tripoli.[150]

Like the National Committee of Dialogue in Lebanon, in Egypt *Bayt al-'ā'ila*, which issued an official statement condemning 'The Innocence of Muslims' around 16 September 2012, was established by Shaykh al-Azhar Ahmad al-Tayyib in response to the terror attacks on the Coptic Orthodox Two Saints Church in Alexandria on 1 January 2011, which killed twenty-three persons. The committee includes both Christian and Muslim figures and aims to prevent conflict.[151] The statement issued by the late Mahmūd 'Azab in the name of the *Bayt al-'ā'ila* describes 'The Innocence of Muslims' as a 'criminal event that took place in the United States of America' and triggered the anger of 'the Egyptian Churches, the Egyptian Christians, like their Muslim brothers'. Still, the statement offers slight criticism of the violent reactions and simply summarises the statements of al-Azhar and the Coptic Orthodox Church. Besides this statement, the institution did not play any visible or vocal role at all. One of its members, an azhari scholar, gave a speech at the festival for inter-religious understanding in Nag Hammadi.[152]

In all other joint reactions, the task of contributing to cultivating and strengthening Christian–Muslim relations took place outside institutionalised frameworks. These efforts did not necessarily take place on a high-ranking level. Instead, as in Lebanon, especially in northern Akkar, local individual initiatives were the rule.

Conclusion

At first glance the search for proximity seems shallow and without further implications. Yet, this search embodied stakes with a significant potential for pressure. It is, however, necessary to highlight that Christians and Muslims exhibited different approaches to this issue, which illustrate their different positions in society. Christians to a larger extent engaged in the ambiguity of this search for proximity to Muslims, whereas for Muslims it was an efficient way to improve their position and stake their claims for leadership. This entailed a moderation of their attitude that was further enhanced by their fear of *fitna*, whose limits I will explore in the next chapter. For Christians, in particular the Greek Orthodox in Lebanon and Christians in Jordan, the search for proximity was coupled with a subtle yet powerful means to pressure Muslims to live up to what Islam supposedly embodied. It is noteworthy that religious references were made without forsaking Christian religious values.

5

THE CORE OF PEACEFUL RELATIONS: RITUALS OF SOLIDARITY AND AVOIDANCE

Introduction

So far, this study has shown how many Muslim and Christian figures, including non-institutional lay Christian and Islamist figures, engaged in the controversy to pursue their personal interests and, at the same time, materialised Christian–Muslim relations. Some claimed to embody the moderate voice of Islam (official Islam, the Hashimite monarchy), others sought proximity with local Christians (*al-Gamā'a al-Islāmiyya*, Ahmad al-Asīr, Hezbollah), and yet others expressed proximity to Muslims through a shared Arab identity, while the overall interests actually were to strengthen one's political credentials, one's political and personal position, political equality and the renegotiation of Christian–Muslim relations. Proximity was thus a key ingredient of inter-communal relations.

But the corollary of this search for proximity was avoidance, denial, silence and highly ritualised language and behaviour. In fact, except for the Egyptian Salafi organisation *al-Da'wa al-Salafiyya*, Fādī Yūsuf of the Coptic youth organisation Coalition of Egypt's Copts and the Greek Orthodox Bishop George Khodr, hardly anyone had seen the video. The reactions were thus often merely based on the idea of an offence and used repetitive, ritualised language. Both Christians and Muslims used terms such as *isā'a* (offence, harm) and *izdirā'* (spite) repeatedly, even in a condemnation no longer than one or two sentences only. Consequently, Christian condemnations, in particular those by the Churches in Lebanon, seemed at times *pro forma* rather than genuine condemnations of 'The Innocence of Muslims'. Quite often it was unclear what the condemnation was about. These reactions could all too easily be dismissed as shallow and repetitive – mere rituals.

For Yvonne Yazbek Haddad and Rahel Fischbach, however, rituals constitute one key dimension of inter-religious dialogue in Lebanon[1] – and, as I will show, Christian–Muslim relations in general. It was precisely this level of dialogue and the ritualised condemnations in joint protests and conferences that ensured a de-escalation and encouraged reciprocity. In her analysis of violence during the Lebanese War, Élizabeth Picard notes:

> Throughout the centuries these societies not only developed avoidance behaviour coded by highly subtle customs, but they are capable of inverting or controlling the effects of hostile relations by rules of hospitality, asylum, and, more generally, neighbourhood, whose security virtues compete with those of armed protection.[2]

In this chapter, I want to make a further-reaching claim than simply a mere description of one dimension of Christian–Muslim relations: rituals and avoidance did, in fact, have tremendous implications. It was precisely by avoiding, denying and engaging in rituals that enabled these societies to avoid a violent backlash against Christians and also allowed for all of these actors – both Christians and Muslims – to exert the full potential of their agency. For Christians, it was rituals in various forms that enabled them to put additional pressure on Muslims. For Muslim figures, in particular the Egyptian Muslim Brotherhood, rituals meant that, through a series of manoeuvres, they were able to get around the limits put on their agency (discussed in Chapter One) and instead to re-join the political game. Third, a tacit element of rituals is reciprocity – that is, reciprocated acknowledgement or value of rituals, offences, feasts and equality. I will thus test the limits of Islamist moderation discussed in the previous chapter.

My argument runs counter general assumptions about agency, most often seen as unfolding in subversion, outspoken language and antagonising action. As Saba Mahmood notes, there is a 'tendency among scholars to look at expressions and moments of resistance'.[3] Following her vision, agency is 'not simply [as] a synonym for resistance to social norms but [. . .] a modality of action'[4] – or, in the present case, speaking and acting in an ambiguous way.

I will first explore rituals of reciprocity through language, followed by behaviour, then thirdly digress on the issue of Christmas – a footnote that really highlights what is at stake with rituals. Finally, I will look at claims of national unity as a ritual to exert pressure.

Ritualised and Avoidant Language: Rituals of Solidarity

The outcry over 'The Innocence of Muslims' was about something nobody had seen and hardly anyone had named. If it were not for the context, it would have been unclear what the condemnations – whether elaborate or in the form of only one sentence – were about. Of all those reacting, only three actors stated that they had actually watched the video and discussed its content. Moreover, the video was very rarely mentioned by its title, but usually referred to as 'the offending film', or simply 'the offence'.

This repetitive, seemingly shallow language has greater implications, however. Ritualisation comprised not only the level of language (to be discussed in the present section) but also behaviour (see next section). The use of words such as *isā'a* (offence, harm) and *izdirā'* (spite), almost *ad nauseum*, should not hide the fact that it was a tool for both Christians and Muslims to put pressure on the other community. However, it suggested solidarity while also entailing expectations of reciprocity. For Christians, the condemnation of offences targeting Islam *entailed* the expectation towards Muslims that they would condemn offences targeting Christianity – no matter who committed it. The Council of Churches in Jordan expressed it as follows: 'If Muhammad was for all Arabs, then all Arabs are for Muhammad'.[5]

The Coptic Orthodox Church has often been criticised for this ritualised language, criticisms which are often met with denial. As mentioned in Chapter Two, the term *fitna tā'ifiyya* to refer mostly to violence against Copts, is a prime example of this ritualised language of avoidance. Yet, the late Coptic Orthodox Patriarch Shinūda III rejected the term altogether, affirming in the 1990s that 'Egypt does not have a sectarian problem. Muslims and Christians share a long history [. . . and] you cannot distinguish between the Copt and the Muslim'.[6] This comment marked a clear shift from the earlier stance of Shinūda III. When a Coptic church was burnt in 1952, the then priest wrote: 'The burning is nothing new for us, our history [of] persecution is full of such examples concerning abomination and cruelty. Christianity in Egypt has been walking a narrow path throughout the generations since the martyrdom of the apostle Mark'.[7] When he was elected patriarch, Shinūda III initially adopted an attitude antagonising President al-Sadat for Egypt's Islamist turn and was exiled, but after President Mubarak had welcomed him back, the patriarch supported the regime, realising that '[t]his non-confrontational attitude allowed the Pope to gain significant access to the executive and gave him leeway to approach officials about issues dear to the Church'.[8] But this was not an attitude of mere denial or submission, as his comment on the term *fitna tā'ifiyya* might suggest. Instead of using outspoken language, he invested in rituals and came to 'master the art of signify anger and sadness'.[9] Following violent clashes between the police and Coptic protesters in al-Umraniyya in November 2010 (see Chapter Three), Shinūda III retreated to the monasteries of the Wadi al-Natrun to obtain the release of 133 imprisoned Copts.[10] This is how we should understand his call to his flock to pray and fast following the Maspero Massacre in October 2011. But after 2011 there was a clear shift; the Coptic Orthodox Church continued to resort to these seemingly apolitical rituals, whereas the young Coptic activists chose to forsake them and rejected this ritualised language and behaviour. They refused to comply with the patriarch's call and did not cancel a march on the fortieth day after the Maspero massacre, when they marched from St Mark's Cathedral in al-Abassiya to Tahrir Square.[11] Thus, in September 2012 there clearly occurred a clash between these two types of approaches. While the Coptic Orthodox Church under Bishop Bākhūmyūs continued to resort to ritualisation, the young Coptic associations were much more outspoken, a stance to be explored further in this chapter.

For some Christian figures in the region, condemning 'The Innocence of Muslims' was therefore an opportunity to connect it to offences targeting Christian content and symbols. As mentioned in Chapter Two, the Churches and clerics used exactly the same language and arguments as when facing *The Da Vinci Code*, *Jesus Christ Superstar*, or the novel *Azazeel*. For the Churches in Egypt, *The Da Vinci Code* by the American author Dan Brown seemed to 'despise religion and its spiritual and moral values'.[12] The film was viewed as 'propagat[ing] Zionist thought'. According to Bishop Athanāsyūs, both *The Da Vinci Code* and the offending video shared the same goal: 'a battle between humanity'.[13] It is noteworthy that this sharp criticism does include perceived offences against Christianity by an Egyptian Muslim author. Bishop Bishoy of Damietta and Kafr al-Shaykh, known for his controversial positions,[14] published a 300-page-long refutation of the novel *Azazeel* and sent out a call to Muslims: 'Do Muslims in Egypt agree with the distortion of the Islamic religion and creed and its religious symbols in early times by means of lies in form of a novel which, at its end, calls for the denial of the existence of God and Satan?'[15]

Similarly, in September 2012, Christianity was swiftly targeted, too, as was mentioned above with regard to the burning of a copy of the Gospel by the Salafi preacher Abū Islām. There was therefore a clear expectation on the Christian part towards Muslims to condemn this. In his declaration to *al-Ahrām* on 22 September 2012, Bishop Bākhūmyūs began by repeating the Church's condemnation of the video and its solidarity with Muslims, but went on to condemn harshly the 'disgraceful act' of the burning of the Bible by 'Abū Islām'.[16] In doing so, the bishop used the discourse of national unity: '[t]his does not serve our religious and national causes'. Quite interestingly, in appealing to 'political and religious forces' to take the necessary measures so as to prevent new backlashes against Christians and Christianity, he 'Islamised' Christianity 'to stop these attacks on religions, their symbols, their sacred items and their revealed books (*kutubihā al-samāwiyya*)'. In short, the Bible, especially the Gospels, were defined as 'revealed books' like the Qur'an, which is not quite accurate. In doing so, Bishop Bākhūmyūs was attempting to make the Bible worthy of respect and to protect it from Islamist and Salafi forces. Yet even before 'The Innocence of Muslims' gained wider relevance, Nādir Bakkār of the Nur Party expressed the need to enshrine the criminalisation of blasphemy in the new constitution in a speech at a conference on 10 September 2012. Bakkār explained: 'For example, if a Muslim exposes the Lord Christ (*al-sayyid al-Masīh*) to foulness', this was considered a crime under Islamic rule, because it is not 'permissible to offend any of the prophets sent by God'.[17] Such an article of criminalisation was justified, according to Nādir Bakkār, by the very nature of Egypt, as the country 'of the noble al-Azhar and of the Egyptian Church'.

This allows us to go further than in Chapter Two, which highlighted how both Muslims and Christians proceeded to create a hierarchy of the targets' value. While offending religious symbols attracted more condemnation than targeting the families of the video's makers, there were higher stakes here. Paradoxically, the issue of religion is wrought the most with denial and avoidance. This level of dialogue is the most difficult, according to George Sabra.[18]

Yet, the position of the Coptic Orthodox bishops, in particular the example of Bākhūmyūs concerning 'The Innocence of Muslims' or of Bishop Bishoy concerning *Azazeel*, suggests that, on the contrary, religion is an area where negotiating Christian–Muslim relations is possible and where, crucially, most pressure for the sake of reciprocity – and thus equality – is possible. For if solidarity when Islam is offended implies reciprocity when Christianity is targeted, then Islam and Christianity are to be defended and protected *equally* – in short, they are *equal*. The comment by Nādir Bakkār above initially supports this idea. By the same token, this trickles down to the followers of these religions: Christians and Muslims. Strikingly, we touch on the very element preventing full equality between Christians and Muslims for Islamists and Salafis: a person's *Christian* belonging.

Behaviour and the Expectation of Reciprocity

Besides language and expressions of reciprocity, ritualisation also included actions and behaviour. As for discourse, this level implied the expectation of reciprocity. In this regard, the way in which the controversy unfolded reveals the tremendous amount of pressure that both Muslim and Christian actors were able to exert on the other community. This section will show how useful rituals are for Muslim actors, too. On the one hand, like Christians, they engaged in rituals as a way to pressure Christians to endorse their stance. On the other hand, engaging in these rituals allowed Muslim actors – in particular, the Muslim Brotherhood in Egypt – to get around the limits imposed on their agency, as discussed in Chapter One, and came to play a prominent role once again. Strikingly, all of this happened in a non-institutional framework. Instead, rituals entirely rested on personal relations – including between Churches and Islamist figures – that materialised in September 2012, despite the upheavals of the Arab Spring.

Joint protests in south Lebanon against 'The Innocence of Muslims' illustrated how Islamist actors recognized the benefit of Christian–Muslim rituals and used them to pressurise Christians into displays of solidarity. Since the Civil War, Christian–Muslim relations have deteriorated in southern Lebanon, a mainly Shi'i area that also includes a large number of Sunni and various Christian communities. In the turmoil of the Civil War in the 1970s, Israel had taken three Christian villages (among them Rmeich), from which the Israeli army put pressure on Bint Jbeil, and Bint Jbeil's invasion and destruction by Israel led to a massive exodus of the population.[19] This area remained under occupation by Israel and the Southern Lebanese army until 2000. The city of Bint Jbeil and its surroundings were particularly affected by the Civil War and the war against Israel in 2006.

During the controversy in 2012, joint Christian–Muslim protests took place in Tyre, Nabatieh, Hasbaya and Arkoub. The Hezbollah/Amal protest in Bint Jbeil on 22 September 2012 gathered lower-ranking Christian clerics; Father Bāsīl Nāsif, the head of the Maronite monastery of the Lady of the Annunciation; Father Shukr Allāh Shūfānī, the dean of Kaslik University, section Rmeich; and Father Maryūs Khayr Allāh, the priest of the Greek Catholic parish in Ayn Ibl and Yaroun.[20] The participation of Christian representatives from the villages of Rmeich and Ayn Ibl in this protest is extremely significant, as the University of Kaslik played a leading role in formulating a more militant vision of Maronitism during the Civil War.[21] As a result, unsurprisingly, the two MPs ʻAlī Bazzī of the Amal Movement and Nawwāf al-Mūsawī of Hezbollah emphasised the unity of this area in their speeches. ʻAlī Bazzī stated that this area was 'one village in unity, faith and love, in the power and defence of the pride of Lebanon, of its dignity, and sovereignty'. To some extent, the speech of MP Nawwāf al-Mūsawī expressed a sense of expectation towards Christians to show solidarity. Given that the day before that protest, 'we' were at a Christian mass, on that day they were defending Islam.[22]

This ritualisation quickly materialised into joint reactions and thus displays of unity that needed no further institutionalisation – despite the upheavals of the Arab Spring. The attempted storming of the US embassy in Cairo occurred on 11 September 2012; only three days later, on Friday, 14 September 2012, joint Christian–Muslim actions were already taking place. As mentioned earlier, the bishop of Giza, Theodosius, sent nearly a hundred Coptic demonstrators to a protest that started at a mosque in al-Muhandisin.[23] He also sent delegations from three parishes to the same or another protest organised by the Muslim Brotherhood, in which Salafi youths and members of *al-Gamāʻa al-Islāmiyya* also participated.[24] In Lebanon, on Sunday, 16 September 2012, Hezbollah leader Hasan Nasr Allāh announced a series of protests to start the following day, which were then joined by high-ranking Christian religious and lay people. Few of these reactions relied on a permanent institution or body for

Christian–Muslim relations. They were the fruit of political alliances, as well as interactions grounded in ritualised or personal relations.

The fact that in many of the joint Christian–Muslim reactions in Egypt – often initiated by Coptic Orthodox bishops – the Muslim Brotherhood constituted the 'Islamic' contingent (more so than al-Azhar, which only participated in the event in Nag Hammadi) shows the flexibility of Christian–Muslim relations, despite or rather *alongside* their ritualised dimensions. Paradoxically, the Coptic Orthodox Church contributed to the re-integration of the Muslim Brotherhood into the controversy, after the latter initially had to scale back its mobilisation. Although the late Patriarch Shinūda III had repeatedly warned against an upcoming Islamist accession to power, which was the main reason for his opposition to the 25 January 2011 Revolution, the Church as a whole displayed a significant capacity for adaptation in the way in which it adapted to the new political circumstances. In particular, Bishop Būlā of Tanta (and speaker of the Church) was known for his fairly good relations with the Muslim Brotherhood and Salafi leaders, and thus his nomination as the representative of the Coptic Orthodox Church in the constituent assembly caused anger among the Copts.[25] The bishop organised a conference (mentioned in Chapter Two) that attracted the governor of Gharbiyya, as well as members of the Freedom and Justice Party and several other political actors.[26]

Before closing this section, it is worth noting that Christians very much used these rituals to pursue their interests as well. In Suez, a Catholic delegation comprised of the Coptic Catholic bishop and two Latin priests used a visit to the governor on 4 October 2012 to assert Christian–Muslim unity and to ask him for sustained contact.[27] In his speech during the Hezbollah/Amal protest in Bint Jbeil, MP Nawwāf al-Mūsawī made a casual comment with significant implications for Christian–Muslim relations: he mentioned the presence of this Islamist party at a Christian mass the day before. In fact, this constitutes a test of the willingness of Islamist and Salafi movements to fully engage in Christian–Muslim relations after the Arab Spring.

Excursus: The Issue of Christmas

Chapter Four has addressed the consistent effort of *al-Gamāʻa al-Islāmiyya* throughout the controversy to display proximity to local Christians. For *al-Gamāʻa al-Islāmiyya*, like al-Asīr, Hezbollah and the Egyptian Muslim

Brotherhood, this was a valuable means to prove their position. Yet, this search for proximity necessarily extended to include a number of rituals, such as displaying solidarity when religious symbols and contents were offended. As discussed above, both Christians and Muslims engaged in these rituals with a level of expectation towards the other community. These rituals, however, include the religious feasts of each community. The post-Arab Spring period marked a novelty in that Islamists in Egypt, including the Muslim Brotherhood, which had just entered politics, started to engage in such rituals officially.

Religious feasts such as Christmas, Easter and *iftār* are a key dimension of Christian–Muslim relations. As mentioned in the introduction to this chapter, for Yvonne Yazbeck Haddad and Rachel Fischbach this constitutes one significant level of relations – that is, '[t]he ritualistic and ceremonial interfaith dialogue model, in which religious leaders participate in each other's religious ceremonies, or laypeople collaborate in organizing their religious festivities, such as *iftār* dinners, and so on'.[28]

The willingness to attend Christmas services and to extend wishes for Christmas and Easter was pivotal, because it implied a certain respect for Christian practices on the Muslims' part. Also, the social pressure to do so was undeniable. In addition to Amal Khoury's description, this ritual possesses a valuable political and symbolic potential which helped to increase the political credentials of Islamists – and is, as demonstrated earlier, connected to a visible search for proximity to Christians. But this level of inter-communal relations and dialogue has larger social and political implications in terms of defining consequences for Christians. Beyond the claims of moderation by Islamist and Salafis, their willingness to extend their wishes for Christmas or Easter and to attend religious celebrations reveal their core attitudes after the Arab Spring towards Christians – Christians as fellow citizens, or Christians as infidels.

There are two ways to look at this issue. One is seeing it as part of traditional social practices. In this regard, Catherine Mayeur-Jaouen highlights a 'marked decline in the traditional exchanges of greeting between neighbors or acquaintances that once took place on the main feast days of both religions'.[29] But it also has a political, *realpolitik* dimension that is more consequential here. At the end of the 1990s, Patriarch Shinūda described this in the following way: 'When the tradition began of inviting [Muslims] to the *iftar* celebration at dusk during Ramadan, the idea spread to all corners of [Egypt . . .]. People sit together in a spirit of love, exchanging understandings, mixing together, living together'.[30] This implies a clear distinction between these two religions, recognizing Christianity as Christianity, valuing Islam as Islam. Thus, I think, it is more useful to consider it as part of a larger political shift starting in the nineteenth century to redefine the status of Christians within the Islamic realm, removed from the derogatory attitude emanating from a supremacist kind of Islam (see Chapters Four and Five). As Heather Sharkey notes, Sultan Abdulmajid, under whose rule the 1856 *Hatt-i Hümayun* was issued, started attending Christian feasts, such as a Greek Orthodox wedding, in the 1850s.[31] At the same time, the issue grew increasingly controversial within Salafi circles, which have constantly called on fellow Muslims not to extend wishes or attend Christian religious feasts. In 2007, *al-Daʿwa al-Salafiyya* issued a fatwa forbidding Muslims from extending wishes to Christians for their religious festivities.[32] By contrast, official Islam – al-Azhar and the mufti – have consistently fought against Salafi pressure and religiously sanctioned this practice. It is noteworthy that 7 January has been a national holiday in Egypt since 2003.[33] However, this is an issue primarily in Egypt. By contrast, in the wider Middle East, Muslim figures have long since discovered and made use of the advantages of the proximity to Christians. On his path to empower the Shiʿi Lebanese community, Musa Sadr relied on the symbolic representation of his proximity to Christians, such as preaching in a church with a crucified Jesus Christ behind him.[34]

In Egypt, after the Arab Spring, the issue of exchanging wishes developed into a controversy ahead of the Coptic Christmas celebrations in January 2012. The Muslim Brotherhood was highly divided on the issue. For the first time, on invitation of Patriarch Shinūda III, it sent a high-ranking delegation to the Coptic Orthodox cathedral, but it was careful to leave before the actual liturgy started.[35] However, at Easter in April 2013, ʿAbd al-Rahman al-Birr issued a fatwa, forbidding Muslims from extending wishes, whereas ʿIsām al-ʿAryān from the FJP wished Christians a happy Easter on his Facebook page.[36] In the meantime, Mursī's controversial decision regarding the constituent assembly had antagonised large parts of Egyptian society, including the Coptic Orthodox Church, which had withdrawn from the assembly. *Al-Daʿwa al-Salafiyya* and *al-Gamāʿa al-Islāmiyya* refused to extend wishes. Yāsir Burhāmī, deputy secretary of *al-Daʿwa al-Salafiyya*, claimed that 'the pious forefathers forbade extending wishes to the unbelievers for their festivities which are connected to dogmatic matters, like the birth of Christ or his death and crucifixion because they comprise the endorsement of the correctness of a corrupted creed'.[37] Al-Birr conveyed the same idea when he justified his rejection of wishing people Happy Easter: '[T]he Qur'an provides no proof for celebrating Easter because Jesus was not crucified'.[38] These are all references to *tahrīf*, the idea that Christians have corrupted the revelation that they received (see Chapter Four). Thus, despite the comments of moderation and the willingness to engage in some aspects of reciprocity (such as offences against religious symbols), the Nur Party and *al-Gamāʿa al-Islāmiyya* had not forsaken their fundamental attitude towards Christian Egyptians whom they still vilified and considered to be infidels and polytheists.

Yet, for Christians, this type of ritual is very important because it proves to them the extent to which the Muslim side regards Christians as equally valuable. It is noteworthy that the Coptic Orthodox Church published in its magazine *al-Kirāza* in May 2012 a long list of all the parties, politicians and other actors (professional associations) who had extended Easter wishes.[39] Yet, the Christian leadership also discerned the political and symbolic benefit of attending Muslim feasts, as suggested by the comment of Patriarch Shinūda III above. All in all, however, actors of official Islam were very outspoken against the Salafi stance. In January 2013, the Egyptian Mufti ʿAlī Gumʿa defined Christmas as follows: '[T]he birth of Christ, peace be upon him, has always been and will always be a birth of goodness, peace and mercy, not only for our Christian brothers, but for Muslims and the whole of humankind everywhere'.[40] Nevertheless, for Salafis the existence of Christian religious feasts and, worse, attending and celebrating them posed a threat to Muslims' piety and to their very Islamic identity. Muslims should therefore avoid any contact with Christians. However, for al-Azhar this constituted a threat to Egypt's social fabric. ʿAbd al-Majīd Hāmid Subh wrote in *Majallat al-Azhar* during the Christmas controversy:

> And we say: realising the truth and stating Islamic sharīʿa in word and deed [...] as it means brotherhood in faith connecting the Muslim with his Muslim brother, it also means brotherhood in humanity, connecting humankind, as it also means brotherhood in the nation, connecting the children of the one nation with their different creeds.[41]

Thus, for all these Muslim actors, Christian–Muslim relations were intimately connected with the question of politics, personal interests and the nation – crucially, just as they were for Christians.

A Powerful Ritual: The United Egyptian Nation

Finally, the idea of nation has come to the forefront. Before discussing its political implications in Chapter Six, this final section will discuss claims of national unity, in particular Egyptian national unity, as a ritual allowing Christians to exert pressure on Muslims. This contradicts earlier scholarship on Egyptian nationalism, which highlights it as void, empty and a diversion from the actual problems affecting Copts. Yet, the controversy highlighted how, by engaging differently with this narrative, the Coptic Orthodox Church and the young Coptic activists were able to build varying degrees of effective pressure.

The narrative of Egyptian national unity has attracted greater scholarly attention than the narratives of Lebanese or Jordanian national unity.[42] One reason behind this interest is that, historically, a sense of Egyptian nationhood developed earlier on, in connection with the emergence of the modern state from an Ottoman province to a khedival state under British occupation. After the monarchy was overthrown in 1952, as the Jews, Greeks and Syro-Lebanese left, Egypt turned to a Coptic–Muslim 'face-à-face' 'with a strong tendency, on both sides, for monolithic and totalising visions'.[43] Copts and Muslims have both accepted this narrative. The issue at stake is the terms of the social contract.[44] For Vivian Ibrahim, it has been a key element in making Christians 'invisible': '[A]ll Copts and all Muslims are assumed to have a shared an "authentic" [sic] experience of "Egyptian-ness". Yet this narrative denies the Copts, or any other faction be it religious or class based, self-agency to promote a different version of events'.[45]

In September 2012, the nature of the Egyptian nation was a matter of ongoing heated discussion. Crucially, there was no strong state that would monopolise the discussions. Although unity was promoted by a broad range of both Christian and Muslim figures, some did not buy into it.

The Coptic Orthodox Church adhered to the narrative of national unity, enshrined in an inherent difference. While its representatives framed it with the usual 'vagueness and ritualistic character',[46] the young Coptic organisations and activists approached it more critically. The Church used the usual tropes and images associated with this narrative – shared values, shared history, biological unity – using repeated slogans, such as the Holy Synod's description of the Muslims as 'partners in the nation and humanity' and Bishop Bisantī's 'we are one people' who only differ in prayer.[47] The systematic differentiation between Christians and Muslims elaborated here in the same 'fabric', yet different 'places of worship', is important and basic to the Christians' Egyptianness: 'Our Coptism teaches us the preservation of the feelings of our partners in the nation',[48] claimed Bishop Mūsā, the bishop for the youth. The secretary general of the Coalition of Egypt's Copts, Fādī Yūsuf, justified the participation of his organisation at the protests at the US embassy on 11 September 2012 in similar, ritualistic terms: the need to counter the video with a 'true national unity between the children of the Egyptian people, Muslims and Christians', otherwise it would divide the two religions.[49]

Many Muslim figures likewise accepted this narrative, including representatives of official Islam. In his interview with *al-Ahrām*, Muftī 'Alī Gum'a asserted: 'The brotherly relations between the children of the united nation, Muslims and Christians, are governed by respect and mutual brotherhood. They grow in firmness and strength, generation after generation, and have become a model followed as an example in all states of the world'.[50] Similarly, the newly elected president, Muhammad Mursī, in a statement published on 12 September 2012, one day after the failed storming of the US embassy in Cairo, said that 'the Egyptian people, [in] its Muslims and Christians, have already rejected this attack on sacred items'.[51] The FJP asserted that 'the Egyptian people in its two components, Muslims and Copts, was, continues to and will remain united against these mean attempts'.[52]

The Egyptian media carried this narrative, reinforcing the idea of unity between Christians and Muslims, enshrined in a systematic differentiation. In the case of the governorate of Minya, *al-Masrī al-Yawm* reported that roughly 300 people and 100 Copts joined a march with banners reading: 'No to the offence of Muslim brothers'.[53] In reports of the second statement of the Coptic Orthodox Church on the video, the media emphasised the solidarity expressed by the Church: the description of Muslims as 'partners in the nation and humanity' was widely quoted, including in *al-Masrī al-Yawm*[54] and *al-Shurūq* on 11 September 2012.[55] The Church's *'abnā' al-watan al-wāhid'* – may it be 'a high offence for Islam, its noble Prophet and the children of the united nation' – was quoted in *al-Ahrām* on September 12.[56]

Beyond the surface of this repetitive and ritualistic narrative, however, there were subtler issues. For one thing, despite all its repetitiveness and seemingly insincere reliance on it, the Coptic Orthodox Church nonetheless pressured the issue and discussed who was in fact legitimately Egyptian. Ahead of the urgent meeting of the Coptic Orthodox Church, the Salafi Front, which had caused it, sent a report to the general prosecutor, comprising a list of three clerics, among them the bishop of Los Angeles, Bishop Serapion, as well as six other persons, allegedly involved in the making of 'The Innocence of Muslims'.[57] In response, a restricted Holy Synod met on Friday 21 September 2012.[58] At the subsequent press conference, the Church's spokesman, Bishop Būlā, rejected all accusations against the three clerics and accused the Salafi Front, which levered accusations of being enemies of the Egyptian nation: '[W]e completely reject the attempts at slander between the children of the united nation and the spread of discord [. . .] they are the enemies of our nation in which we have lived for fourteen centuries, crushing the most conscious example of unity'.[59] Similarly, Bishop Bākhūmyūs condemned the burning of a copy of the Bible by 'Abū Islām' (without naming him) as a 'disgraceful act', declaring: 'These matters do not serve our religious and national causes'.[60] By contrast, on 10 September 2012, the coordinator of the Coptic youth organisation Copts Without Restrictions formulated this criticism in more outspoken terms, vilifying what he called the 'double standards' of Egyptian society. He asked: 'Why are these voices not raised to condemn the more extremist positions of institutions and media trumpets in Egypt against the Christians, their sacred items and symbols?'[61] Similarly, during the events leading to the Maspero Massacre in October 2011, the MYU drew attention to a sectarian incident in southern Egypt, accusing the governor of Aswan and Salafi leadership of fuelling the violence, something that the Salafi Front countered with a reference to 'the Nazarene extremists [who] rapidly increased the issue in the media'.[62]

Conclusion

Through several examples of rituals, this chapter has demonstrated just how far-reaching such rituals of reciprocity can be. They bore so much authority because their opposite – that is, *fitna*, or strife – evoked so much fear. The corollary of rituals was an expectation of reciprocity in which *al-Daʿwa al-Salafiyya* and *al-Gamāʿa al-Islāmiyya* were not willing to engage, despite their claims of moderation, while on the Christian side some were able to cast doubt on the former's loyalty to the nation. We thus have reached a point where the controversy was used as an occasion for renegotiating the terms of Christian–Muslim relations.

6

RENEGOTIATING THE PROMISES OF THE ARAB SPRING

Introduction

The preceding chapters have gradually brought greater clarity to the understanding of Muslim and Christian motivations during this controversy. Besides the desire to promote themselves, many of the Christian reactions to 'The Innocence of Muslims' expressed a desire for equality. As for Islamists, the controversy illustrated their uneven political maturity since, in their desire to defend Islam, some actually antagonised local Christians (especially the Nur Party), whereas others managed to incorporate them into their responses (Hezbollah, Ahmad al-Asīr, *al-Gamāʿa al-Islāmiyya*). As the chapters have progressed, the book has touched on the deeper layers of the controversy: underneath the official condemnations and joint mobilisations, beyond the subtle rituals and the careful and avoidant language, there were ambiguous reactions and actions. Thus, even though, say, the Coptic Orthodox bishops may not have elaborated a clear political vision or made calls for equality, the use of ritualised language was grounded in an expectation of reciprocity leading towards equality.

This chapter is concerned with the visions of Christian–Muslim relations as visions of polity and the question of the extent to which full equality was deemed possible for all these actors. This chapter takes the various questions of the previous chapters as a starting point for discussion. First, when condemning the video, claims of unity between Christians and Muslims were formulated in ways that often mingled religious, political and national references. I will explicate who made such claims and how they connected these three types of references. Second, the Coptic Orthodox Church as well as Christian Jordanians and Greek Orthodox figures all actually carved out a similar position of negotiation with Muslims: they claimed unity and proximity to Muslims through differentiation – that is, by positioning themselves as Christians as the foundation for a new social contract. In this chapter, I will explore the risks of this differentiation, along with the reasons for this choice. Third, the comment by ʿAbd al-Majīd Ḥāmid Subh at the end of the previous chapter echoes Christian strategies to a certain extent:

> And we say: realising the truth and stating Islamic sharīʿa in word and deed [. . .] as it means brotherhood in faith connecting the Muslim with his Muslim brother, it also means brotherhood in humanity connecting humankind, as it also means brotherhood in the nation connecting the children of the one nation with their different creeds.[1]

This raises the question of the ontological continuity within Christian–Muslim relations between their religious, national and political dimensions. For the Egyptian Salafis, the Christians' political status was predicated on their theological status, whereas the connection that may exist in a national context did not translate into political equality. By contrast, for other actors, ideas of equality were possible in all circumstances.

Writing this chapter presented difficulties, because all the tension and expectation of reciprocity building up so far would presumably lead us to clear visions of political Christian–Muslim relations that would vary depending on how the various actors engaged with mechanisms of Christian–Muslim relations, one may think. However, once one has reached the issue of polity, they do not quite fit the connection, and the vision is not clear. Also, on a political level, other issues have been more extensively discussed, such as the political role of the Coptic Orthodox Church. These issues mean that it is difficult to connect the present chapter to the existing literature.

Discussions about the political terms of Christian–Muslim relations have, for the most part, been precisely that: *political* discussions with references to the religious, more specifically Islamic, nay Islamist underpinnings, whenever they came up.² These have often been discussions in terms of 'tolerance', 'citizenship' and 'democracy',³ an approach that may not have been that useful, as Rachel Scott concedes: the 'concept of citizenship – in a variety of manifestations and interpretations – has been broadly – and readily – embraced: Islamist ideology, for example, has shown an impressive flexibility at internalising – and naturalising – the concept of citizenship'.⁴ However, as Chapter Five has shown, the possibility of equality does not always take the road of 'tolerance' or citizenship but quite often manifests itself in ambiguous social and religious rituals of reciprocity. The present chapter aims to look at the political implications of these rituals. All these difficulties may be another argument backing the concept of ambiguity, the idea of *at the same time*.

I will first reconsider the Arab Spring. The chapter will then proceed with the question of whether a political system should include Christians as Christians and Muslims as Muslims. Is a religious characteristic sufficient to establish the inherent difference between Christians and Muslims? I will then go on to explore the national, religious and political foundations of unity.

Old and New Fears

In theory, there was no need for a renegotiation of Christian–Muslim relations as, according to the constitutions of these countries, all citizens were equal already. Egypt was in the midst of producing a new constitution. But the reactions betrayed a sense of uncertainty and dissatisfaction on the part of the Christians, especially in the context of the Arab Spring.

Although this period was hailed with much hope, there was also resistance and fear of change. Its uncertain consequences had attracted initial condemnation by the Churches in Egypt. Bishop Murqus of Shubra al-Khayma, near Cairo, said: 'We do not know the goal of these protests, nor the details, nor who is behind it'.⁵ The Coptic Orthodox Church only issued a statement praising the 'revolution of the youth' on 15 February, one day after the departure of Mubarak.⁶ As mentioned earlier, after the revolution, Shinūda III continued to express his fears by listing all the assaults on Coptic individuals and churches in *al-Kirāza*.⁷ In contrast, the magazine issued by the Coptic Catholic Church, *al-Salāh*, criticised the 'production of fear' in connection with the reportedly high figure for Coptic emigration following the 2011 revolution, allegedly aimed at emptying Egypt of its Copts.⁸ Later on, the

Coptic Catholic patriarch Antūnyūs Naguīb expressed his praise of the revolution, which 'revealed a new image of the Christians; full of energy, boldness, perseverance'.⁹ These fears were not far-fetched, as Islamist and Salafi forces quickly made significant political gains and the controversy over 'The Innocence of Muslims' showed how quickly Coptic Egyptians could come under suspicion and be pressured to prove their loyalty. Unsurprisingly, for Muhammad Badīʿ the reason for 'The Innocence of Muslims' rested in its timing: the 'hate against the revival of humanity, spiritual vigilance, and the emergence of the Arab Spring which again calls for the return of Islam; a model for life and a message of light'.¹⁰ The fear of an Islamist takeover was also to be found among the figures of official Islam, as Mufti ʿAlī Gumʿa asserted the need for a moderate Islam (see Chapter Three).

When al-Azhar convened representatives of various religious and political forces for a discussion of Egypt's future in June 2011, its final statement affirmed its task in 'preserving [Islamic principles] from misuse by various deviant movements who have already raised the religious, sectarian or ideological banner [. . .] and contradicted the essence of Islam in terms of liberty, justice and equality'.¹¹ Dominique Avon asserts that the key motivation behind this initiative was to 'rehabilitate an institution that had been discredited by its silence [concerning the revolution] six months earlier and establish it as "the sole relevant authority representing a reference in Islamic matters"'.¹²

Fear of instability and Islamisation also affected Christians in countries where the Arab Spring had no or almost no impact, such as Lebanon and Jordan. The existential threat posed to the Christian presence in Iraq after 2003 had traumatised Christians in the region. As a result, the Maronite Patriarch Bishāra Butrus al-Rāʿī repeatedly expressed his opposition to the 'Arab Spring', motivated by the example of Iraq, where 'democracies have become civil wars and led to the emigration of Christians'.¹³ During a press conference ahead of the visit of Pope Benedict XVI in September 2012, he therefore demanded the separation 'of religion and state in order to secure democracy [. . .] it is not possible to talk of replacing democracy by religious theocratic states'.¹⁴ On that occasion, he also mentioned 'The Innocence of Muslims' very briefly and praised the pope's visit as 'a message against the clash of civilisations'. Fr Antoine Daw, who joined one of the Hezbollah/Amal protests, produced a long comment in *al-Safir*, in which he condemned 'the misuse of religion in political conflict', demanding 'an honest commitment to the Arab Islamic-Christian awakening'.[15] He accused the video of contradicting the teachings and values of Christianity and Islam and of attacking the 'culture of Christian–Muslim brotherhood, living together, the partnership in love and the unity in diversity'.

Even in Christian reactions expressing proximity to Islam, one finds dissatisfaction with how the situation may evolve. The Council of Churches in Jordan ended its statement addressing fellow Muslims with a reference to the 2010 Special Synod for the Middle East:

> Together, we will work on building civil societies founded on citizenship, religious freedom, and the freedom of creed. Together, we will co-operate to strengthen justice, peace, human rights, and the values of life and family. It is (truly) our shared responsibility to build our nations.

This suggests that citizenship, religious freedom and freedom of creed were not fully achieved.

What Level of Differentiation?

Before moving on to reflections on unity, one has to wonder: should a political system include Christians as Christians and Muslims as Muslims? Should religious references and communal belonging feature in any way? Is a religious characteristic sufficient to establish the inherent difference between Christians and Muslims, which would be the basis for narratives of unity? The behaviour of most Christians during the controversy, for example, the Coptic Orthodox or Christian Jordanians, highlighting their Christian belonging, suggests that it is. This is a far cry from the slogan voiced during the 1919 Revolution in Egypt, of *al-dīn li-llāh wa-l-waṭan li-l-jamīʿ* (Religion is for God, the Homeland is for all), and it is even further removed from the claim of the khedive of Egypt, Muḥammad ʿAlī (mentioned in Chapter Four) who affirmed: 'I do not wish there to be any difference between my subjects based on difference of religion, the only difference is the way they pray in their temples'.[16] To a certain extent, this positioning contradicts the founding principle of the modern state, as Saba Mahmood explains:

> Th[e Christians'] enfranchisement was predicated upon their willingness to privatize their Christianity, precisely because their religious difference was

deemed to be inconsequential to their public, political, and legal status. This circumscription of Coptic Christianity to the private domain went hand in hand with the enshrinement of Islam as the collective identity of the nation.[17]

Most of the Christian reactions to the video, however, expressed a desire to establish their difference as Christians as a starting point for any discussion of Christian–Muslim relations and political terms. But there was by no means a consensus regarding the extent to which Egyptians who happened to be Christians were indeed a separate community. The Coptic Catholic Church discussed this issue in an article published in 2012 in its patriarchal magazine, minimising the differences and arguing that Christian Egyptians were not a minority:

> [N]ot in an ethnic sense as in the case of the Kurds of Iraq or the Berbers of the Arab Maghreb, nor in a sectarian sense like the Druze or Armenians in Israel and Lebanon, nor in a religious sense alone, and this is the secret of the Egyptian specificity throughout human experience.[18]

This quote seems a verbatim reproduction of Muhammad Haykal's reflections on the Copts:

> What amazes me and continues to amaze me is that Egypt's Copts cannot be counted among the minorities of the Arab world and the Middle East, neither in an ethnic (*'irqī*) sense, such as the Kurds in Iraq and the Berbers in the Maghreb, nor in a sectarian (*ṭā'ifī*) sense, like the Druze or the Armenians in Israel or Lebanon, not even in a religious sense (*wa-lā bi-l-ma'nā ad-dīnī waḥdihi*). This is the secret of the Egyptian distinctiveness, all along the human history of this land (*waṭan*).[19]

Yet, the Coptic Catholic Church went further, claiming in its article that the term 'Copt', originally from the Greek, started being used by Europeans in the sixteenth century to designate Christian inhabitants of Egypt.[20] The Coptic Catholic Church, which numbers between 300,000 and 400,000 followers,[21] condemned 'The Innocence of Muslims' (see Chapter One), but in a way that differed from the Coptic Orthodox Church, using a more neutral language. As a minority within a minority, the Coptic Catholics are nevertheless part of the global Roman Catholic Church, something that impacts its positioning in Egypt, as evident in the comments quoted here. The Coptic Orthodox Church long considered its Catholic pendant 'betrayers or parias, unfaithful to the Orthodox cause'.[22]

Positing a difference that is too far-reaching between Egypt's Christians and Muslims could have problematic implications for the Copts, as Paul Sedra observes:

> To identify a *Coptic Christian community in Egypt today – one distinct* from the Egyptian national community – is to enter into an intensely political debate. The notions that a distinctly Coptic identity exists, that Copts share a consciousness of their ethnicity, and that referring to the Copts as a community is credible and meaningful, strike at the *core of Egyptian national identity* and, in turn, at the security of the Egyptian state [my emphases].[23]

A distinct 'Coptic' community thus too quickly leads to the idea of a 'minority'. In the context of the West, this term is randomly used to designate the Christian inhabitants of the Middle East, as Cardinal Jean-Louis Tauran did ahead of the visit of Benedict XVI to Lebanon, calling on Christians in the region to remain an 'active minority'.[24] In the Middle East, however, the term is very controversial, and Patriarch Shinūda III opposed its use: 'We are not a minority in Egypt. We do not like to consider ourselves a minority and do not like others to call us a minority'.[25] Similarly, Maronite Bishop Mgr. Chucrallah Nabil al-Hage said:

> [T]he concept of minorities is foreign to our societies [...] the Christians do not constitute minorities in their countries [...]. The concept of minority therefore destroys the Christians' ability to witness the Gospel and craft the Kingdom in their human environment.[26]

The term 'minority' is problematic for several reasons. First, it is historically constructed. Benjamin White argues that it became relevant only in the context of the League of Nations after the First World War, noting that it had no entry in the 1910/11 Encyclopaedia Britannica, but that in the 1929 edition it occupied eleven pages.[27] By contrast, Elizabeth Monier dates its emergence to the last decades of the Ottoman Empire, when 'the need to reformulate

Ottoman collective identity by incorporating non-Muslims on a more equal basis [...] set the stage for the invisibilisation of minority framing or representation in subsequent nation-state projects'.[28] Second, Géraldine Chatelard wonders as 'to which identity norm must be referred to determine a majority [in Jordan]: Islam, Arabism, "Jordanianness", sedentarity?'[29]

As al-Hage's comments suggest, 'minority' is understood in a way that goes beyond international law and resonates with local Christian experiences. As quoted earlier, Bishop Mārūn Lahhām describes Christians in Muslim-majority countries as having a 'minority mentality'. Therefore, by acknowledging a difference between Christians and Muslims, Christians risk ending up as *dhimmī*, something that gained new relevance when Islamists and Salafis entered the political game in Egypt. Although discussions of the *dhimma* had always remained part of Islamist discourses, they now pervaded mainstream discussions, even more so with the drafting of the Egyptian constitution, then underway in September 2012.

Thus, why would Christian figures insist on their distinct Christian identity as much as they did, despite the risks of alienation and minoritisation? There are three responses to this issue. For one, there is a clear generational gap. When the Coptic youth organisation Christian Brothers was founded in July 2012, the former Egyptian MP Gamāl Asʿad and member of an older generation of Coptic activists (or rather activists who happened to be Christian) expressed his worries, seeing it as a dangerous step towards sectarianism in Egypt:

> Such an association is certainly not in the interest of Copts; on the contrary, it benefits radical Islamists promoting a religious state [...] [I]f the Copts aspire to a civilian state based on citizenship, they need to define themselves as Egyptians and not as a Christian minority.[30]

Gamāl Asʿad used the controversy over 'The Innocence of Muslims' to promote his views, claiming on 10 September 2012 on *al-Nahār TV* that the problems faced by Christians in Egypt have nothing to do with religion but are linked to 'social relations with Muslims'; meaning that the 'Islamic stream rules the majority in the street'.[31] At a conference organised by the Association of Lawyers that included Coptic Orthodox Bishop Mārtīrūs, Gamāl

As'ad argued that 'Copts have a right to defend themselves, but in a political framework and not a sectarian one'.³² For figures like Gamāl As'ad, the SSNP and George Ishāq, the acknowledgement of and references to such a difference, especially in the political context, should be kept to a minimum, and the shared national political interests and values should be stressed. Yet, for the Coptic Orthodox Church, and the young generation of Coptic activists who had grown up within its walls, establishing a difference was crucial for negotiating with the Muslims from a position of strength. As Candace Lukasik explains, the young Coptic activists 'demand equality through the expression of a distinctive Coptic identity'.³³ Countering Gamāl As'ad's criticism of the Christian Brothers quoted above, the movement's leader, Mīkhā'īl Fahmī, asserted that its aim was precisely to ground and revive the concept of citizenship.³⁴ During the 25 January 2011 revolution, Coptic participants advertised their presence as Christians by including Christian symbols such as chanting in Coptic.³⁵ In an interview with the author, Minā Magdī explained this overall sectarian approach by noting that Copts 'must ha[ve] people to speak about them, to defend their case and they must be from this group itself, [. . .] we are not a religious group, we are a political group' – the latter referring to the fact that the leader of the political office was a Coptic Catholic.³⁶

Second, the move towards differentiation is also a result of the dynamics of the twentieth century, which explains why Christian Jordanians of all denominations as well as Greek Orthodox have come to insist more strongly on their Christian belonging, despite also avowing their Arabness. Yet, it is precisely this shared Arab identity (or Egyptian nation) which has manifested its shortcomings over recent years and decades. Fiona McCallum explains:

> It was not until Islam was given a more prominent role that Arab nationalism became a populist ideology. [. . .] Consequently, although Islam was a major component in Arab nationalism, the belief that a common language and culture also contributed to Arab identity meant that this nationalist movement provided the first opportunity for Eastern Christians to participate on equal terms with Muslims concerning their political future.³⁷

However, the idea of a secular golden age in Egypt needs to be tempered, as 'simultaneously, the underlying Islamic current in Egyptian politics became prominent once more with the founding of the Muslim Brotherhood in 1928'.[38] In the case of the Greek Orthodox of Lebanon, who have always prided themselves in being able to differentiate between a political national identity and a religious identity – '*Nous sommes d'empire* [...] The Orthodox do not mix their religious affiliation with their civil governance', explained Metropolitan George Khodr[39] – things have changed. During the Civil War, the Greek Orthodox did not form militias (although some did join other communities' militias). In recent years, however, this non-sectarian position has increasingly been questioned. Since the end of the Civil War, the Greek Orthodox have complained about their lack of representation in the confessional system. In 2012, several delegations visited Patriarch Ignatius IV Hāzim and, in cooperation with Lebanese bishops, submitted demands to form an institution that would include former deputies, ministers, officers and former diplomats.[40] This initiative was strongly condemned by the Orthodox Youth Movement, because it would 'entrust the community's affairs to politicians and men of wealth and influence'.[41] Maxilian Felsch offers two reasons to explain this change of heart:

> First, there are no longer any significant secular alternatives to the sectarian system, since pan-Arab movements have declined in favour of pan-Islamic ones; and second – perhaps even more significantly – the Orthodox communities have been major victims of anti-Christian violence in many Arab states since the start of the Arab uprisings.[42]

Similarly, in the case of Jordan, in the context of 'The Innocence of Muslims' Christian figures and organisations did indeed establish their Christian belonging as a starting point from which to promote a narrative of national unity and, in doing so, surprisingly came to use the same discourse of distinction as the Coptic Orthodox, although they usually have different approaches to Muslims. Lise Paulsen Galal's explanation of the Coptic Orthodox Church's assertion of distinctiveness shows how it could work without compromising the claim for full equality:

> As an aspect of identity formation in general, constructions of sameness and difference are, unsurprisingly, simultaneous processes [...], but the interesting issue is how the two narratives interact in practice. How do the Egyptian and

Coptic identities *meet, conflate* and *support each other*, and not simply remain in binary opposition or only become situational identities? [...]. Yet the difference in faith is equally important for the Coptic Orthodox Church in order for it to defend and promote its Christian identity, and in so doing it is negotiating, reconciling, balancing, and mediating the antithetical potentialities of being the same as or different from the national, Muslim majority.[43]

Largely due to a changing regional context, a heightened differentiation between Christians and Muslims was the zeitgeist.

The Egyptian, Lebanese and Jordanian Nations

While Chapter Five has explored Egyptian national unity as a ritual, this chapter is interested in its political implications. I will examine the differences between the claims to Egyptian, Lebanese and Jordanian unity, whether the Christian take on them differed from the Muslim one, and, finally, how national, political and religious references coexisted. Yet, we will see that all three narratives required a third element to make the Christian–Muslim binomial function.

In September 2012, the nature of the Egyptian nation was a matter of ongoing heated discussion. Although unity was promoted by a broad range of both Christian and Muslim figures, the issue was whether Islamist and Salafi figures were willing to fully engage in it, despite the implied equality between Christians and Muslims. For the Coptic Orthodox Church, this was a tool to exert pressure on fellow Muslims. I have demonstrated how it helped Bishop Būlā cast doubt on their loyalty over the Salafi Front. The core element of the Coptic Orthodox' nationalism is its miaphysite faith and the land of Egypt. Candace Lukasik notes:

> Coptic Orthodox Christianity does make a difference, for Copts and some Muslims alike, as it constructs the membership of Copts in the Egyptian nation by virtue of their Christian identity – where Coptic Orthodoxy stands as a faith connected to the land of Egypt, which withstood 'foreign', Byzantine (Roman) persecution and accusations of 'monophysitism' following their dissent to the Council of Chalcedon in 451 AD.[44]

Figures of the Coptic Orthodox Church vividly connect the land of Egypt with Coptic Christianity. Patriarch Shinūda III said in an Al-Jazeera documentary: 'Egypt is not a nation, which we live in. Egypt is a nation, which lives within us'.[45] In reaction to 'The Innocence of Muslims', Bishop Mūsā asserted that 'our Coptism teaches us the preservation of the feelings of our partners in the nation'.[46] Coptic Christianity is the very condition and foundation for coexistence with Muslims. One can find elements of this in comments by the Salafi movement. As mentioned in Chapter Five, Nādir Bakkār described Egypt as the country 'of noble al-Azhar and of the Egyptian Church'.[47] Overall, they seemed to support the narrative of national unity, at least at times. During the parliamentary elections in December 2011, Nur Party spokesman Yusrī Hammād stated: 'The Nur Party's position on Copts is clear and outspoken in considering them partners in the nation; they are an original part of Egypt's sons [...] my right is his right and my destiny is his destiny'.[48] However, *al-Daʿwa al-Salafiyya* rejected the implicit equality conveyed by the narrative of national unity:

> Regarding the term 'national unity': If it means peaceful coexistence and participation in one nation, and that we live together under the shadow of legality (*sharʿ*), then the meaning is good. If it means equality of religious communities (*milal*) and the endorsement of their validity, then the meaning is false and vile.[49]

Discussions about Lebanese national identity have historically been more discussions of Lebanon as a Christian homeland, dominated by Maronite figures who have promoted the idea of Phoenicianism, claiming an origin with the ancient Phoenicians, and who have tried to prove Lebanon's exceptionalism and distinction from the larger Arab environment. After the Civil War, a narrative built on John Paul II's claim that Lebanon was a message of peaceful coexistence gained traction.[50] In the context of 'The Innocence of Muslims', this narrative was not as pervasive as in Egypt and coexisted with the claim of Arab unity, as elaborated in Chapter Four by Greek Orthodox figures. Yet, Muslim figures in particular used this narrative, which relies on the terms *taʿāyush* (coexistence) and *al-ʿaysh al-mushtarak* (shared life),[51] and they connected it to Benedict XVI's visit. The Sunni Mufti Qabbānī, for instance, demanded a national Lebanese response to the video: 'We repeat our call to Muslim and Christian Lebanese to be united in the refusal of offence [...] so that Lebanon remains [a] message and [a] model of coexistence between all religions'.[52] At the Hezbollah/Amal protest in Baalbek, the Maronite Bishop 'Aṭā' Allāh explained that he was participating in this protest as the representative of his parish so that 'Lebanon remains a light for human civilisation'.[53] The minister of agriculture and member of Hezbollah, Husayn al-Ḥājj al-Ḥasan, condemned the video and praised Benedict XVI's visit during an educational event in the Nabatieh province: '[F]rom the viewpoint of the position of original *muhammadian* Islam, of resisting Islam, of Lebanese citizenship (*al-muwātiniyya*), of belonging to the Arab and the Islamic communities (*ummatayn*), from all these positions, our message is that Lebanon is the nation of message (*watan al-risāla*)'.[54] This message was further explained as being one of 'coexistence, love, and living together. It is the nation (*watan*) of resistance against occupation'. In addition, Husayn al-Ḥājj al-Ḥasan defined Lebanon as the 'civilisational and intellectual connection between Islam and Christianity'. But, like the Egyptian narrative, this Lebanese national narrative needed a third element to make it work. And thus, Lebanon was best expressed by what it was *not*: a counter-model to Zionism and Israel. Lebanon is thus an illustration of another function of violence as pointed out by Élizabeth Picard: that is, maintaining the group's cohesion,[55] by pushing the past violence outside the imagined boundaries of Lebanon. Because there was an enemy, Lebanon existed. Druze leader Walid Jumblatt illustrated this well, by saying: 'It is not possible not to make Israel responsible'.[56] The timing of the release during Benedict XVI's visit caused Jumblatt to reflect on Lebanon as a 'diverse democracy in contrast to the monolithic Israeli model'.[57]

In Jordan, a narrative of national unity was exclusively conveyed by Christian Jordanian figures and institutions. It consisted of unity between Christians and Muslims under the leadership of the Hashimite King – here the third element of this equation. The Jordanian case has two unique features. First, this narrative starkly contrasts with previous studies on Jordanian nationalism, in which the status of Jordanians of Palestinian origin is extensively discussed: that was not an issue at all here. Second, Christian Jordanians insisted on the Hashimite monarchy. Previous studies on Jordanian nationalism, such as those by Joseph Massad and Luisa Gandolfo, emphasise the dichotomy between Jordanians of Palestinian and Transjordanian origin, as well as the role that the monarchy has played in cultivating this dichotomy: the 'presence of Palestinians [is] crucial to the emergence of a specific configuration of Jordanian national identity and national culture that became increasingly exclusivist'.[58] Luisa Gandolfo describes Jordan as a '"large extended family", while during periods of crisis the media produces images of Jordan as the small, beleaguered tribe'.[59] In particular, in recent years the idea that Jordan could become a country of 'substitution' (*al-waṭan al-badīl*) for Palestine has caused controversies: Christian Transjordanians, like Nāhid Hattar who was killed in 2016 (see Chapter Three), have been some of the most outspoken advocates of an exclusivist Jordanian nation.[60]

The monarchy featured prominently in the reactions from Christian Jordanians. As the Council of Evangelical Churches put it, '[w]e in Jordan, Christians and Muslims, we stand side by side, with a united view, and we will not accept the shattering of our unity, as one Jordanian people that lives in a country beloved in our hearts under its wise Hashimite leadership led by His Majesty, King Abdullah II'.[61] Comments such as these were displays of loyalty to a monarchy which, since its establishment, has always relied on Transjordanian Christian tribes.[62] 'I love the King', said Bāssim Farrāj in an interview with the author, mentioning that he had been filling out his income tax just before the interview.[63] During protests against the Greek Orthodox Patriarchate in Jordan in 2014, for instance, anger was directed at the Jordanian government, but never the king, who was called upon to 'correct' the perceived injustices.[64] In the case of Jordanian Islamists, there was a consistent effort to react outside Islamist circles, including Christians, as discussed in Chapter One. In an article titled 'Christians and Citizenship', published in October 2013, Ruhayl al-Gharāyiba of the IAF claimed that 'the Christians are an original part of the national texture, and original Arabs, they already shared in the civilisational Arab Islamic achievement with their Muslim brothers, and they had a valuable preserving role that is not possible to ignore or neglect, and this is proven by the true documented history'.[65]

The common thread running through these three narratives is that they all have a third element tying the Christian–Muslim equation together. In the case of Egypt, it is the land of Egypt; for Lebanon, it is the Zionist/Israeli enemy; and for Jordan, it is the king. In all these cases, whether this third element completes or antagonises, it is vital to the Christians and Muslims forming a unity, as it mediates Christian–Muslim relations.

The Religious Foundations of Unity

I have already on several occasions touched on the religious attitudes towards the other community. *Al-Daʿwa al-Salafiyya* and *al-Gamāʿa al-Islāmiyya* held on to their concept of *tahrīf*, despite their apparent moderation. Some Christian figures, especially those claiming proximity to Muslims through a shared Arab identity (see Chapter Four), 'smuggled' in religious references which constituted the foundation of their vision of unity. Similarly, ʿAbd al-Majīd Ḥāmid Subh offered an understanding of how Islamic religious references could constitute the basis for coexistence. The key here is that the terms of a (new) political contract were not formulated in a political or politicised language of rights, duties, democracy, citizenship and so on; instead, one can extract political visions from an avoidant, ritualised language in terms of 'coexistence'. Even in instances where religious references are avoided altogether, it is still possible to extract a vision.

As discussed earlier, a number of both Muslim and Christian actors sought to find in Christianity and Islam the premises for a peaceful coexistence of reciprocity and thus equality. I have previously mentioned Metropolitan George Khodr, ʿAbd al-Majīd Ḥāmid Subh and a 'Common Word'. This type of approach rested on three discursive strategies to find common ground: the similarity of both religions is highlighted; the diversity of religions is taken as a value in itself; or there is a common divine origin. The idea of a common origin and thus continuity was elaborated by Bishop George Khodr who advanced that all of humanity stems from the same divine source (see Chapter Four). Similarly, ʿAbd al-Amīr Qabalān, the vice-president of the Higher Islamic Shiʿi Council, claimed in a talk at the Université Saint-Joseph in 2003: 'Islam decided the unity of the human origin'.[66] From there, it is only a quick step to claiming that all religions likewise come from God. George Khodr considered the Holy Spirit to be working 'both inside and outside the visible church' (see Chapter Four). In an article by the late Islamic scholar Muhammad ʿAbd Allāh Dirāz, published in *Majallat al-Azhar* after the 2011 revolution, Islam exists in continuity with Judaism and Christianity:

> As the word 'Judaism' or Mosaism concerns the law of Moses and what derives from it and the word of Nazarism or Christianity concerns the law of ʿIsā and what is affiliated with it [. . .] The Gospel certifies and supports the Torah, and the Qur'an certifies and supports the Gospel and the Torah.[67]

Fawzī Fāḍil al-Zafzāf, member of the Council for Islamic Research at al-Azhar, echoed positions voiced earlier by Greek Orthodox clerics when he asserted in an article published in December 2011 – during the parliamentary elections and the controversy over Christmas – that 'the revealed religions come from God' and that 'the sources of all revealed religions are one and no religion differs in this from another, as the proofs of the existence of God, the call to believe in Him, His unicity, His veneration, and the belief in His books and messengers, His angels and the Day of Judgement'.[68] This echoes the comments made by Fr Nāyif Istifān at one of the conferences in Akkar, when he formulated a shared Christian-Islamic creed resting on the Islamic idea that there is no distinction between the various prophets and messengers: 'Muslims and Christians, we believe in God, His angels and in His revelation, in the resurrection. We do not distinguish in this between one and the other in any of the ways of the prophets'.[69] Similarly, in his speech at the Université Saint-Joseph, 'Abd al-Amīr Qabalān quoted from the Qur'an: 'We do not distinguish between any of them'.[70]

From there, again, it is an easy step to claiming that Christianity and Islam share the same core values and *features*. Referring to 'A Common Word', the Council of Churches in Jordan calls on Muslims: 'We say to our Muslim citizens that we are truly brothers, and God wants us to live together, united in the faith of the One God and the commandment of the love of God and the love of one's Neighbour'.[71] But this approach through similarity presents one key problem: it negates key differences and glosses over the self-understanding of these two religions. For one, this Islamic approach does not look at Jesus Christ as Christians see him. Johnny Awwad, professor at the Near East School of Theology in Beirut, criticised 'A Common Word' for just that, claiming that the document shows a 'Jesus [who] remains within the boundaries of Judaism'.[72] Yet, in Christianity, Jesus Christ is the site of revelation, the incarnated word of God. Moreover, often these comments do not use the Qur'anic verses that explicitly name Christians – which are polemical – but rather Qur'anic verses that generally convey the ideas of the plurality of humankind and Jesus Christ as a prophet. Yūsuf al-Qaraḍāwī, who has inspired many Jordanian Islamists promotes the idea that polemical Islamic verses regarding the 'People of the Book' refer either to the polytheists of that time or to 'non-Muslims who were actively hostile to the early Islamic community'.[73]

Another different strategy is to take the diversity of humankind as God-wanted and not an accident of history. For Lebanese Islamic scholars, 'each human is provided the opportunity of faith and has the right and responsibility to choose his/her own religious faith. *Sura* 2:256 [no compulsion in matters of religion] then becomes the legal cornerstone for a pluralist social organization'.[74] Similarly, 'Abd al-Amīr Qabalān used this verse to claim that the 'distinction of humankind in its colours, races, languages is [indeed] a sign of the greatness of the creator and His strength'.[75]

A clue as to how Muslim figures overall envision the place of Christians in society is provided by looking at the way in which they name Christians. In the context of 'The Innocence of Muslims', Muslim figures in Egypt variously used the terms 'Christians' (*masīhiyyūn*) and 'Nazarenes' (*nasārā*, to be explained further below). Shaykh al-Azhar Ahmad al-Tayyib referred to Christian Egyptians as '*masīhiyyūn*'.[76] Mufti 'Alī Gum'a wrote that there were 'brotherly relations between the children of the united nation, Muslims and Christians'.[77] The Supreme Guide of the Muslim Brotherhood, Muhammad Badī', referred to 'our Christian brothers (*ikhwāninā al-masīhiyyūn*)'.[78] Muhammad Mursī spoke of 'the Egyptian people, [. . .] its Muslims and Christians'.[79] The secretary general of the Nur Party, 'Imād 'Abd al-Ghaffūr, called them 'the Christians of Egypt (*masīhiyyī Misr*)'.[80] By contrast, in its long statement issued on 11 September 2012, *al-Da'wa al-Salafiyya* used terms derived from 'Nazarenes' ('*al-nasrāniyya*', '*misrī nasrānī*') and 'Copt' ('many of the Church and political and popular Coptic leaders'), but not the word 'Christian' (*masīhiyyūn*). Similarly, Wisām 'Abd al-Wārith, preacher on the channel *al-Hikma*, described the video as an example of a 'Nazarene provocation' towards the stream of political Islam in Egypt.[81] In Lebanon, all Muslim and Islamist figures, including Hezbollah and Ahmad al-Asīr, used '*masīhiyyūn*'. One exception was Māhir Hammūd, one of the Sunni supporters of Hezbollah, who, in an analysis of Christian–Muslim relations undertaken on the occasion of Benedict XVI's visit, called Christians '*ahl al-kitāb* and *al-nasārā, in accordance with their Islamic historical designation* [my emphasis]'.[82] In Jordan, the use of '*masīhiyyūn*' prevailed: *Hizb al-du'ā*' spoke of 'Islamic and Christian revealed beliefs',[83] and the Agricultural Engineers of 'Muslims and Christians'.[84]

The use of '*nasārā*' as opposed to '*masīhiyyūn*' has serious implications. *Nasārā* is the Qur'anic term, but its exact origin is not clear.[85] In general, the scientific community has too easily translated *nasārā* as 'Christians'. Until recently, Christian sources and actors used *nasrāniyya* for Christianity, too. In 1933, for instance, the Syriac Orthodox Patriarch Ighnātiyūs Afrām I gave a lecture at the American University in Beirut in which he used *nasrāniyya* for 'Christianity'.[86] Starting in the early 1960s, however, the patriarchate's magazine gradually ceased using it,[87] and Christians in the Middle East have increasingly come to consider *nasārā* and *nasrāniyya* offensive. Fr Rafiq Khoury from the Latin Patriarchate explained to the author: 'We do not accept this term, neither do we accept 'Īsā. But more and more Muslims say 'Yasū' al-Masīh' and '*al-masīhiyyūn*' and not 'Īsā. Yasū' and 'Īsā have the same root. [However,] it is not the etymology that matters but the memory'.[88] Similarly, 'Āmir al-Hāfī, the vice-director of the Royal Institute for Inter-Faith Studies in Amman, criticised this insistence on the part of Muslims on referring to Christians as '*nasārā*', noting that the Qur'an had adopted this term because this was what Christians called themselves in the time of Muhammad.[89] Nowadays, however, Christians no longer use this term, so '*masīhiyyūn*' is more accurate, explained al-Hāfī.

From there one can make two assumptions. Firstly, those who do not use *nasārā* can be assumed to forsake the idea of *tahrīf*. In this regard, there was a recurring insistence on the idea that Islam equally embraces all prophets, including Jesus Christ and *thus* Christianity. The Tribes of the Tafileh Governorate Province Demanding Reform in Jordan referred to local Christians within this Islamic framework:

> We as Muslims, we do not complete our faith except through our faith in God, His books, His Messengers, where our brothers from the revealed religions lived and continue to live among us. To them that which is for us and upon them which is upon us.[90]

The Jordanian *Dā'irat al-iftā'* once again praised Islam by issuing a reminder of the inherent tolerance of Islam which compels Muslims to respect all prophets, messengers and the other revealed religion, quoting Qur'an 2:285.[91] The IAF promoted the same view (see Chapter Four). In the case of Hezbollah, there is a sort of compromise reached in the way in which Jesus Christ is designated, with Hasan Nasr Allāh using Yasū' al-Masīh and '*mashiyyūn*' in his speeches, thus combining the Islamic term for Jesus with the Christian Arab term for Christ. As a result, Islamists such as the Jordanian Muslim Brotherhood have taken the Qur'an's endorsement of peaceful relations as the foundation of social relations.[92]

In the case of the Egyptian Salafis, the use of *nasārā* is indeed ideologically justified and explicitly endorsed. In a fatwa issued in July 2011, *al-Daʿwa al-Salafiyya* explicitly rejected the use of the word *masīhiyyūn* to designate contemporary Christians: '[Even] if it were not forbidden to use the term "Christian" [to refer to them] because it connects to Christ – Peace be upon him – and he has nothing to do with them nor they with him, [it would be forbidden] because they are from a different community (*milla*)'.[93] *Al-Daʿwa al-Salafiyya* used '*masīhiyyūn*' only once, in the context of the Maspero Massacre in October 2011.[94] The organisation has conveyed the idea that Christians have distorted and falsified the revelation that Jesus Christ allegedly received in terms of content (*tahrīf al-maʿnā*) by introducing the creed of the Trinity, Incarnation, and, in terms of text (*tahrīf al-nass*), the Gospel,[95] considering it 'texts inherited over generations from which [the Nazarenes] corrupted their religion from a noble monotheism into a distressing paganism'.[96] This is an idea that Yāsir Burhāmī voiced again during the controversy when he condemned Abū Islām's burning of the Bible: 'It is never permissible', conceding, however, that 'it is correct that the Gospel contains paragraphs and parts of the revealed Gospel, and there is monotheism and proof of the prophecies which assert the correctness of its meaning'.[97]

These accusations have far-reaching and dangerous implications. For one, in the Qur'an the 'Nazarenes' are not simply a community which allegedly falsified a revelation, but they are a quintessential and perpetual enemy to the community of believers – the Muslims – and present a permanent danger to their faith, as illustrated by Yusrī Hammād's comment in the context of 'The Innocence of Muslims'. Haranguing Muslims, he said:

> Where are your loud voices now? You are now silent like the dead and you remain quiet [about] Copts of the diaspora who were announcing that God is love; and when they left your country, they declared enmity for you and abuse your religion and your Prophet.[98]

Thus, Christians live under the sword of Damocles. *Al-Daʿwa al-Salafiyya* ominously stated: 'We consider peaceful coexistence among Muslims, Jews and

Nazarenes in the country of Islam the foundation of social relations between us and them *as long as* they do not fight us in religion [my emphasis]'.[99]

The sharpest divergence was thus between Salafis in Egypt, on the one hand, and all other actors, on the other hand, including Christians. Forsaking the accusation of *taḥrīf* – or, at least, silencing it – puts Muslim figures immediately into a different position towards Christians, with contrasting political implications. As illustrated so far, the articles published in *Majallat al-Azhar* in the aftermath of the Arab Spring were the strongest opponents to Egyptian Salafis. Even non-Egyptian Salafis turned on Egyptian Islamists. In March 2013, in an interview with the Egyptian independent newspaper *al-Shurūq*, Ahmad al-Asīr called on Islamists in Egypt to stop saying 'Islam is the solution', for 'it is possible to put forward a reform programme but without saying "Islam is the solution" [...] because at its core Islam is a message of predication'.[100]

The Political Sources of Unity

Overall, it seems that Islamists and Salafis in Jordan and Lebanon displayed a higher level of flexibility in their understanding of Islam. For instance, Ruhayl al-Gharāyiba of the IAF rejected the idea of 'applying the sharīʻa' altogether 'because the latter is not a book whose rulings one can easily apply'.[101] As a result, the sharīʻa 'should constantly change with the place and time in which the *umma* finds itself'.[102] There was however a shared vision of the values of Islam. As mentioned in Chapter Three, Egyptian Mufti ʻAlī Gumʻa praised Muhammad for 'how he founded a state based on the rule of law, justice and equality', 'how this religion preserved the rights of women', and 'how Islam reversed the big and was merciful with the small'.[103] Similarly, during the parliamentary elections, Yusrī Hammād of the Nur Party defined the principles of sharīʻa in a similarly abstract way as 'justice, equality, and dignity'.[104] In May 2011, ʻIsām Darbāla of *al-Gamāʻa al-Islāmiyya* defined *ḥudūd* as 'a legal system governed by a specific philosophy which is the protection of life, honour, and property'.[105] There was even some mutual ground when it came to Islam as a political system. The extent to which it should constitute the basis for polity was debated in the region. In June 2011, al-Azhar endorsed the position that 'Islam does not know, neither in its law, nor its civilisation or history [...] the religious theocratic state', a position shared by Yāsir Burhāmī: '[T]he word religious state is a western term and taken from the theocratic state, this is a state Islam fights'.[106]

The key difference between Egyptian Salafis and all the other figures mentioned here was that, for the latter, the values of Islam should be translated into polity, but *not be* the basis of polity. There were fundamental disagreements over the nature of the state, the sources of law and the communal or individual foundation of belonging. For al-Azhar, the law stemmed from the legitimacy of the elected representatives of the people supporting the foundation of a 'national, constitutional, democratic, modern state founded on a constitution and with a separation between the authorities of the state and its legal institutions ruling [in which] the legal power belongs to the representatives of the people'. By contrast, for *al-Daʿwa al-Salafiyya*, '[t]he Christians in Egypt are one part of the woven fabric of Egyptian society, and their rights [. . .] are guaranteed by the commitment of the Muslim majority to Islam [. . .] forbidding attacks on them and guaranteeing their freedom of belief and practice'.[107] Christians' rights were therefore safeguarded by the Muslim majority and not an independent body of legislation.

When it comes to the communal or individual source of belonging, there were in fact no major differences between the Salafis and the Coptic Orthodox Church, with *al-Daʿwa al-Salafiyya* declaring: 'We recognize to non-Muslims of the People of the Book their rights: they should not be forced in terms of religion (Q 7.54) [but the reference should be Qur'an 2:256]; they are a part of society which has rights and duties as God gave them in matters of personal status such as marriage and divorce'.[108] It is noteworthy that the Coptic Orthodox Church did not fundamentally disagree in this regard, as in its statement issued in March 2012, it demanded the application of canon law in matters of personal status for the '*ahl al-kitāb*', using Islamic terminology.[109] The 2012 constitution introduced an article enshrining the application of canon law, reportedly to please the Coptic Orthodox Church.[110] In 2014, the article was maintained, something that constituted a 'new constitutional commitment' and enshrined the 'communal status of citizenship', according to Rachel Scott.[111]

The term citizenship has attracted a lot of interest over the past years, both in the scholarly community and in public discourse in the Middle East. But there is no consensus as to what it actually entails. For Christians in the Middle

East, the term carried much hope; as Paola Pizzo notes, 'the Copts as a religious minority utilize citizenship discourses to gain social visibility and political legitimacy'.[112] However, for the 'Christian Brothers' citizenship has a more sectarian undertone; as we have seen earlier in this chapter, its goal was to ground and revive the concept of citizenship. The Coptic Catholic Church, on the other hand, designated it as the 'equality of opportunities [. . .] It does not matter to me *if he is Christian or Muslim*, what matters is that [it produces] an effect which respects his conscience and serves all. Citizenship therefore means that *every individual* feels esteem and respect and that dialogue is the means to achieve peace'.[113] Interestingly, Islamists such as the Muslim Brotherhood in Egypt and Jordan have started using this term, even fully endorsing it: the 'Islamist ideology [. . .] has shown an impressive flexibility at internalising – and naturalising – the concept of citizenship'.[114] As Joas Wagemakers notes, 'the Jordanian Brotherhood have increasingly discussed religious minority rights in terms of citizenship, not *dhimma*, using the latter as a source of authentically Islamic inspiration rather than as a functional concept for today's society'.[115]

The notion of citizenship has been connected to the Islamic adage '*lahum mā lanā wa 'alayhum mā 'alaynā*' (community of rights and duties).[116] Mariz Tadros argues that this supposedly *fiqh* principle rests on only 'weak or inauthentic' hadith that Muhammad reportedly said in relation to recently converted Muslims.[117] According to Gudrun Krämer, for modern Islamic thinkers, this adage, which suggests some sort of equality, actually acknowledges the autonomy of non-Muslim communities in matters of personal status.[118] However, taken the other way around, it conveys the very idea of reciprocity, which is paramount to Christian–Muslim relations. As Ruhayl al-Gharāyiba explains in his article, this is a community of rights and duties because '[Christians] are partners in the land and the nation, partners in authority and responsibility, partners in property and wealth'.[119] Therefore, equality is possible, even if 'some positions should be off-limits to non-Muslims'.[120]

Conclusion

This chapter has discussed claims of unity in terms of polity. An unclear picture has emerged: while for the Egyptian Salafis the political status of Christians was predicated on their theological status, for all the other actors, the ideals of peaceful coexistence and equality enshrined in Islam and Christianity did not necessarily translate into a clear political vision. Nevertheless, religious unity was deemed a political unity. As a result, the sharpest difference occurred between Egyptian Salafis and all the other actors mentioned in this book.

More than anything, these discussions highlighted the deep fears of political upheavals and looming political instability, especially for Christians. This fear was nurtured by a cross-regional vision of their place in society, so that the plight of Iraqi Christians was directly felt by Christians elsewhere. This betrays a deep mistrust of the state and the state's capacity to uphold and defend the rights of its citizens. The insistence on speaking as Christians and the high level of differentiation was thus a testimony to the distrust of the secular project(s) of the twentieth century.

CONCLUSION
THE REQUIREMENTS FOR
THE IDEAL ISLAMIC SOCIETY

From early September until early October 2012, a video deemed offensive to Islam provoked controversy in the Middle East. Although the video denounced a specific situation in Egypt, the uproar it caused was not confined to Egypt but spread throughout the wider region.

Except for *al-Daʿwa al-Salafiyya*, one Coptic activist in Egypt, and the Greek Orthodox Metropolitan of Mount Lebanon, George Khodr, nobody had actually watched 'The Innocence of Muslims'. It was very rarely mentioned by its title, but usually referred to as 'the offending film' or simply 'the offence'. Nevertheless, the reactions were vocal in ascribing a specific aim to the video. The controversy unfolded differently in the various countries. In Egypt, Muslim figures navigated a path between fuelling the outcry and de-escalating it to prevent a backlash against local Christians. In Lebanon, the controversy was dominated by Hezbollah – in particular, by Hasan Nasr Allāh – and its allies, the Amal Movement and the Syrian Socialist National Party, as well as its opponents (the March 14 Alliance with Samīr Geagea and Amin Gemayel, and the Salafi preacher Ahmad al-Asīr) who accused Nasr Allāh of diverting public attention from his involvement in the Syrian conflict. In Jordan, besides the government and institutions of official Islam, the defence of Islam was taken on by actors with no explicit Islamic outlook: the professional associations, the tribes and some political parties. Yet, in terms of mobilisation, the professional associations were more active than Islamist and Salafi actors. Overall, Christians and Muslims were often quite similar in their reactions, and the sharpest differences were those between official Islam and Egyptian Salafis. Looking at the Christian reactions, one can discern an interesting move on the part of Christian Jordanians who, like the Coptic Orthodox, engaged in the controversy by positioning both their Christian and Arabic belongings as equally important.

This book used this short but intense outcry as an entry point into the mechanisms of Christian–Muslim relations in Egypt, Jordan and Lebanon, by offering a thorough comparison between the reactions and going beyond the condemnations, tackling what was at stake for the various actors weighing in. The short comments paraphrased in the media, the long, elaborate statements reflecting on the history of Christian–Muslim relations and the current political situation, as well as the speeches given at conferences, whether in the small town of Akkar, Lebanon, or major cities, could all too easily be dismissed as shallow and repetitive – mere rituals. The discussion of such outcries in the media or academia have usually rested on the level of tensions and suspicions. I chose, however, to follow the condemnations and mobilisations wherever they occurred and whoever initiated them. A more complex picture of Christian–Muslim relations emerged as a result of that approach.

In particular, this book has taken all the apparent 'anomalies' of the controversy as an impetus for further study: the conspiracies and claims of Christian–Muslim unity, the Christian affirmations to Islam, and Islamists searching for proximity to Christians. Most importantly, an occasion for violence turned into an occasion for cooperation: Christians and Muslims as a society found a way out.

I thus constructed a theoretical framework based on an approach inspired by micro-history – one single event – combined with a comparative approach – three countries, Christian–Muslim relations, and institutional and non-institutional actors. I have argued for the need to connect our understanding of violence to agency, considered here as an ambiguous mode of behaviour and language. This book has explored the reactions as being multi-layered, combining several motivations at the same time: genuine condemnations of an offence, fear, self-promotion and a means to build pressure. It explored the possibility that violence was avoided by choice, not mere chance.

How was violence avoided? First, the focus of this book – the numerous condemnations rather than the incidents of violence – reduced the overall relevance of violence by contextualising it in relation to the other events of this controversy, such as joint Christian–Muslim protests. Second, the focus on condemnations and actually *listening* to them implied that we followed the actors in where they located violence: the *potential* violence that the video could have caused. Third, a key factor of avoiding violence was denial. Denying that there was an anti-Christian backlash, denying that there was an overall recurrence of Christian–Muslim violence. Fourth, the claims of unity and joint reactions certainly created the impression that cooperation outweighed tensions. Fifth, the many conspiracies crafted by both Christians and Muslims played a crucial role as they helped the Christians to position themselves as victims, nay the prime victims of a larger conspiracy of which 'The Innocence of Muslims' was but one of many examples.

What was the benefit for these various actors of condemning the video? The idea of agency as ambiguity helped us unearth the various rationales at play. Introducing agency in the case of Islamist and Salafi figures was useful, as it showed the constraints to which they were actually subjected: loyalty to their ideological position, but the need to fulfil the political requirements of the new political game. The Nur Party antagonised local Christians, whereas Hezbollah, *al-Gamā'a al-Islāmiyya* and Ahmad al-Asīr searched for proximity to Christians and as a result strengthened their own positions. This shows that a sound Islamist ideology, particularly if it is based on *taḥrīf*, or a strong organisation does not suffice to cement leadership, especially if a group aspires to national relevance. They had to take local Christians into account. More importantly, the latter could serve as powerful political tools and, as the case of the Egyptian Muslim Brotherhood shows, the Coptic Orthodox Church helped the latter get around the limits of its ability to mobilise and be part of the political game again. The controversy also revealed the flexibility of all these actors who did have or sought to have personal relations with members of the other community.

Even though the benefits for Christians were not evident at first sight, the reasons for their engagement went beyond the fear of a backlash. It was an occasion to strengthen personal relations (for example, the Coptic Catholic Church with the new governor of Suez), to promote themselves, or to tackle larger issues. A fascinating feature was that, through the claim of proximity and unity, Christians were actually exerting subtle pressure on Muslims and the Muslim rulers to live up to those ideals. This was putting the *dhimma* upside down. Yet, agency was clearly limited, due to the fact that a number of actors felt the need to react *as* Christians, even though they did not aspire to be token Christians.

Overall, as we followed all these diverse actors in their ambitions and interests, we managed to restore the agency of *individuals*, not merely communities – specifically the Christian communities. All the various positions on Christian–Muslim relations, Islam and Christianity that we encountered were the results of personal choices and, as such, exhibited great variety.

The controversy brought deeper mechanisms of inter-communal relations to the fore: avoidance and proximity, the expectation of reciprocity through rituals, as well as the fear of *fitna*, strife. The controversy was a fascinating moment, as it unfolded as a movement of both proximity and avoidance, both denial and cooperation. This seemingly contradictory movement actually showed us two sides of the same coin. By avoiding certain topics and refraining from using outspoken language, the highest level of proximity was possible. The condemnations of the video were rituals that actually had tremendous implications, since they implied pressure on the other community, and the expectation of reciprocity conveyed great authority. Reciprocity entailed the mutual acknowledgement or value of rituals, offences, feasts and, crucially, equality. Rituals, as this book has shown, carried so much authority because their opposite, *fitna*, or strife, conveyed so much fear. Thus, the opposite of Christian–Muslim relations – the opposite of this very hyphen – was *fitna*: sedition, division, violence, chaos. Herein lies perhaps the greatest limitation on Muslim agency: the ideal of an Islamic society can be reached only in so far as public order is maintained.

It is my hope that I have been able to show how fruitful it is to break down the walls between Islamic Studies and Minority Studies or Middle Eastern Christian Studies, areas where scholars have worked separately so far. Although probably leaving many questions unanswered (such as on Jordanian Salafis and other Christian communities, for instance), this book has offered glimpses into the fact that there exists a lot of interaction between the diverse set of Muslim and Christian actors – both tension and cooperation.

NOTES

Introduction

1. Copts Today, أمن الدولة' تحقق في واقعة تمزيق الإنجيل أثناء أحداث السفارة الأمريكية, 22 September 2012: http://www.coptstoday.com/Copts-News/Detail.php?Id=34184 (accessed 23 May 2016).
2. Angie Heo, *The Political Lives of Saints: Christian–Muslim Mediation in Egypt* (Berkeley: University of California Press, 2018), 2.
3. The New York Times, 'Protesters in Beirut Set Danish Consulate on Fire', 5 February 2006: http://www.nytimes.com/2006/02/05/international/middleeast/05cnd-beirut.html?_r=0 (accessed 22 March 2023).
4. Bård Helge Kårtveit, *Dilemmas of Attachment: Identity and Belonging among Palestinian Christians* (Leiden: Brill, 2014), 105.
5. Copts Today, مؤامرة شيطانية... الفيلم المسىء للرسول... بقلم القس فيلوباتير جميل عزيز, 12 September 2012: http://www.coptstoday.com/Copts-News/Detail.php?Id=32517 (accessed 22 March 2023). See Chapter Two for more information on this priest.
6. Yvonne Haddad and Joshua Donovan, 'Good Copt, Bad Copt: Competing Narratives on Coptic Identity in Egypt and the United States', *Studies in World Christianity* 19:3 (2013), 208–32; Nadia Marzouki, 'The U.S. Coptic Diaspora and the Limit of Polarization', *Journal of Immigrant & Refugee Studies* 14:3 (2016), 261–76.
7. Haddad and Donovan, 'Good Copt, Bad Copt', 209.
8. Bernard Heyberger, *Les chrétiens au Proche-Orient: De la compassion à la compréhension* (Paris: Manuels Payot, 2013), 17.

9. See Fiona McCallum, 'Muslim-Christian Relations in Egypt: Challenges for the Twenty-First Century', in Emma Loosley and Anthony O'Mahony (eds), *Christian Responses to Islam and Muslim-Christian Relations in the Modern World* (Manchester: Manchester University Press, 2008), 66–84.
10. Some Christian communities have benefitted more from this renewed scholarly attention than others. In particular, studies on the Coptic Orthodox community using historical and ethnographic methods have produced a more nuanced image of the Christian community and thus of Christian–Muslim relations. In the case of Jordan, studies are rarer: the only comprehensive one is that by Géraldine Chatelard in French which, with more attention paid to the Coptic Orthodox, reveals significant differences in Christian–Muslim relations. Interestingly, there is no comprehensive study on Christians in Lebanon; studies are instead split along denominational divisions. Except for Chatelard's study, which discusses the experience of all Christian communities in Jordan, studies on Christians in Egypt or Lebanon often highlight just one particular community – the Coptic Orthodox, or the Maronites – neglecting other Christian communities that are equally Egyptian or Lebanese. For studies on the Coptic Orthodox community, see Wolfram Reiss, *Erneuerung in der koptisch-orthodoxen Kirche: Die Geschichte der koptisch-orthodoxen Sonntagsschulbewegung und die Aufnahme ihrer Reformansätze in den Erneuerungsbewegungen der koptisch-orthodoxen Kirche der Gegenwart* (Hamburg: LIT, 1998); and the edited volumes by Nelly van Doorn-Harder, *Between Desert and City: The Coptic Orthodox Church Today*, ed. with Kari Vogt (Oslo: Novus Forlag, 1997; Portland: Wipf and Stock Publishers, 2004) and *Copts in Context: Negotiating Identity, Tradition, and Modernity* (Columbia: University of South Carolina Press, 2017). On historical aspects, see Febe Armanios, *Coptic Christianity in Ottoman Egypt* (New York: Oxford University Press, 2011); Vivian Ibrahim, *The Copts of Egypt: The Challenges of Modernisation and Identity* (London: I. B. Tauris, 2013); Brigitte Voile, *Les coptes d'Égypte sous Nasser: Sainteté, miracles, apparitions* (Paris: CNRS Éditions, 2004). For more recent developments, see Sebastian Elsässer, *The Coptic Question in the Mubarak Era* (New York: Oxford University Press, 2014); Laure Guirguis, *Les Coptes d'Égypte: Violences communautaires et transformations politiques (2005–2012)* (Paris: Karthala, 2012); Mariz Tadros, *Copts at the Crossroads: The Challenges of Building Inclusive Democracy in Contemporary Egypt* (Cairo: American University in Cairo Press, 2013); Heo, *The Political Lives of Saints*; Saba Mahmood, *Religious Difference in a Secular Age: A Minority Report* (Princeton: Princeton University Press, 2016). For another approach to Christians in Egypt, see Mayeur-Jaouen on

the Coptic Catholic Church: *Voyage en Haute-Égypte: Prêtres, coptes et catholiques* (Paris: CNRS, 2019). For studies on Christians in Jordan, see Géraldine Chatelard, *Briser la mosaïque: Les tribus chrétiennes de Madaba, Jordanie, XIX–XXe siècles* (Paris: CNRS, 2004); Anna Hager, 'The Orthodox Issue in Jordan: The Struggle for an Arab and Orthodox Identity', *Studies in World Christianity* 24:3 (2018), 212–33; Julia Droeber, '"We are different!" Similarities between Christian and Muslim Women in Jordan', *Islam and Christian–Muslim Relations* 23:1 (2012), 59–78; Paolo Maggiolini, 'Christian Churches and Arab Christians in the Hashemite Kingdom of Jordan', *Archives de Sciences Sociales des Religions* 171 (2015): http://journals.openedition.org/assr/27010 (accessed 23 February 2023), 37–58. For studies on Christians in Lebanon, see Ussama Makdisi, *The Culture of Sectarianism: Community, History and Violence in Nineteenth Century Ottoman Lebanon* (Berkeley, Los Angeles, London: California University Press, 2000); Franck Salameh, *Language, Memory, and Identity in the Middle East: The Case for Lebanon* (Lanham: Lexington Books, 2010); Fiona McCallum, *Christian Religious Leadership in the Middle East: The Political Role of the Patriarch* (Lewiston: The Edwin Mellen Press, 2010); Alexander D. M. Henley, 'Politics of a Church at War: Maronite Catholicism in the Lebanese Civil War', *Mediterranean Politics* 13:3 (2008), 353–69.

11. Laura Robson, 'Recent Perspectives on Christianity in the Modern Arab World', *History Compass* 9:4 (2011), 312.
12. American Historical Review, 'AHR Conversation: Religious Identities and Violence', December 2007, 1433.
13. Heo, *The Political Lives of Saints*, 6.
14. Élizabeth Picard, 'La violence milicienne et sa légitimation religieuse', in Thomas Scheffler (ed.), *Religion between Violence and Reconciliation* (Beirut: Orient-Institut Beirut; Würzburg: Ergon-Verl., 2002), 323–24.
15. Peter E. Makari, *Conflict and Cooperation: Christian–Muslim Relations in Contemporary Egypt* (Syracuse: Syracuse University Press, 2007), xiii.
16. Ibid, 190.
17. Ibid, xvii.
18. AHR, 'AHR Conversation', 1469.
19. Paul S. Rowe, 'The Middle Eastern Christian as Agent', *International Journal of Middle East Studies* 42:3 (2010), 472. See also Robson, 'Recent Perspectives on Christianity in the Modern Arab World'.
20. Anh Nga Longva and Anne Sofie Roald (eds), *Religious Minorities in the Middle East: Domination, Self-Empowerment, Accommodation* (Leiden, Boston: Brill,

2012), 4; in Paola Pizzo, 'The "Coptic Question" in Post-Revolutionary Egypt: Citizenship, Democracy, Religion', *Ethnic and Racial Studies*, 38:14 (2015), 2598.
21. Saba Mahmood, *Politics of Piety: The Islamic Revival and the Feminist Subject* (Princeton: Princeton University Press, 2011), 8.
22. Ibid, 34.
23. Ibid, 157. More recently, the Palestinian theologian Mitri Raheb published *The Politics of Persecution: Middle Eastern Christians in an Age of Empire*, in which '[i]n opposition to portrayals of Christian death and ruin in the Middle East, Raheb lays the foundation for a new way of looking at Christian communities in the region – not merely as objects of analysis, but as actors telling their own stories. Raheb argues that Christian persecution in the Middle East is a construction of the West and that the idea of persecution says more about the West than it does about Middle Eastern Christians'. Candace Lukasik, '*The Politics of Persecution: Middle Eastern Christians in an Age of Empire.* By Mitri Raheb', *Journal of Church and State* 64:4 (2022), 745.
24. 'Ein Phänomen kultureller Ambiguität liegt vor, wenn über einen längeren Zeitraum hinweg einem Begriff, einer Handlungsweise oder einem Objekt gleichzeitig zwei gegensätzliche oder mindestens zwei konkurrierende, deutlich voneinander abweichende Bedeutungen zugeordnet sind [. . .]'. Thomas Bauer, *Die Kultur der Ambiguität: Eine andere Geschichte des Islams* (Berlin: Verlag der Weltreligionen im Insel Verlag, 2011), 27. This idea is inspired by a concept increasingly used in comparative literature. See Oliver Auge and Christiane Witthöft (eds), *Ambiguität im Mittelalter: Formen zeitgenössischer Reflexion und interdisziplinärer Rezeption* (Berlin, Boston: de Gruyter, 2016), 3: 'To identify ambiguity, there is a need for an interpretation that incoporates the text's, the speaker's, and the actor's intention as well as a contextual knowlege about behavorial norms and values'.
25. Chatelard, *Briser la mosaïque*, 29.
26. Jillian Schwedler, 'Islamists in Power? Inclusion, Moderation, and the Arab Uprisings', *Middle East Development Journal* 5:1 (2013), 4.
27. See Gudrun Krämer, 'Dhimmi ou citoyen: Réflexions réformistes sur le statut des non-musulmans en société islamique', in Alain Roussillon (ed.), *Entre réforme sociale et mouvement national: Identité et modernisation en Égypte (1882–1962)* (Cairo: CEDEJ, 1995), 577–90: https://books.openedition.org/cedej/1446 (accessed 23 February 2023); Rachel Scott, *The Challenge of Political Islam: Non-Muslims and the Egyptian State* (Palo Alto: Stanford University Press, 2010); Mariz Tadros, *The Muslim Brotherhood in Contemporary Egypt: Democracy Redefined or Confined?*

(London: Routledge, 2012); Anna Hager, 'From "Polytheists" to "Partners in the Nation": Islamist Attitudes towards Coptic Egyptians in Post-Revolutionary Egypt (2011–2013)', *Islam and Christian–Muslim Relations* 29:3 (2018), 289–308.
28. Krämer, 'Dhimmi ou citoyen'.
29. David D. Grafton, *The Christians of Lebanon: Political Rights in Islamic Law* (London: Tauris Academic Studies, 2003), 9.
30. See Pizzo, 'The "Coptic question" in Post-Revolutionary Egypt'. Norig Neveu, *Le Prince Hasan, Hérault du rapprochement islamo-chrétien en Jordanie* (Unpubl. MA thesis, Paris IV-Sorbonne, 2004–5).
31. Carlo Ginzburg, 'Microhistory: Two or Three Things that I Know about It', trans. John and Anne C. Tedeschi, *Critical Inquiry* 20:1 (1993), 22.
32. Heo, *The Political Lives of Saints*, 5–6.
33. Robson, 'Recent Perspectives on Christianity in the Modern Arab World', 320.
34. George Sabra, 'The "Common Word" Letter in the Context of Christian–Muslim Dialogue', *NEST Theological Review* 30:1 (2009), 89–90.
35. Yvonne Yazbeck Haddad and Rahel Fischbach, 'Interfaith Dialogue in Lebanon: Between a Power Balancing Act and Theological Encounters', *Islam and Christian–Muslim Relations* 26:4 (2015), 424.
36. These institutions include in Beirut the Orient Institut Beirut, the CEMAM and the library of the Faculty of Religious Science at the Université Saint-Joseph, the NEST and the Ifpo; in Cairo, the Dominican Institute for Oriental Studies, the Franciscan Center of Christian Oriental Studies Library and the Netherlands-Flemish Institute; in Amman, the library of the University of Jordan and the Ifpo; and in Princeton, the Princeton University Library.
37. The website of the Lebanese Islamist organisation *Harakat al-Tawḥīd al-Islāmī*, altawhid.org, was especially valuable because it cited numerous statements, comments and reactions.

Chapter 1

1. See Risto Kunelius (ed.), *Reading the Mohammed Cartoons Controversy: An International Analysis of Press Discourses on Free Speech and Political Spin* (Bochum: Projekt Verlag, 2007); Mahmood, *Religious Difference in a Secular Age*, Chapter Five: Secularity, History, Literature.
2. This is the topic of Chapter Five in Saba Mahmood's *Religious Difference in a Secular Age*.
3. Zoltan Pall, *Salafism in Lebanon: Local and Transnational Movements* (Cambridge: Cambridge University Press, 2018), 106.

4. Tadros, *The Muslim Brotherhood in Contemporary Egypt*, 84.
5. Stéphane Lacroix, 'Sheikhs and Politicians: Inside the New Egyptian Salafism', Brookings Doha Center, 2012: http://www.brookings.edu/~/media/research/files/papers/2012/6/07-egyptian-salafism-lacroix/stephane-lacroix-policy-briefing-english.pdf (accessed 20 February 2023), 1.
6. Al-Ahram Hebdo, 'Un deuxième bastion islamisé', 7–13 March 2012 (number 912, year 18), 6.
7. Al-Ahram Hebdo, 'Les tentacules se déploient', 28 March–3 April 2012 (number 915, year 18), 3. In September 2012, the future constitution was fiercely debated, eventually leading to the withdrawal of the secular and Christian representatives in November 2012.
8. Mariz Tadros, 'Participation not Domination: Morsi on an Impossible Mission?' in Kraetzschmar and Rivetti (eds), *Islamists and the Politics of the Arab Uprisings*, 23.
9. Asef Bayat, *Post-Islamism: The Changing Faces of Political Islam* (Oxford: Oxford University Press, 2013), 4.
10. See Gudrun Krämer, *Hasan al-Banna* (Oxford: Oneworld Publication, 2010).
11. Grégoire Delhaye, 'Contemporary Muslim-Christian Relations in Egypt: Local Dynamics and Foreign Influences', in Anh Nga Longva and Anne Sofie Roald (eds), *Religious Minorities in the Middle East: Domination, Self-Empowerment, Accommodation* (Leiden, Boston: Brill, 2012), 83.
12. To avoid confusion with the Lebanese *al-Jamāʿa al-Islāmiyya*, the Lebanese branch of the Muslim Brotherhood, I am using the colloquial 'g' to designate the Egyptian *al-Gamāʿa al-Islāmiyya*.
13. Mahmood, *Politics of Piety*, 3–4.
14. Delhaye, 'Contemporary Muslim-Christian Relations in Egypt', 75.
15. Voile, *Les coptes d'Égypte sous Nasser*, 56.
16. Bernard Haykel, 'On the Nature of Salafi Thought and Action', in Roel Meijer (ed.), *Global Salafism: Islam's New Religious Movement* (Oxford: Oxford University Press, 2014), 34–35.
17. Richard Gauvain, *Salafi Ritual Purity: In the Presence of God* (London: Routledge, 2013), 14.
18. Hager, 'From "Polytheists" to "Partners in the Nation"', 291.
19. Gauvain, *Salafi Ritual Purity*, 14.
20. Lacroix, 'Sheikhs and Politicians', 2.
21. Hager, 'From "Polytheists" to "Partners in the Nation"', 292.
22. Lacroix, 'Sheikhs and Politicians', 1.

23. Ibid, 3.
24. Tadros, 'Participation not Domination', 19.
25. Al-Ahrām, عماد عبد الغفور مساعد رئيس الجمهورية, 12 September 2012 (number 45936, year 137), 4.
26. Lacroix, 'Sheikhs and Politicians', 3.
27. 'Imād 'Abd al-Ghaffūr established a separate party in January 2013.
28. Esen Kirdiş, *The Rise of Islamic Political Movements and Parties: Morocco, Turkey and Jordan* (Edinburgh: Edinburgh University Press, 2019), 14.
29. See Hager, 'From "Polytheists" to "Partners in the Nation"', 291.
30. Ibid, 292.
31. Al-Ahrām, الغضب يجتاح مصر احتجاجا على الفيلم المسيء للرسول, 13 September 2012 (number 45937, year 137), 5.
32. Al-Ahrām, هدوء حذر يسود محيط السفارة بعد اشتباكات عنيفة, 16 September 2012 (number 45940, year 137), 5.
33. Al-Ahrām, قوات الأمن تحكم سيطرتها على ميدان التحرير, 16 September 2012 (number 45940, year 137), 5.
34. BBC, 'Obama: Egypt is Not US Ally, Nor an Enemy', 13 September 2012: http://www.bbc.com/news/world-middle-east-19584265 (accessed 20 February 2023).
35. Khairat El-Shater, '"Our Condolences", the Muslim Brotherhood Says', *The New York Times*, 13 September 2012: http://www.nytimes.com/2012/09/14/opinion/our-condolences-the-muslim-brotherhood-says.html?_r=1 (accessed 23 May 2016).
36. Al-Ahrām, استمرار ردود الفعل الغاضبة على الفيلم المسيء: الأزهر يطالب بالالتزام بضوابط الاحتجاج والبعد عن العنف, 14 September 2012 (number 45938, year 137), 6.
37. Al-Ahram Hebdo, 'Morsi ne sait pas sur quel pied danser', 19–25 September 2012 (number 940, year 18), 6.
38. Al-Ahrām, ومسيرات عارمة لنصرة الرسول في المحافظات, 15 September 2012 (number 45939, year 137), 4.
39. Al-Ahrām, غضب شعبي من الإساءة للرسول, 12 September 2012 (number 45936, year 137), 1 and 5; Al-Ahrām, استمرار ردود الفعل الغاضبة على الفيلم المسيء: الأزهر يطالب بالالتزام بضوابط الاحتجاج والبعد عن العنف.
40. Al-Ahrām, النواب يطالبون أمريكا لاعتذار لمشاعر مليار ونصف مسلم, 13 September 2012 (number 45937, year 137), 4.
41. Al-Yawm al-Sābi', عبد الوارث: الفيلم المسيء للرسول تحرش نصرانى بتيار الإسلام السياسى, 7 September 2012: http://www.youm7.com/story/2012/9/7/%D8%B9%D8%A8%D8%AF-%D8%A7%D9%84%D9%88%D8%A7%D8%B1%D8%AB--%D8%A7%D9%84%D9%81%D9%8A%D9%84%D9%85-%D8%A7%D9%84%D9%85%D8%B3%

D9%89%D8%A1-%D9%84%D9%84%D8%B1%D8%B3%D9%88%D9%84-%D8%AA%D8%AD%D8%B1%D8%B4-%D9%86%D8%B5%D8%B1%D8%A7%D9%86%D9%89-%D8%A8%D8%AA%D9%8A%D8%A7%D8%B1-%D8%A7%D9%84%D8%A5%D8%B3%D9%84%D8%A7%D9%85-%D8%A7/778969#. VjI_Nm5OfVJ (accessed 31 January 2023).

42. Gauvain, *Salafi Ritual Purity*, 241. See Chapter Six.
43. Al-Masrī al-Yawm, "النور" و"الجبهة السلفية" ينضمانلوقفةأمامالسفارةالأمريكيةضدالفيلمالمسيء 10, September 2012: http://www.almasryalyoum.com/news/details/162864 (accessed 31 January 2023).
44. Copts Today, أمن الدولة ' تحقق في واقعة تمزيق الإنجيل أثناء أحداث السفارة الأمريكية, 22 September 2012.
45. Al-Masrī al-Yawm, عمرو موسى: من أعد "الفيلم المسيء" فئة حاقدة وباغية ومريضة, 12 September 2012: http://www.almasryalyoum.com/news/details/163163 (accessed 31 January 2023).
46. Al-Yawm al-Sābiʿ, سياسيون ينتقدون صناع الفيلم المسيء للرسول ويهاجمون القس المتطرف تيري جونز وزقلمة وموريس صادق... رضوان: لن نسمح لهم بإهانة الدين... باسل عادل: الأديان السماوية خط أحمر... السادات: هؤلاء دعاة فتنة وتقسيم.., 8 September 2012: http://www.youm7.com/story/2012/9/8/%D8%B3%D9%8A%D8%A7%D8%B3%D9%8A%D9%88%D9%86_%D9%8A%D9%86%D8%AA%D9%82%D8%AF%D9%88%D9%86_%D8%B5%D9%86%D8%A7%D8%B9_%D8%A7%D9%84%D9%81%D9%8A%D9%84%D9%85_%D8%A7%D9%84%D9%85%D8%B3%D9%89%D8%A1_%D9%84%D9%84%D8%B1%D8%B3%D9%88%D9%84_%D9%88%D9%8A%D9%87%D8%A7%D8%AC%D9%85%D9%88%D9%86_%D8%A7%D9%84%D9%82%D8%B3_%D8%A7%D9%84%D9%85%D8%AA/779069#.VjHXf25OfVJ (accessed 31 January 2023).
47. Al-Shurūq, إسلاميةمسيحيةضدالإساءةللرسول "ثورةغضب", 12 September 2012 (number 1320, year 4), 5.
48. Al-Hurra, الأقباط في دائرة الاتهام ... الفيلم المسيء للإسلام, 19 September 2012: http://www.alhurra.com/content/video-islam-copts-situation-egypt/212035.html (accessed 23 May 2016).
49. This ʿĀb Yūtā' is a Coptic cyber-activist who rose to fame in 2008 when he wrote a response to the novel *Azazeel* by Yusef Ziedan. However, according to Sebastian Elsässer, this 'Father Yūtā' may not exist. Elsässer, *The Coptic Question*, 204.
50. Al-Yawm al-Sābiʿ, القصص "ساويرس" يتصل بنادر بكار لحذف ما نشرته مواقع سلفية ضده, 13 September 2012: http://www.youm7.com/story/2012/9/13/%D8%A7%D9%84%D9%82%D9%85%D8%B5-%D8%B3%D8%A7%D9%88%D9%8A%D8%B1%D8%B3-%D9%8A%D8%AA%D8%B5%D9%84-%D8%A8%D9%86%D8%A7%D8%AF%D8%B1-%D8%A8%

D9%83%D8%A7%D8%B1-%D9%84%D8%AD%D8%B0%D9%81-%D9%85%D8%A7-%D9%86%D8%B4%D8%B1%D8%AA%D9%87-%D9%85%D9%88%D8%A7%D9%82%D8%B9-%D8%B3%D9%84%D9%81%D9%8A%D8%A9-%D8%B6%D8%AF%D9%87/784996#.VjDYa25OfVJ (accessed 31 January 2023).

51. Arab West Report, عبد الغفور في خطبة الجمعة بالاسكندرية: حرق البعض للإنجيل تصرف غير محسوب ومحرم, *Al-Shurūq al-Jadīd*, 15 September 2012: http://arabwestreport.info/ar/lsn-2012/lsbw-37/76-bd-lgfwr-f-khtb-ljm-blskndry-hrq-lbd-llnjyl-tsrf-gyr-mhswb-wmhrm (accessed 29 January 2016).

52. Al-Yawm al-Sābi', برهامي: لا يجوز حرق "الإنجيل" ... وتمزيقه إهانة لشيء فيه ذكر الله, 14 September 2012: https://www.youm7.com/story/2012/9/14/%D8%A8%D8%B1%D9%87%D8%A7%D9%85%D9%89-%D9%84%D8%A7-%D9%8A%D8%AC%D9%88%D8%B2-%D8%AD%D8%B1%D9%82-%D8%A7%D9%84%D8%A5%D9%86%D8%AC%D9%8A%D9%84-%D9%88%D8%AA%D9%85%D8%B2%D9%8A%D9%82%D9%87-%D8%A5%D9%87%D8%A7%D9%86%D8%A9-%D9%84%D8%B4%D9%89%D8%A1-%D9%81%D9%8A%D9%87-%D8%B0%D9%83%D8%B1/786012 (accessed 2 February 2023).

53. Al-Ahrām, بديع: الإساءة للرسول وحدت المصريين. ولا نحمل المسيحيين وزر سفهاء الخارج, 21 September 2012 (number 45945, year 137), 7.

54. Al-Shurūq, حرب البيانات بين الكنيسة والجبهة السلفية, 23 September 2012 (number 1331, year 4), 3. See Chapter Five for more information.

55. Al-Ahrām, باخوميوس: التعدى على الأديان يحتاج لموقف حازم, 22 September 2012 (number 45946, year 137), 3.

56. Copts United, الكنيسة الأرثوذكسية ترفض الفيلم المسيء للإسلام، وتؤكد: هذا يخالف تقاليد المسيحية, 10 September 2012: http://www.copts-united.com/Article.php?I=1288&A=69777 (accessed 3 February 2023).

57. Coptic Catholic Patriarchate, بيان الكنيسة الكاثوليكية بشأن ما تنشره وسائل الإعلام عن ظهور فيلم يسيء للإسلام, 11 September 2012: http://coptcatholic.net/p12776/ (accessed 3 February 2023).

58. YouTube, كلمة نصر الله عن الفيلم المسيء للرسول (ص), 17 September 2012: https://www.youtube.com/watch?v=EjGlC1LbZHE (accessed 17 May 2016).

59. Al-Nahār, من زيارة البابا إلى تصاعد الاحتجاجات تظاهرة تتردّد في السفارة الأميركية, 18 September 2012 (number 24852, year 80), 1 and 12.

60. Michael Kerr, 'Before the Revolution', in Are Knudsen and Michael Kerr (eds), *Lebanon after the Cedar Revolution* (London: Hurst, 2012), 27.

61. Are Knudsen and Michael Kerr, 'Introduction', in *Lebanon after the Cedar Revolution*, 10.

62. Emma Aubin-Boltanski, 'La Vierge, les chrétiens, les musulmans et la nation', *Terrain* 51 (2008): http://journals.openedition.org/terrain/10943 (accessed 16 February 2023).
63. This movement should not be confused with the Egyptian *al-Gamāʿa al-Islāmiyya*. Al-Jamāʿa al-Islāmiyya was founded in 1964 as the Lebanese branch of the Muslim Brotherhood and has participated in parliamentary elections after the Civil War, winning only a few seats. It can be considered moderate because it promotes a 'moderate Islamic ideology' and has accepted the confessional system in Lebanon. After the withdrawal of the Syrian army, it sided with the March 14 Alliance, something that caused internal divisions, and so its influence over the Sunni population was limited. Pall, *Salafism in Lebanon*, 9, 70.
64. Sabrina Mervin, 'Le lien iranien', in Sabrina Mervin (ed.), *Le Hezbollah: État des lieux* (Arles: Actes Sud, 2008), 83. He is one of the two representatives of Chamenei in Lebanon.
65. Nicholas Noe (ed.), *Voice of Hezbollah: The Statements of Sayyed Hassan Nasrallah* (London: Verso, 2007), 57.
66. Rola El-Husseini, *Pax Syriana: Elite Politics in Postwar Lebanon* (Syracuse: Syracuse University Press, 2012), 73.
67. Noe, *Voice of Hezbollah*, 69.
68. Maya Mikdashi, 'Blaming Others: A History of Violence in Lebanon', *Jadaliyya*, 5 June 2012: https://www.jadaliyya.com/Details/26160/Blaming-Others-A-History-of-Violence-in-Lebanon (accessed 23 February 2023).
69. Kårtveit, *Dilemmas of Attachment*, 103.
70. Knudsen and Kerr, *Lebanon after the Cedar Revolution*, 7.
71. Mikdashi, 'Blaming Others: A History of Violence in Lebanon'.
72. Hannes Baumann, 'The "New Contractor Bourgeoisie" in Lebanese Politics: Hariri, Mikati and Fares', in Knudsen and Kerr, *Lebanon after the Cedar Revolution*, 141.
73. Schwedler, 'Islamists in Power?' 10.
74. Sabrina Mervin, 'Charisme et distinction: L'élite religieuse chiite', in Franck Mermier and Sabrina Mervin (eds), *Leaders et Partisans au Liban* (Paris: Karthala, IFPO, ISSMM, 2012), 343.
75. Youtube, السيد حسن نصرالله: مسيرة الولاء للنبي محمد (ص), 17 September 2012: https://www.youtube.com/watch?v=7Tv8YGVZycY (accessed 17 May 2016).
76. Leftist Baathists introduced Kerbala as an occasion for political mobilisation. Musa Sadr used Kerbala to form the Lebanese resistance against Israel. See Sabrina Mervin, 'La religion du Hezbollah', in Mervin (ed.), *Le Hezbollah: État des lieux*, 195–98.

77. YouTube, (ص) كلمة نصر الله عن الفيلم المسيء للرسول.
78. Ibid.
79. YouTube, (ص) السيد حسن نصرالله: مسيرة الولاء للنبي محمد.
80. YouTube (ص) كلمة نصر الله عن الفيلم المسيء للرسول .
81. Al-Anwar, الأحرار: الفيلم المسيء للمسلمين عمل طائش وللحوار شروط كي لا يصبح ملهاة وغطاء, 22 September 2012 (number 18148, year 53): http://www.archive.alanwar.com/article.php?articleID=173042&issuedate=20120922 (accessed 17 May 2016).
82. Al-Anwar, الجميل استنكر في مؤتمر صحافي الاساءة للإسلام وخطف مواطن: خطاب نصرالله بتوقيته ضرب وفاقاً أوجدته زيارة البابا, 18 September 2012 (number 18144, year 53): http://www.archive.alanwar.com/article.php?articleID=172576&issuedate=20120918 (accessed 17 May 2016).
83. Al-Akhbar English, 'Lebanon-Syria Border: A Weapons Market Boom', 5 May 2012: http://english.al-akhbar.com/content/lebanon-syria-border-weapons-market-boom (accessed 15 July 2017).
84. Al-Akhbar English, 'A Shadow State in Lebanon for the Syrian Opposition', 9 October 2012: http://english.al-akhbar.com/content/shadow-state-lebanon-syrian-opposition (accessed 15 July 2017).
85. New York Times, 'Hezbollah Aids Syrian Military in a Key Battle', 19 May 2013: http://www.nytimes.com/2013/05/20/world/middleeast/syrian-army-moves-to-rebel-held-qusayr.html?pagewanted=all&_r=0 (accessed 15 July 2017).
86. Al-Akhbar English, 'Tripoli Clashes: Keeping Conflict Alive', 14 February 2012: http://english.al-akhbar.com/content/tripoli-clashes-keeping-conflict-alive (accessed 15 July 2017).
87. Al-Akhbar English, 'Tripoli Clashes: Keeping Conflict Alive'.
88. See International Crisis Group, 'Popular Protest in North Africa and the Middle East (IX): Dallying with Reform in a Divided Jordan', 12 March 2012, Middle East/North Africa Report Number 118: https://d2071andvip0wj.cloudfront.net/118-popular-protest-in-north-africa-and-the-middle-east-ix-dallying-with-reform-in-a-divided-jordan.pdf (accessed 31 May 2022).
89. See Joas Wagemakers, *The Muslim Brotherhood in Jordan* (Cambridge: Cambridge University Press, 2020), 88–89.
90. Marion Boulby, *The Muslim Brotherhood and the Kings of Jordan 1945–1993* (Atlanta: Scholars Press, 1999), 84.
91. Jillian Schwedler, *Faith in Moderation: Islamist Parties in Jordan and Yemen* (New York: Cambridge University Press), 65.
92. See Schwedler, 'Islamists in Power?' 11; Wagemakers, *The Muslim Brotherhood in Jordan*, 99.

93. Wagemakers, *The Muslim Brotherhood in Jordan*, 104.
94. Schwedler, 'Islamists in Power?' 11.
95. Wagemakers, *The Muslim Brotherhood in Jordan*, 104.
96. Ibid, 106.
97. Kirdiş, *The Rise of Islamic Political Movements and Parties*, 151.
98. Wagemakers, *The Muslim Brotherhood in Jordan*, 112.
99. Al-Dustūr, مسيرات واعتصامات تندد بالإساءة للرسول الكريم, 15 September 2012 (number 16228), 29.
100. Al-Ghad, الجرشيون يندون بالفيلم المسيء للرسول, 15 September 2012: http://www.alghad.com/articles/607348-%D8%A7%D9%84%D8%AC%D8%B1%D8%8A%D9%88%D9%86-%D9%8A%D9%86%D8%AF%D8%AF%D9%88%D9%86-%D8%A8%D8%A7%D9%84%D9%81%D9%8A%D9%84%D9%85-%D8%A7%D9%84%D9%85%D8%B3%D9%8A%D8%A1-%D9%84%D9%84%D8%B1%D8%B3%D9%88%D9%84 (accessed 21 May 2016).
101. Kirdiş, *The Rise of Islamic Political Movements and Parties*, 151.
102. Al-Ghad, عجلون: فعاليات شعبية تنتصر للرسول وتطالب بالاصلاح, 15 September 2012: http://www.alghad.com/articles/607357-%D8%B9%D8%AC%D9%84%D9%88%D9%86-%D9%81%D8%B9%D8%A7%D9%84%D9%8A%D8%A7%D8%AA-%D8%B4%D8%B9%D8%A8%D9%8A%D8%A9-%D8%AA%D9%86%D8%AA%D8%B5%D8%B1-%D9%84%D9%84%D8%B1%D8%B3%D9%88%D9%84-%D9%88%D8%AA%D8%B7%D8%A7%D9%84%D8%A8-%D8%A8%D8%A7%D9%84%D8%A7%D8%B5%D9%84%D8%A7%D8%AD?s=e3ac7a8af367d7f51c818fe724336e38&search=%D8%A7%D9%84%D9%81%D9%8A%D9%84%D9%85%20%D8%A7%D9%84%D9%85%D8%B3%D9%8A%D8%A1 (accessed 21 May 2016). The Movement of Kufranja for Reform and Change is a locally based movement of local politicians, national figures and, probably, the tribes as well. See Ajloun News, حراك كفرنجة للإصلاح يعقد إجتماعا لمناقشة سبل تطوير عمل الحراك الشعبي, 6 January 2012: http://www.ajlounnews.net/index.php?module=news&id=7546&category=71 (accessed 21 May 2016). Ahmad 'Ināb was a deputy in the Jordanian parliament; he was apparently very outspoken during the Arab Spring in Jordan. Enjaz News, الدكتور احمد عناب ... قائد يتمتع بحنكة استثنائية, http://www.enjaznews.com/details.aspx?id=26852 (accessed 21 May 2016).
103. Al-Dustūr, الحكومة تعرب عن ادانتها الشديدة ورفضها القاطع للإساءة لرسول الله ص, 14 September 2012 (number 16227), 3.
104. The Amman Message, 'The Amman Message', 2004: https://ammanmessage.com/the-amman-message-full/ (accessed 22 March 2023).

105. Al-Dustūr, الحكومة تعرب عن ادانتها الشديدة ورفضها القاطع للإساءة لرسول الله ص, 14 September 2012.
106. See Katja Hermann, *Aufbruch von Unten: Möglichkeiten und Grenzen von NGOs in Jordanien* (Hamburg: Lit, 2000), 57. The Muslim Brotherhood is heavily involved in the professional associations. Wagemakers, *The Muslim Brotherhood in Jordan*, 93.
107. Renate Dietrich, *Transformation oder Stagnation? Die jordanische Demokratisierungspolitik seit 1989* (Hamburg: Deutsches Orient Institut, 1999), 294.
108. Hermann, *Aufbruch von Unten*, 57–58.
109. Ibid, 58, 59.
110. Al-Jazeera, دور النقابات المهنية في الحياة السياسية بالأردن., 12 May 2015: https://www.youtube.com/watch?v=5mcmtPXtXp8 (accessed 22 February 2023).
111. Al-Dustūr, تواصل الادانة والاستنكار للفيلم المسيء لرسول الله, 16 September 2012 (number 16229), 9.
112. Al-Dustūr, الأردنيون يواصلون التنديد بالفيلم المسيء للرسول, 18 September 2012: http://www.addustour.com/16612/%D8%A7%D9%84%D8%A3%D8%B1%D8%AF%D9%86%D9%8A%D9%88%D9%86+%D9%8A%D9%88%D8%A7%D8%B5%D9%84%D9%88%D9%86+%D8%A7%D9%84%D8%AA%D9%86%D8%AF%D9%8A%D8%AF+%D8%A8%D8%A7%D9%84%D9%81%D9%8A%D9%84%D9%85+%D8%A7%D9%84%D9%85%D8%B3%D9%8A%D8%A1+%D9%84%D9%84%D8%B1%D8%B3%D9%88%D9%84.html (accessed 21 May 2016). The imams are mentioned here as part of the professional associations because they are employed by the state and because the state has been increasing its control over Islamic institutions in Jordan since the 1970s. See Chatelard, *Briser la mosaïque*, 277.
113. Al-Dustūr, الحكومة تعرب عن ادانتها الشديدة ورفضها القاطع للإساءة لرسول الله ص, 14 September 2012.
114. Al-Dustūr, مسيرات واعتصامات تندد بالإساءة للرسول الكريم, 15 September 2012; Al-Ghad, معان: دعوة لحملة لمقاطعة البضائع والمنتجات الأميركية, 15 September 2012: http://www.alghad.com/articles/607351-%D9%85%D8%B9%D8%A7%D9%86-%D8%AF%D8%B9%D9%88%D8%A9-%D9%84%D8%AD%D9%85%D9%84%D8%A9-%D9%84%D9%85%D9%82%D8%A7%D8%B7%D8%B9%D8%A9-%D8%A7%D9%84%D8%A8%D8%B6%D8%A7%D8%A6%D8%B9-%D9%88%D8%A7%D9%84%D9%85%D9%86%D8%AA%D8%AC%D8%A7%D8%AA-%D8%A7%D9%84%D8%A3%D9%85%D9%8A%D8%B1%D9%83%D9%8A%D8%A9?s=e3ac7a8af367d7f51c818fe724336e38&search=%D8%A7%D9%84%D9%81%D9%8A%D9%84%D9%85%20%D8%A7%D9%84%D9%85%D8%B3%D9%8A%D8%A1 (accessed 21 May 2016).

115. Al-Dustūr, .الحكومة تعرب عن ادانتها الشديدة ورفضها القاطع للإساءة لرسول الله ص, 14 September 2012.
116. Al-Dustūr, تواصل الادانة والاستنكار للفيلم المسيء لرسول الله ., 16 September 2012.
117. Al-Ghad, لجنة بلدية الطفيلة تستنكر الفيلم المسيء للرسول الكريم, 17 September 2012: http://www.alghad.com/articles/607214-%D9%84%D8%AC%D9%86%D8%A9-%D8%A8%D9%84%D8%AF%D9%8A%D8%A9-%D8%A7%D9%84%D8%B7%D9%81%D9%8A%D9%84%D8%A9-%D8%AA%D8%B3%D8%AA%D9%86%D9%83%D8%B1-%D8%A7%D9%84%D9%81%D9%8A%D9%84%D9%85-%D8%A7%D9%84%D9%85%D8%B3%D9%8A%D8%A1-%D9%84%D9%84%D8%B1%D8%B3%D9%88%D9%84-%D8%A7%D9%84-%D9%83%D8%B1%D9%8A%D9%85?s=e3ac7a8af367d7f51c818fe724336e38&search=%D8%A7%D9%84%D9%81%D9%8A%D9%84%D9%85%20%D8%A7%D9%84%D9%85%D8%B3%D9%8A%D8%A1 (accessed 21 May 2016).
118. Ibtissam al-Attiyat, Musa Shteiwi and Suleiman Sweiss, *Building Democracy in Jordan: Women's Political Participation, Political Party Life and Democratic Elections* (Stockholm: International Institute for Democracy and Electoral Assistance & the Network for Development, 2005): https://www.idea.int/sites/default/files/publications/building-democracy-in-jordan.pdf (accessed 22 March 2023), 88.
119. Al-Dustūr, تواصل الإدانة والاستنكار للفيلم المسيء لرسول الله, 17 September 2012: http://www.addustour.com//16611/%D8%AA%D9%88%D8%A7%D8%B5%D9%84+%D8%A7%D9%84%D8%A5%D8%AF%D8%A7%D9%86%D8%A9+%D9%88%D8%A7%D9%84%D8%A7%D8%B3%D8%AA%D9%86%D9%83%D8%A7%D8%B1+%D9%84%D9%84%D9%81%D9%8A%D9%84%D9%85+%D8%A7%D9%84%D9%85%D8%B3%D9%8A%D8%A1+%D9%84%D8%B1%D8%B3%D9%88%D9%84+%D8%A7%D9%84%D9%84%D9%87.html (accessed 21 May 2016)..
120. Al-Dustūr, الحكومة تعرب عن ادانتها الشديدة ورفضها القاطع للإساءة لرسول الله ص, 14 September 2012.
121. See the comment of the Council of Evangelical Churches in Jordan (Al-Rai, مجلس ومجمع الكنائس يستنكران الفيلم المسيء, 15 September 2012: http://www.alrai.com/article_m/539017.html [accessed 21 May 2016]), and that of the Jordan Theological Evangelical Seminary (JETS) (in Al-Dustūr, تواصل الادانة والاستنكار للفيلم المسيء لرسول الله, 16 September 2012). The Council of Evangelical Churches in Jordan (*majma' al-kanā'is al-injīliyya*) comprises five Evangelical Churches that are not officially recognized by the state but are registered as 'associations': the Free Evangelical Church, the Baptist Church, the Nazarene Church, the Christian and Missionary Alliance and the Assemblies of

God Church. Wolfram Reiss, J. Kriener and K. Hock, *Die Darstellung des Christentums in Schulbüchern islamisch geprägter Länder, 3: Libanon und Jordanien* (Berlin: EB-Verlag, 2012), 305–6.
122. Ḥannā Kildānī, Personal Interview, 8 April 2015, Marj al-Hammam, Amman.
123. Linga, مجلس رؤساء الكنائس في الأردن هو المرجعية الوحيدة لكل الشؤون المسيحية!!!, 27 January 2009: https://www.linga.org/local-news/MjMx (accessed 16 March 2023).
124. Abouna, بيان شجب واستنكار من مجلس رؤساء الكنائس في الأردن, 14 September 2012: http://www.abouna.org/node/1164 (accessed 21 May 2016); Ḥannā Kildānī, Personal Interview.

Chapter 2

1. The Coptic Orthodox priest Fīlūbātir Gamīl 'Azīz is a somewhat controversial figure in Egypt. In 2004, he co-founded the journal *al-Katība al-Tibiyya*, which was distributed in churches and chronicled all incidents of violence against Copts (Jayson Casper, 'The Coptic Movements: Coptic Activism in a Revolutionary Setting', *Arab West Report*, 15 May 2013: http://www.arabwestreport.info/sites/default/files/pdfs/AWRpapers/paper44.pdf [accessed 22 March 2023], 5).
2. Copts Today, مؤامرة شيطانية ... الفيلم المسيء للرسول .. بقلم القس فيلوباتير جميل عزيز, 12 September 2012.
3. The New York Times, 'Protesters in Beirut Set Danish Consulate on Fire', 5 February 2006.
4. Kårtveit, *Dilemmas of Attachmen*, 105. Catherine Mayeur Jaouen notes that the controversy over the Regensburg lecture was the only time in recent history that Coptic Catholics felt particularly vulnerable. See her *Voyage en Haute-Égypte*, 326.
5. POC 63:1–2 (2013), 170.
6. The video was quickly removed from YouTube, but the author was able to secure it.
7. Heo, *The Political Lives of Saints*, 23.
8. Reiss, *Erneuerung in der koptisch-orthodoxen Kirche*, 289.
9. Elsässer, *The Coptic Question*, 68; Ibrahim, *The Copts of Egypt*, 159.
10. Voile, *Les coptes d'Égypte sous Nasser*, 55–56.
11. Elsässer, *The Coptic Question in the Mubarak Era*, 50.
12. See The World Bank, 'Population, Total: Egypt, Arab Rep.', [n. d.]: https://data.worldbank.org/indicator/SP.POP.TOTL?locations=EG (accessed 23 February 2023).
13. Wolfram Reiss, 'Die Situation der Kopten in der Gegenwart', in A. Hölscher, A. Middelbeck-Varwick and M. Thurau (eds), *Kirche in Welt: Christentum im Zeichen kultureller Vielfalt* (Frankfurt: Peter Lang Verlag, 2013), 64.

14. Reiss, *Erneuerung in der koptisch-orthodoxen Kirche*, 81.
15. Ibid, 99.
16. Catherine Mayeur-Jaouen, 'What Do Egypt's Copts and Muslims Share? The Issue of Shrines', in Albera Dionigi and Maria Couroucli (eds), *Sharing Sacred Spaces in the Mediterranean: Christians, Muslims, and Jews at Shrines and Sanctuaries* (Bloomington: Indiana University Press, 2012), 150.
17. Mayeur-Jaouen, *Voyage en Haute-Égypte*, 20.
18. Ibid, 345, 341.
19. Heo, *The Political Lives of Saints*, 244.
20. Youssef Sidhom, 'Code Name: Sectarian Strife', *Watani*, 15 May 2011 (number 2577, year 53/number 543, year 11).
21. Guirguis, *Les Coptes d'Égypte*, 43.
22. Ibid.
23. Ibid, 37.
24. Mahmood, *Religious Difference in a Secular Age*, 86.
25. Ahram Online, 'Church-State Relations Yet to Change in Morsi's Egypt', 18 November 2011: http://english.ahram.org.eg/NewsContent/1/64/58089/Egypt/Politics-/-Churchstate-relations-yet-to-change-in-Morsis-Egy.aspx (accessed 23 February 2023).
26. Guirguis, *Les Coptes d'Égypte*, 43.
27. Aïda Kanafani-Zahar, *Liban, la guerre et la mémoire* (Rennes: Presses Universitaires de Rennes, 2011), 77, 78, 79.
28. Elizabeth Iskander, 'The "Mediation" of Muslim-Christian Relations in Egypt: The Strategies and Discourses of Official Egyptian Press during Mubarak's Presidency', *Islam and Christian–Muslim Relations* 23:1 (2012), 33.
29. Al-Ahrām, مفتي الجمهورية للأهرام: نصرة النبي تتحقق باتباع منهجه . . . والإسلام يرفض العنف وإرهاب الآمنين, 21 September 2012 (number 45945, year 137), 40.
30. Tadros, *Copts at the Crossroads*, 46.
31. Ibid, 46.
32. Anthony Shenoda, 'Reflections on the (In)visibility of Copts in Egypt', *Jadaliyya*, 18 May 2011: http://www.jadaliyya.com/pages/index/1624/reflections-on-the-%28in%29visibility-of-copts-in-egyp (accessed 8 February 2023).
33. Shenoda 'Reflections on the (In)visibility of Copts in Egypt'.
34. Gauvain, *Salafi Ritual Purity*, 241.
35. Ibid.
36. Shenoda, 'Reflections on the (In)visibility of Copts in Egypt'.
37. Gauvain, *Salafi Ritual Purity*, 241.
38. Sidhom, 'Code Name: Sectarian Strife'.

39. POC 63:1–2 (2013), 170–71.
40. Ibid, 170.
41. Copts United, بالفيديو والصور الأنبا كيرلس أسقف نجع حمادي: لا لازدراء الاديان . . . واحترسوا من الثعالب الصغيرة, 14 September 2012: http://www.copts-united.com/article.php?I=1292&A=70190 (accessed 21 May 2016). On *Bayt al-ʿāʾila*, see Chapter Four.
42. Shenoda, 'Reflections on the (In)visibility of Copts in Egypt'.
43. Watanī, المصريون 'يدينون' الفيلم المسيء للرسول, 16 September 2012 (number 2647, year 54/number 613, year 12), 9.
44. Elsässer, *The Coptic Question in the Mubarak Era*, 50.
45. Heo, *The Political Lives of Saints*, 245.
46. See *Majallat al-Azhar*, January 2011, pages *waw-zayn*, which publishes the condemnations of Shaykh al-Azhar Ahmad al-Tayyib, Mufti ʿAlī Gumʿa and the minister of Islamic Endowments. Ahmad al-Tayyib claimed that 'the targets are not only the Christians, but all Egyptians. Whoever targets a church, targets a mosque'.
47. Heo, *The Political Lives of Saints*, 244.
48. Ibid, 245.
49. Bauer, *Die Kultur der Ambiguität*, 27.
50. Al-Yawm al-Sābiʿ, أقباط المهجر يشعلون الفتنة بإنتاج فيلم مسيء للرسول . . سياسيون يهاجمون القس الأمريكي تيري جونز و"صادق" و"زقلمة" ويطالبون بالملاحقة القانونية للفيلم. . رضوان: المسيحيون المصريون قبل المسلمين ضد الفيلم, 9 September 2012: http://www.youm7.com/story/0000/0/0/-/780136#.Vjhs7m5OfVI (accessed 16 March 2023).
51. Ibid.
52. Al-Shurūq, "ثورة غضب" إسلامية مسيحية ضد الإساءة للرسول, 12 September 2012.
53. Copts Today, حركة "أقباط بلا قيود" نرفض الإساءة للمقدسات الإسلامية ونطالب بوضع حد للإساءات لرموزنا المسيحية, 10 September 2012: http://www.coptstoday.com/Copts-News/Detail.php?Id=32279 (accessed 23 May 2016).
54. L'Orient le Jour, 'Geagea: Le Hezbollah n'est pas prêt au dialogue et utilise le film islamophobe pour se créer la dimension politique qu'il espère', 18 September 2012 (number 13557), 3.
55. Mīnā Magdī, Personal Interview, 21 January 2015, Cairo.
56. Hannā Kildānī, Personal Interview.
57. Mārūn Lahhām, Personal Interview, 20 April 2015, Amman.
58. Bishop Benedict, Personal Interview, 24 April 2015, Amman; Bāssim Farrāj, Personal Interview, 27 April 2015, Amman.
59. Al-Dustūr, مختصون مسلمون ومسيحيون: الفيلم المشبوه مؤامرة على التعايش السلمي بين الأديان, 22 September 2012: http://www.addustour.com/16616/%D9%85%D8%AE%D8%AA

%D8%B5%D9%88%D9%86+%D9%85%D8%B3%D9%84%D9%85%D9%88%D9%86+%D9%88%D9%85%D8%B3%D9%8A%D8%AD%D9%8A%D9%88%D9%86+%3A+%D8%A7%D9%84%D9%81%D9%8A%D9%84%D9%85+%D8%A7%D9%84%D9%85%D8%B4%D8%A8%D9%88%D9%87+%D9%85%D8%A4%D8%A7%D9%85%D8%B1%D8%A9+%D8%B9%D9%84%D9%89+%D8%A7%D9%84%D8%AA%D8%B9%D8%A7%D9%8A%D8%B4+%D8%A7%D9%84%D8%B3%D9%84%D9%85%D9%8A+%D8%A8%D9%8A%D9%86+%D8%A7%D9%84%D8%A3%D8%AF%D9%8A%D8%A7%D9%86.html (accessed 21 May 2016)..

60. AHR, 'AHR Conversation: Religious Identities and Violence', 1444.
61. YouTube, مناظرة وسام عبد الوارث وجمال أسعد الفيلم المسيء للرسول, 9 September 2012: https://www.youtube.com/watch?v=sqhRj3ArQRQ (accessed 23 May 2016).
62. Al-Safīr, القاهرة فيلم يفجّر غضباً اقتحام السفارة الأمريكية, 12 September 2012 (number 12281, year 39), 1 and 17.
63. Al-Shurūq, السفارة الأمريكية تحت الحصار, 12 September 2012 (number 1320, year 4), 1.
64. The Guardian, 'Protests in Cairo and Benghazi over American Film', 11 September 2012: http://www.theguardian.com/world/2012/sep/11/egypt-protest (accessed 23 February 2023).
65. Jayson Casper, 'Salafis, Muslim Youth Protest anti-Muhammad Film at US Embassy', *A Sense of Belonging*, 11 September 2012: http://asenseofbelonging.org/2012/09/11/salafis-muslim-youth-protest-anti-muhammad-film-at-us-embassy/ (accessed 22 March 2023). Another report suggests that the police negotiated with the protesters who eventually descended from the US embassy. Al-Safīr, القاهرة فيلم يفجّر غضباً اقتحام السفارة الأمريكية, 12 September 2012.
66. Al-Shurūq, السفارة الأمريكية تحت الحصار.
67. Watanī, تظاهرات أمام السفارة الامريكية لإدانة الفيلم المسيء للرسول, 11 September 2012: http://www.wataninet.com/%D8%A3%D8%AE%D8%A8%D8%A7%D8%B1-%D9%85%D8%AA%D9%86%D9%88%D8%B9%D8%A9/%D8%AA%D8%B8%D8%A7%D9%87%D8%B1%D8%A7%D8%AA-%D8%A3%D9%85%D8%A7%D9%85-%D8%A7%D9%84%D8%B3%D9%81%D8%A7%D8%B1%D8%A9-%D8%A7%D9%84%D8%A7%D9%85%D8%B1%D9%8A%D9%83%D9%8A%D8%A9-%D9%84%D8%A5%D8%AF%D8%A7%D9%86/142794/ (accessed 12 July 2017).
68. Copts Today, وصول مسيرة قبطية الي السفارة الامريكية وهتافات . . . مسلم مسيحى ايد واحدة, 12 September 2012: http://www.coptstoday.com/Copts-News/Detail.php?Id=32628 (accessed 3 March 2015).
69. Copts Today, مؤامرة شيطانية . . . الفيلم المسيء للرسول . . بقلم القس فيلوباتير جميل عزيز, 12 September 2012.

70. Al-Safīr, طرابلس: إحراق 'كنتاكي' و 'هارديز' يوقع قتيلاً و25 جريحا, 15 September 2012 (number 12284, year 39), 6.
71. Ibid.
72. Ibid.
73. Copts Today, السلفيون يتجمهرون أمام منزل " جوزيف نصر الله " صاحب قناة الطريق, 18 September 2012: http://www.coptstoday.com/Copts-News/Detail.php?Id=33564 (accessed 3 March 2014).
74. Copts Today, فيديو . . . حرق منزل موريس صادق بالقاهرة في وجود الشرطة المصرية. 13 September 2012: http://www.coptstoday.com/Copts-News/Detail.php?Id=32652 (accessed 3 March 2014).
75. Al-Ahrām, 200 متظاهر يحاصرون منزل أحد منتجي الفيلم المسيء للرسول الكريم, 19 September 2012: http://www.ahram.org.eg/archive/The-First/News/171900.aspx (accessed 23 May 2016). However, because *al-Ahrām* mentioned that Niqūlā Bāsilī Niqūlā had emigrated to the United States ten years earlier – which was not correct – it is not certain that this really was Niqūlā Bāsilī Niqūlā.
76. Le Monde, 'Dans la diaspora copte, des extrémistes minoritaires mais très actifs', 20 September 2012: https://www.lemonde.fr/afrique/article/2012/09/19/dans-la-diaspora-copte-des-extremistes-minoritaires-mais-tres-actifs_1762299_3212.html (accessed 31 May 2020).
77. Copts Today, أمن الدولة' تحقق في واقعة تمزيق الإنجيل أثناء أحداث السفارة الأمريكية, 22 September 2012.
78. Al-Balad, 'مسلم مسيحي إيد واحدة' . . . وترفع لافتة مطرانية المنوفية تستنكر الإساءة للرسول, 15 September 2012: http://www.el-balad.com/265222 (accessed 21 May 2016).
79. Al-Shurūq, أمن الدولة تستدعى "أبو إسلام" المتهم بتمزيق الإنجيل, 25 September 2012 (number 1333, year 4), 6.
80. Al-Hayāt, اشتباكات بين إسلاميين وأقباط في محاكمة سلفي أحرق الإنجيل, 1 October 2012 (number 18077), 6.
81. Watanī, الحكم بالسجن لابو إسلام 11 سنة ولابنه ثمان سنوات, 12 June 2013: http://www.watani-net.com/%D8%A3%D8%AE%D8%A8%D8%A7%D8%B1-%D9%85%D8%AA%D9%86%D9%88%D8%B9%D8%A9/%D8%A7%D9%84%D8%AD%D9%83%D9%85-%D8%A8%D8%A7%D9%84%D8%B3%D8%AC%D9%86-%D9%84%D8%A7%D8%A8%D9%88-%D8%A5%D8%B3%D9%84%D8%A7%D9%85-11-%D8%B3%D9%86%D8%A9-%D9%88%D9%84%D8%A7%D8%A8%D9%86%D9%87-%D8%AB%D9%85/121024/ (accessed 12 July 2017).
82. Al-Ahrām, اليوم أولى جلسات محاكمة 'أبو إسلام' المتهم بحرق الإنجيل أمام السفارة الأمريكية, 30 September 2012 (number 45954, year 137), 22.
83. Arab West Report, أسقف بني مزار يعتذر للمسلمين عن الإساءة مؤكدا مخالفتها لسماحة المسيحية, 17 September 2012: http://www.arabwestreport.info/ar/lsn-2012/lsbw-37/73-sqf-bn-mzr-ytdhr-llmslmyn-n-ls-mwkd-mkhlfth-lsmh-lmsyhy (accessed 2 November 2015).

84. See Guirguis, *Les Coptes d'Égypte*, 144–47.
85. Dan Brown, *Da Vinci Code* (Paris: JC Lattès, 2004).
86. Middle East Council of Churches, بيان من رؤساء الكنائس المسيحية بمصر حول فيلم شيفرده دافمسي, Muntada, July-September 2006, 26.
87. See Guirguis, *Les Coptes d'Égypte*, 145.
88. Yūsif Zaydān, عزازيل (Cairo: Dār al-Shurūq, 2008).
89. Mahmood, *Religious Difference in a Secular Age*, 195, 182.
90. New York Times, 'Cultural Clash Fuels Muslims Angry at Online Video', 16 September 2012: http://www.nytimes.com/2012/09/17/world/middleeast/muslims-rage-over-film-fueled-by-culture-divide.html?_r=0 (accessed 23 May 2016).
91. Hannā Kildānī, Personal Interview.
92. Mahmood, *Religious Difference in a Secular Age*, 112.
93. See Guirguis, *Les Coptes d'Égypte*, 75–77.
94. Mahmood, *Religious Difference in a Secular Age*, 114.
95. Ibid, 141.
96. Alexander Pollack establishes six categories of Anti-semitism: dishonesty, alienation, inherent, economic Jewry, corruption and the impulse to corrupt, and the Jewish world conspiracy. See his 'Antisemitismus: Probleme der Definition und Operationalisierung eines Begriffs', in John Bunzl and Alexander Senfft (eds), *Zwischen Antisemitismus und Islamophobie: Vorurteile und Projektionen in Europa und Nahost* (Hamburg: VSA, 2008), 21.
97. Picard, 'La violence milicienne et sa légitimation religieuse', 323.
98. The Guardian, 'Muhammad Film: Director Goes into Hiding after Protests', 12 September 2012: http://www.theguardian.com/world/2012/sep/13/anti-islamic-film-us-nakoula?INTCMP=SRCH (accessed 23 February 2023).
99. The Guardian, 'Anti-Islamic Film Search Leads to Coptic Christian in California', 12 September 2012: http://www.theguardian.com/world/2012/sep/13/anti-islamic-film-us-nakoula?INTCMP=SRCH (accessed 23 February 2023). In 2010, Niqūlā Bāsilī Niqūlā was sentenced to twenty-one months in prison for having used fake identity cards and social security numbers to open credit accounts. The New York Times, 'Man of Many Names is Tied to a Video', 13 September 2012: http://www.nytimes.com/2012/09/14/us/origins-of-provocative-video-are-shrouded.html?_r=0 (accessed 12 July 2017).
100. Los Angeles Times, 'Christian Charity, Ex-Con Linked to Film on Islam', 13 September 2012: http://articles.latimes.com/2012/sep/13/local/la-me-filmmaker-20120914 (accessed 22 March 2023).

101. RT, 'Law Enforcement Confirms Convicted Fraudster behind Anti-Muslim Movie', 13 September 2012/2 October 2012: https://www.rt.com/usa/nakoula-confirmed-anti-muslim-movie-063/ (accessed 12 July 2017).
102. Le Monde, 'Dans la diaspora copte, des extrémistes minoritaires mais très actifs'.
103. The New York Times, 'Updates on Rage over Anti-Islam Film', 12 September 2012: http://thelede.blogs.nytimes.com/2012/09/12/latest-updates-on-rage-over-anti-islam-film/ (accessed 12 July 2017).
104. Le Monde, 'Dans la diaspora copte, des extrémistes minoritaires mais très actifs'.
105. Al-Safīr, القاهرة فيلم يفجّر غضباً اقتحام السفارة الأمريكية, 12 September 2012.
106. Copts United, الكنيسة الأرثوذكسية ترفض الفيلم المسيء للإسلام، وتؤكد: هذا يخالف تقاليد المسيحية, 10 September 2012.
107. Gate al-Ahram, الأنبا بولا: الفيلم المسيء فكرة شيطانية صهيونية لضرب الأديان . . ويبطله عميلا للموساد, 15 September 2012: http://gate.ahram.org.eg/News/251298.aspx (accessed 21 May 2016).
108. M. H. Yousef, with R. Brackin, *Son of Hamas* (Carol Stream, Israel: Tyndale Momentum, 2011).
109. Al-Yawm al-Sābi', انتفاضة المؤسسات الدينية ضد الفيلم المسيء للرسول… "الأزهر": الداعون لإنتاجه هدفهم إشعال الفتنة.. "الإفتاء": ليس من الحرية ويمس أقدس رمز للمسلمين.. و"أقباط المهجر": نتبرأ من موريس صادق وزقلمة, 11 September 2012: https://www.youm7.com/story/2012/9/11/%D8%A7%D9%86%D8%AA%D9%81%D8%A7%D8%B6%D8%A9-%D8%A7%D9%84%D9%85%D8%A4%D8%B3%D8%B3%D8%A7%D8%AA-%D8%A7%D9%84%D8%AF%D9%8A%D9%86%D9%8A%D8%A9-%D8%B6%D8%AF-%D8%A7%D9%84%D9%81%D9%8A%D9%84%D9%85-%D8%A7%D9%84%D9%85%D8%B3%D9%89%D8%A1-%D9%84%D9%84%D8%B1%D8%B3%D9%88%D9%84-%D8%A7%D9%84%D8%A3%D8%B2%D9%87%D8%B1-%D8%A7%D9%84%D8%AF%D8%A7%D8%B9%D9%88%D9%86-%D9%84%D8%A5%D9%86%D8%AA%D8%A7%D8%AC%D9%87/782099 (accessed 31 January 2023).
110. Al-Yawm al-Sābi', انتفاضة المؤسسات الدينية ضد الفيلم المسيء للرسول… "الأزهر": الداعون لإنتاجه هدفهم إشعال الفتنة.. "الإفتاء": ليس من الحرية ويمس أقدس رمز للمسلمين.. و"أقباط المهجر": نتبرأ من موريس صادق وزقلمة, 11 September 2012.
111. 'Indeed, those who disbelieve spend their wealth to avert [people] from the way of Allah. So they will spend it; then it will be for them a [source of] regret; then they will be overcome. And those who have disbelieved – unto Hell they will be gathered. / [This is] so that Allah may distinguish the wicked from the good and place the wicked some of them upon others and heap them all together and put them into Hell. It is those who are the losers'. Qur'an 8:36–37: http://quran.com/8 (accessed 31 January 2023).

112. Al-Ahrām, غضب شعبي من الإساءة للرسول, 12 September 2012 (number 45936, year 137), 1 and 5; Al-Ahrām, وزير الأوقاف يطالب بتغليب صوت العقل في التعامل مع إزدراء الأديان, 21 September 2012 (number 45945, year 137), 5.
113. YouTube, كلمة نصر الله عن الفيلم المسيء للرسول (ص), 17 September 2012.
114. Elie Ferzli was an MP from 1992 to 2005 and deputy speaker of parliament, also from 1992 to 2005 (*Who's Who 2007–2008*, s. v. 'Ferzli, Elie Najib').
115. Elie Ferzli, 'Elie Ferzli Blog', 26 September 2012: http://elieferzli.blogspot.co.at/2012_09_01_archive.html (accessed 15 July 2017).
116. Some protests in Jordan demanded a boycott of 'Jewish products', such as in the southern city of Ma'an, where protesters reportedly demanded the closure of the US embassy and the boycott of 'American and Jewish products'. In Al-Ghad, "سلفيو معان ينتصرون للرسول في أسبوع الغضب", 20 September 2012: http://www.alghad.com/articles/606985-%D8%B3%D9%84%D9%81%D9%8A%D9%88-%D9%85%D8%B9%D8%A7%D9%86-%D9%8A%D9%86%D8%AA%D8%B5%D8%B1%D9%88%D9%86-%D9%84%D9%84%D8%B1%D8%B3%D9%88%D9%84-%D9%81%D9%8A-%D8%A7%D8%B3%D8%A8%D9%88%D8%B9-%D8%A7%D9%84%D8%BA%D8%B6%D8%A8?s=e3ac7a8af367d7f51c818fe724336e38&search=%D8%A7%D9%84%D9%81%D9%8A%D9%84%D9%85%20%D8%A7%D9%84%D9%85%D8%B3%D9%8A%D8%A1 (accessed 12 July 2017).
117. Al-Dustūr, فعاليات الوسطية و'عشائر الطفيلة' تستنكر الإساءة إلى النبي الكريم, 19 September 2012 (number 16231), 29.
118. Abouna, بيان شجب واستنكار من مجلس رؤساء الكنائس في الأردن, 14 September 2012.
119. Al-Da'wa al-Salafiyya, بيان من 'الدعوة السلفية' بشأن الفيلم المسيء 'لرسول الله - صلى الله عليه وسلم, 11 September 2012: http://www.anasalafy.com/play.php?catsmktba=35834 (accessed 22 February 2023).
120. Elsässer, *The Coptic Question in the Mubarak Era*, 110.
121. Gudrun Krämer, 'Anti-Semitism in the Muslim World: A Critical Review', *Die Welt des Islams* 46:3 (2006), 270.
122. See Kirsten E. Schulze, *The Jews of Lebanon: Between Coexistence and Conflict* (Brighton: Sussex Academic Press, 2001).
123. Krämer, 'Anti-Semitism in the Muslim World', 265.
124. Kimberley Katz, *Jordanian Jerusalem: Holy Places and National Spaces* (Gainesville: University Press of Florida, 2005), 146, 149.
125. Hager, 'The Orthodox Issue in Jordan', 217.
126. Statement of the Orthodox Society given to the author in May 2015 (see Orthodox Society, بيان شجب إدانة., [n. d.]). The newspaper *Haaretz* explained in its 5 September 2012 issue that the term 'price-tag' was coined by Israeli settlers as

a form of revenge for forced evacuations of settlements in the West Bank and Gaza. See Haaretz, 'Monastery Near Jerusalem Torched; Catholics Blame Israeli "Hatred"', 5 September 2012 (number 28380, volume 92), 1 and 2.

127. Al-Nahār, مفتي الجمهورية: زيارة البابا شهادة للبنان, 19 September 2012 (number 24853, year 80), 2.

Chapter 3

1. Heyberger, *Les chrétiens au Proche-Orient*, 18.
2. Ibid, 17.
3. Ibid.
4. Géraldine Chatelard, 'Les chrétiens en Jordanie, dynamiques identitaires et gestion du pluralisme', *Les Cahiers de l'Orient* 93:1 (2009), 41.
5. Mārūn Lahhām, Personal Interview; 'Āmir al-Hāfī, Personal Interview, 9 April 2015, Amman.
6. Delhaye, 'Contemporary Muslim-Christian Relations in Egypt', 71.
7. Joseph Massad, *Colonial Effects: The Making of National Identity in Jordan* (New York: Columbia University Press, 2001), 233.
8. Schwedler, *Faith in Moderation*, 43.
9. International Crisis Group, 'Jordan's 9/11: Dealing with Jihadi Islamism', 4.
10. ANERA, 'Palestinian Refugees in Lebanon', Volume 3 (June 2012): http://bit.ly/1Ty1RcJ (accessed 5 July 2020), 3.
11. UNHCR, 'Syrian Refugees in Lebanon Surpass One Million', 3 April 2014: https://www.unhcr.org/news/press/2014/4/533c15179/syrian-refugees-lebanon-surpass-million.html (accessed 23 February 2023).
12. Byzantine Catholic Church in America, 'Prelate: Muslim Refugees Place Future of Lebanon's Christians in Jeopardy', 22 August 2015: http://byzcath.org/index.php/news-mainmenu-49/4841-prelate-muslim-refugees-place-future-of-lebanon-s-christians-in-jeopardy (accessed 23 February 2023).
13. Rania Maktabi, 'The Lebanese Census of 1932 Revisited: Who are the Lebanese?' *British Journal of Middle Eastern Studies* 26:2 (1999), 227.
14. Maya Mikdashi, 'What is Political Sectarianism?' *Jadaliyya*, 25 March 2011: http://www.jadaliyya.com/pages/index/1008/what-is-political-sectarianism (accessed 24 February 2023).
15. Mikdashi, 'What is Political Sectarianism?'
16. Alexander D. M. Henley, 'The Maronites', in Paul Rowe (ed.), *Routledge Handbook of Minorities in the Middle East* (Milton: Routledge, 2018), 94.
17. POC 66:3–4 (2016), 409.
18. Chatelard, *Briser la mosaïque*, 182.

19. International Crisis Group, 'Popular Protest in North Africa and the Middle East (IX): Dallying with Reform in a Divided Jordan', 12 March 2012, Middle East/North Africa Report Number 118: https://d2071andvip0wj.cloudfront.net/118-popular-protest-in-north-africa-and-the-middle-east-ix-dallying-with-reform-in-a-divided-jordan.pdf (accessed 31 May 2022), 6.
20. See Mahmood, *Religious Difference in a Secular Age*, 103–5.
21. Guirguis, *Les Coptes d'Égypte*, 211–12.
22. Scott, *The Challenge of Political Islam*, 86.
23. Mahmood, *Religious Difference in a Secular Age*, 9.
24. Chatelard, *Briser la mosaïque*, 156.
25. The 2014 Constitution introduced a quota system of twenty-four seats for Egyptian Christians. Dominique Avon, 'Le nom chrétien sous la plume d'hommes de religion musulmans égyptiens', *Les Cahiers d'EMAM* 32 (2020): http://journals.openedition.org/emam/2669 (accessed 17 February 2023).
26. Dominique Avon, 'Al-Azhar ou l'expression d'un désarroi des autorités sunnites', 2015: https://hal.science/halshs-03263255v1 (accessed 17 February 2023).
27. Makari, *Conflict and Cooperation*, 93.
28. Pierre-Jean Luizard, 'Al-Azhar: Institution Sunnite réformée', in Alain Roussillon (ed.), *Entre réforme sociale et mouvement national: Identité et modernisation en Égypte (1882–1962): Actes du colloque 'Réforme sociale en Égypte' 10-13/12/1992* (Cairo: Institut Français d'archéologie, 1995), 547.
29. Bernard Rougier, *Le jihad au quotidien* (Paris: PUF, 2004), 114–15.
30. Ibid, 119.
31. Ibid, 118.
32. Al-Akhbar English, 'Lebanon's Mufti: The Future Movement Wants My Turban', 16 August 2012: http://english.al-akhbar.com/content/lebanons-mufti-future-movement-wants-my-turban (accessed 17 May 2016).
33. Rougier, *Le jihad au quotidien*, 118.
34. Zoltan Pall, *Lebanese Salafis Between the Gulf and Europe: Development, Fractionalization and Translational Networks of Salafism in Lebanon* (Amsterdam: Amsterdam University Press, 2013), 32.
35. Wagemakers, *The Muslim Brotherhood in Jordan*, 86.
36. Chatelard, *Briser la mosaïque*, 276–77.
37. The Amman Message, 'The Amman Message', 2004
38. Yvonne Yazbeck Haddad and Jane I. Smith, 'The Quest for "A Common Word": Initial Christian Responses to a Muslim Initiative', *Islam and Christian–Muslim Relations* 20:4 (2009), 370.
39. Ibid.

40. Ibid, 371.
41. Makari, *Conflict and Cooperation*, 93. This was evident in the context of this controversy.
42. Pall, *Salafism in Lebanon*, 4.
43. Ibid, 25.
44. Gauvain, *Salafi Ritual Purity*, 3
45. Al-Ahram Hebdo, 'Al-Azhar: Le jeu de la politique et de la religion', 17–23 April 2013 (number 970, year 19), 3.
46. Avon, 'Al-Azhar ou l'expression d'un désarroi des autorités sunnites'.
47. The constituent assembly was dominated by Islamists and Salafis who persisted in influencing the drafting, something that provoked strong opposition from the secular representatives and the representatives of the Churches and led to their withdrawal from the process in November 2012. Muhammad Mursī then issued a highly controversial presidential decree ensuring the constituent assembly's continued work.
48. Al-Ahrām Hebdo, 'Al-Azhar: Le jeu de la politique et de la religion'.
49. Pall, *Salafism in Lebanon*, 67.
50. Māhir Hammūd is a liberal Islamist who maintained a small militia during the Civil War. See Rougier, *Le jihad au quotidien*, 125, 226. According to Bernard Rougier, he has been one of Hezbollah's strongest supporters. See his *Everyday Jihad: The Rise of Militant Islam among Palestinians in Lebanon* (Cambridge, MA, London: Harvard University Press, 2007), 139.
51. Al-Safīr, لقاء علمائي يدعو قباني إلى الاستقالة والسنيورة الى إعادة المال السروق, 17 February 2011 (number 11816, year 37), 2.
52. Ali Gomaa, 'Egypt's Mufti: To Muslims, Prophet Muhammad is "the Mercy to all Worlds"', *Washington Post*, 18 September 2012: http://www.faithstreet.com/onfaith/2012/09/18/prophet-muhammad-is-the-mercy-to-all-worlds-to-muslims-egypts-mufti/10018 (accessed 12 July 2017). The opinion used to be available under www.washingtonpost.com/blogs/guest-voices/post/prophet-muhammad-is-the-mercy-to-all-worlds-to-muslims-egypts-mufti/2012/09/18/a0e7e10a-01ab-11e2-b260-32f4a8db9b7e_blog.html, see https://twitter.com/alhabibali/status/248511310357204992 (accessed 14 May 2023).
53. Gomaa, 'Egypt's Mufti: To Muslims, Prophet Muhammad is "the Mercy to all Worlds"'.
54. Al-Ahrām, مفتي الجمهورية للأهرام: نصرة النبي تتحقق باتباع منهجه . . . والإسلام يرفض العنف وإرهاب الآمنين,.
55. Al-Dustūr, الحكومة تعرب عن ادانتها الشديدة ورفضها القاطع للإساءة لرسول الله ص, 14 September 2012.

56. Al-Ahrām, شيخ الأزهر: الغرب لا يزال يفكر بمنطق عصور الظلام, 28 September 2012 (number 45952, year 137), 4.
57. Al-Yawm al-Sābiʿ, انتفاضة المؤسسات الدينية ضد الفيلم المسيء للرسول... "الأزهر": الداعون لإنتاجه هدفهم إشعال الفتنة.. "الإفتاء": ليس من الحرية ويمس أقدس رمز للمسلمين.. و"أقباط المهجر": نتبرأ من موريس صادق وزقلمة, 11 September 2012.
58. Al-Ahrām, رموز إسلامية ومسيحية تطالب بتجريم ازدراء الأديان, 17 September 2012 (number 45941, year 137), 5.
59. Al-Tawhīd, لبنان: سلسلة واسعة من المواقف المنددة من الأحزاب والجمعيات والشخصيات الإسلامية والمسيحية والوطنية بالإساءة للنبي محمد صلى الله عليه وسلم, 13 September 2012: http://www.altawhid.org/2012/09/13/%D9%84%D8%A8%D9%86%D8%A7%D9%86-%D8%B3%D9%84%D8%B3%D9%84%D8%A9-%D9%88%D8%A7%D8%B3%D8%B9%D8%A9-%D9%85%D9%86-%D8%A7%D9%84%D9%85%D9%88%D8%A7%D9%82%D9%81-%D8%A7%D9%84%D9%85%D9%86%D8%AF%D8%AF%D8%A9-%D9%85/ (accessed 17 May 2016).
60. Al-Nahār, اجتماع بدعوة من قباني دان 'براءة المسلمين'؛ لن يفيد أميركا التنصّل من مسؤولياتها, 21 September 2012 (number 24856, year 80), 6.
61. 'The Messenger has believed in what was revealed to him from his Lord, and [so have] the believers. All of them have believed in Allah and His angels and His books and His messengers, [saying], "We make no distinction between any of His messengers". And they say, "We hear and we obey. [We seek] Your forgiveness, our Lord, and to You is the [final] destination"'. Qurʾan: http://quran.com/2 (accessed 21 May 2016).
62. See Hager, 'The Orthodox Issue in Jordan'.
63. From an ecclesiastical point of view, the Coptic Orthodox and the Armenian Apostolic Churches (as well as the Syriac Orthodox and the Ethiopian Churches) belong to the Oriental Orthodox or miaphysite family of Churches which rejected the Council of Chalcedon in 451 over Christological disputes, whereas the Greek Orthodox (Arabic *rūm*, called 'Chalcedonians' or 'Melkites' during the medieval period), which adopted Chalcedon, split from the Roman Catholic ('Latin' Church) in 1054. The various Protestant Churches appeared in the Middle East in the nineteenth century. There is also the Church of the East (formerly called 'Nestorian', nowadays known as the Assyrian Church) that emerged independently of all these Churches within the realm of the Persian Sasanian Empire. It rejected the idea of Virgin Mary as 'God-bearer' (Greek *theodokos*, Syriac *yoldath Aloho*), considering her instead 'Christ-bearer', something that still attracts the ire of the Coptic Orthodox Church which continues to block the acceptance of the Assyrian Church into the Middle East Council of Churches (MECC).

64. The term 'laity' may be ill-chosen in a Middle Eastern context because it resonates with 'secular'. A more appropriate term may be 'baptised', but this term is not widely used in scholarship. I am therefore using 'laity' as a *terminus technicus*.
65. Maurits H. van den Boogert, 'Millets: Past and Present', in Anh Nga Longva and Anne Sofie Roald (eds), *Religious Minorities in the Middle East: Domination, Self-Empowerment, Accommodation* (Leiden, Boston: Brill, 2012), 31.
66. Heather Sharkey, *A History of Muslims, Christians, and Jews in the Middle East* (Cambridge: Cambridge University Press, 2017), 86.
67. Catherine Mayeur-Jaouen, 'Le christianisme oriental, les chrétiens d'Orient au XIXe siècle: Un renouveau lourd de menace', in Jean-Marie Mayeur, Charles Piétri, Luce Piétri, André Vauchez and Marc Venard (eds), *Histoire du Christianisme, Tome 11, Libéralisme, industrialisation, expansion européenne (1830–1914)* (Paris: Desclée, 1995), 797.
68. Ibrahim, *The Copts of Egypt*, 49.
69. Eugene L. Rogan, *Frontiers of the State in the Late Ottoman Empire: Transjordan, 1850–1921* (Cambridge, New York: Cambridge University Press, 1999), 110–11. See also Hager, 'The Orthodox Issue in Jordan', 214–15.
70. See Mayeur-Jaouen, 'Le christianisme oriental', 808.
71. Ibrahim, *The Copts of Egypt*, 117, 35.
72. Ibid, 49–50.
73. Ibid, 52–53.
74. Mārūn Lahhām, Personal Interview.
75. Bāssim Farrāj, Personal Interview.
76. See Hager, 'The Orthodox Issue in Jordan', 212–33.
77. Ibid, 223. Since then, the conflict seems to have been somewhat resolved with the nomination of the reform-minded Jordanian cleric Christophorus as bishop of Amman in 2018 (Anna Hager, 'Die Christen in Jordanien nach 2011', *Ostkirchliche Studien* 69:1 (2020): 103–16, 109).
78. Hager, 'The Orthodox Issue in Jordan', 224.
79. Hannā Kildānī, Personal Interview.
80. Chatelard, *Briser la mosaïque*, 164.
81. Maggiolini, 'Christian Churches and Arab Christians in the Hashemite Kingdom of Jordan', 52.
82. Metropolitan Bishoy, 'Revival of the Egyptian Church since the Middle of the Nineteenth Century', in Habib Badr (ed.), *Christianity. A History in the Middle East* (Beirut: Middle East Council of Churches, 2005), 775.

83. Catherine Mayeur-Jaouen, *Pèlerinages d'Egypte: Histoire de la piété copte et musulmane, XVe–XXe siècles* (Paris: Éditions de l'École des Hautes Études en Sciences Sociales, 2005), 363.
84. Dina El-Khawaga, 'L'affirmation d'une identité chrétienne copte: Saisir un processus en cours', in Christophe Décobert (ed.), *Itinéraires d'Egypte: Mélanges offerts au père Maurice Martin, s. j.* (Cairo: Institut français d'archéologie orientale du Caire, 1992), 347–48.
85. See Reiss, *Erneuerung in der koptisch-orthodoxen Kirche*, 179. In 1844, there were twelve dioceses, in 1971 seventeen and in 2009 forty-seven. Elsässer, *The Coptic Question*, 55.
86. Reiss, *Erneuerung in der koptisch-orthodoxen Kirche*, 273.
87. Guirguis, *Les Coptes d'Égypte*, 46.
88. S. S. Hasan, *Christians versus Muslims in Modern Egypt: The Century-Long Struggle for Coptic Equality* (Oxford: Oxford University Press, 2003), 184.
89. Guirguis, *Les Coptes d'Égypte*, 112.
90. Heo, *The Political Lives of Saints*, 12. For further information on the Coptic Orthodox reform, see Reiss, *Erneuerung in der koptisch-orthodoxen Kirche*; Voile, *Les coptes d'Égypte sous Nasser*; El-Khawaga, 'L'affirmation d'une identité chrétienne copte'; Hasan, *Christians versus Muslims in Modern Egypt*.
91. Sami E. Baroudi and Paul Tabar, 'Spiritual Authority versus Secular Authority: Relations between the Maronite Church and the State in Postwar Lebanon, 1990–2005', *Middle East Critique* 18:3 (200), 196.
92. Mārūn Lahhām, Personal Interview.
93. Al-Akhbar English, 'Geagea and the Maronite Church: A Battle for Patriarchy', 18 March 2012: http://english.al-akhbar.com/content/geagea-and-maronite-church-battle-patriarchy (accessed 17 May 2016).
94. Paul Sedra, 'The Church, Maspero, and the Future of the Coptic Community', *Jadaliyya*, 19 May 2012: http://www.jadaliyya.com/pages/index/4735/the-church-maspero-and-the-future-of-the-coptic-co (accessed 23 February 2023). It was re-established in 1973 and drew its members from the middle-class.
95. Paul Sedra, 'Religious Difference in a Secular Age: Book Review', 8 May 2016: https://www.madamasr.com/en/2016/05/08/opinion/u/religious-difference-in-a-secular-age-book-review/ (accessed 23 February 2023).
96. See Voile, *Les coptes d'Égypte sous Nasser*, 37.
97. Heo, *The Political Lives of Saints*, 14.
98. Ahram Online, 'Church-State Relations Yet to Change in Morsi's Egypt'.

99. Watani, 'Copts Pushed Back into the Church?' 2 September 2012 (number 2645, year 54/number 611, year 12).
100. Hannā Kildānī, Personal Interview.
101. Linga, ‏مجلس رؤساء الكنائس في الأردن هو المرجعية الوحيدة لكل الشؤون المسيحية!!!‎, 27 January 2009.
102. Jiryis Habāsh, Personal Interview, 28 April 2015, Amman.
103. Various reasons were put forward for this; Fr. Hannā Kildānī recorded that the Greek Orthodox Patriarch of Jerusalem wanted to assume leadership in the council (Hannā Kildānī, Personal Interview, 8 April 2015). Latin Bishop Mārūn Lahhām, however, said that the council was not representative of Christians in Jordan, since the bishops of the other officially recognized Churches, like the Episcopal church, do not reside in Amman and were therefore not members of it (Mārūn Lahhām, Personal Interview, 20 April 2015). As a result, the Council of Jordan and the Holy Land was established and is headed each year alternately by the three Patriarchs of Jerusalem: the Greek Orthodox Patriarch, the Latin Patriarch and the Armenian Apostolic Patriarch (Mārūn Lahhām, Personal Interview, 20 April 2015). All the churches in Jordan are represented in this new council, except for 'some Protestant churches' (Ibid).
104. Al-Ahram Hebdo, 'Encourager l'esprit de citoyenneté', 22–8 December 2010 (number 850, year 17), 3–4.
105. Al-Ahram Hebdo, 'Encourager l'esprit de citoyenneté'.
106. Tadros, *Copts at the Crossroads*, 107–8.
107. See Anna Hager, 'Die Kopten und der Arabische Frühling: Zwischen politischer Emanzipation und Minderheitenstatus', *Études Asiatiques/Asiatische Studien* 72:3 (2018), 806–7.
108. Tadros, *Copts at the Crossroads*, 183.
109. Al-Kirāza, ‏بيان المجمع المقدس الصادر من الكنيسة القبطية الأرثوذكسية‎, November 2011 (numbers 13–14, year 39), 2.
110. Ahram Online, 'Church-State Relations Yet to Change in Morsi's Egypt'.
111. Fādī Yūsuf, Personal Interview, 20 January 2015, Cairo. The Coalition of Egypt's Copts was reportedly founded on 25 February 2011.
112. The organisation Copts Without Restrictions was also founded following the revolution of 25 January 2011, in the aftermath of the Maspero Massacre (Casper, 'The Coptic Movements', 6).
113. Mīnā Magdī, Personal Interview.
114. Ibid. After the Maspero massacre on 9 October 2011, the union was severely criticised by the families of the victims and accused of being 'corrupt and suspicious'.

Daily News Egypt, 'Families of Maspero Victims Attack Maspero Youth Union', 6 October 2012: http://www.dailynewsegypt.com/2012/10/06/families-of-maspero-victims-attack-maspero-youth-union/ (accessed 23 February 2023).

115. Mīnā Magdī, Personal Interview.
116. Al-Ahram Hebdo, 'Une démarche symbolique', 18–24 July 2012 (number 931, year 18), 8.
117. Al-Ahram Hebdo, 'Une démarche symbolique'.
118. Masress, الحقوق المدنية للمسيحيين : نرفض الإساءة للأديان ونطالب بعمل فيلم للرد على المُسيء, 12 September 2012: http://www.masress.com/akhbartoday/36211 (accessed 22 February 2023).
119. Copts Today, حركة "أقباط بلا قيود " نرفض الإساءة للمقدسات الإسلامية ونطالب بوضع حد للإساءات لرموزنا المسحية, 10 September 2012.
120. A copy of the statement was given to the author by Bāssim Farrāj, secretary general of the Orthodox Society.
121. See Hager, 'The Orthodox Issue in Jordan', 225.
122. George Sabra, 'Two Ways of Being a Christian in the Muslim Context of the Middle-East', *Islam and Christian–Muslim Relations* 17:1 (2006), 44.
123. Chatelard, *Briser la mosaïque*, 29.
124. Franck Mermier, 'À l'ombre du leader disparu: Antoun Saadé et le Parti syrien national social', in Franck Mermier and Sabrina Mervin (eds), *Leaders et Partisans au Liban* (Paris: Karthala, IFPO, ISSMM, 2012), 191.
125. *Who's Who in Lebanon 2007-2008* (Munich: Publitec Publications in coedition with K. G. Saur, 2007), s. v. 'Fares, Marwan'.
126. Al-Anwar, حردان: الإساءة الى الإسلام جزء من مخطط أميركي - صهيوني للفتنة, 15 September 2012 (number 18142, year 53): http://www.archive.alanwar.com/article.php?articleID=172297&issuedate=20120915 (accessed 17 May 2016).
127. Al-Masrī al-Yawm, جورج إسحاق يُدين "الفيلم المسيء" ويؤكد: مصر سالمة بنسيجها القوي, 14 September 2012: http://www.almasryalyoum.com/news/details/163642 (accessed 31 January 2013).
128. A clash in the village of Atfīh, in the governorate of Helwan, led to the expulsion of its Coptic inhabitants. The SCAF continued with the practice, followed by the previous regime and convened a peace gathering to resolve the crisis. This gathering was led by a high-ranking delegation that included Islamist figures such as Safwat Higāzī, the secular politicians George Ishāq and 'Amr Hamzawī (Hager, 'From "Polytheists" to "Partners in the Nation"', 296–97).
129. Al-Yawm al-Sābi', الحركات القبطية تنقسم بشأن المشاركة فى تظاهرات الفيلم المسيء للرسول.. "الإخوان المسيحيين": لسنا مطالبين بالتظاهر لتبرئة ساحتنا.. و"أقباط مصر وماسبيرو": نرفض شق الصف ونطالب بمحاكمة دولية

للمسيحين, 11 September 2012: http://www.youm7.com/story/2012/9/11/%D8%A7%D9%84%D8%AD%D8%B1%D9%83%D8%A7%D8%AA_%D8%A7%D9%84%D9%82%D8%A8%D8%B7%D9%8A%D8%A9_%D8%AA%D9%86%D9%82%D8%B3%D9%85_%D8%A8%D8%B4%D8%A3%D9%86_%D8%A7%D9%84%D9%85%D8%B4%D8%A7%D8%B1%D9%83%D8%A9_%D9%81%D9%89_%D8%AA%D8%B8%D8%A7%D9%87%D8%B1%D8%A7%D8%AA_%D8%A7%D9%84%D9%81%D9%8A%D9%84%D9%85_%D8%A7%D9%84%D9%85%D8%B3%D9%89%D8%A1/782863#.Vjx7ZV5OfVJ (accessed 31 January 2023).

130. Massad, *Colonial Effects*, 265.
131. Al-Nahār, مَن هو ناهض حتر؟, 25 September 2016: https://www.annahar.com/article/474242-من-هو-ناهض-حتر- (accessed 22 February 2023). For more information, see Hager, 'Die Christen in Jordanien nach 2011'.
132. Robert Fisk, 'A Year on from the Murder of Christian Writer Nahed Hattar in Jordan, Many Questions Remain Unanswered', *Independent* 21 September 2017: https://www.independent.co.uk/voices/middle-east-jordan-christians-nahed-hattar-murder-king-abdullah-government-a7959026.html (accessed 23 March 2023).
133. Abouna, مطرانية اللاتين تشجب العنف غير المبرر الذي راح ضحيته الكاتب ناهض حتر, 26 September 2016: http://abouna.org/content/-مطرانية-اللاتين-تشجب-العنف-غير-المبرر-الذي-راح-ضحيته-الكاتب-ناهض-حتر (accessed 18 October 2020).
134. Al-Dustūr, رؤساء الكنائس: "مكونات مجتمعاتنا أوعى من الخديعة وأقوى أمام الافتراء", 15 September 2012 (number 16228), 16.
135. Al-Jazeera, انتخاب أول مسيحي في قيادة الحزب الإسلامي الأبرز بالأردن, 20 February 2007: http://www.aljazeera.net/news/reportsandinterviews/2007/2/20/%D8%A7%D9%86%D8%AA%D8%AE%D8%A7%D8%A8-%D8%A3%D9%88%D9%84-%D9%85%D8%B3%D9%8A%D8%AD%D9%8A-%D9%81%D9%8A-%D9%82%D9%8A%D8%A7%D8%AF%D8%A9-%D8%A7%D9%84%D8%AD%D8%B2%D8%A8-%D8%A7%D9%84%D8%A5%D8%B3%D9%84%D8%A7%D9%85%D9%8A-%D8%A7%D9%84%D8%A3%D8%A8%D8%B1%D8%B2-%D8%A8%D8%A7%D9%84%D8%A3%D8%B1%D8%AF%D9%86 (accessed 21 May 2016).

Chapter 4

1. Abouna, بيان شجب واستنكار من مجلس رؤساء الكنائس في الأردن, 14 September 2012.
2. See Krämer, 'Dhimmi ou citoyen'; Scott, *The Challenge of Political Islam*; Tadros, *The Muslim Brotherhood in Contemporary Egypt*; Hager, 'From "Polytheists" to

"Partners in the Nation"'. Richard Gauvain discusses Salafi attitudes, to a limited extent, in *Salafi Ritual Purity*.
3. See Grafton, *The Christians of Lebanon*.
4. Mahmood, *Religious Difference in a Secular Age*, 2.
5. Sidney Griffith, 'Christians and Christianity', in Jane Dammen McAuliffe (ed.), *Enyclopaedia of the Qur'ān* (Leiden: Brill, 2006), 310.
6. Griffith, 'Christians and Christianity'.
7. Krämer, 'Dhimmi ou citoyen'.
8. Ibid.
9. See Albrecht Noth, 'Möglichkeiten und Grenzen islamischer Toleranz', *Saeculum* 29:2 (1978), 190–204.
10. Ibid, 195.
11. Heyberger, *Les chrétiens au Proche-Orient*, 109.
12. See Krämer, 'Anti-Semitism in the Muslim World', 249.
13. Ibid.
14. Sharkey, *A History of Muslims, Christians, and Jews in the Middle East*, 40.
15. Elsässer, *The Coptic Question*, 201.
16. Guirguis, *Les Coptes d'Égypte*, 134.
17. Ibid.
18. Zakaryā Butrus, 'Fr Zakaria Statement Concerning His Relationship to the Making of Mohamed Movie', September 2012: http://www.fatherzakaria.net/main/fr-zakaria-mohamed-movie.htm (accessed 23 March 2024).
19. The video was downloaded by the author.
20. Zakaryā Butrus, 'Les preuves de la Révélation dans l'Islam et dans le Christianisme: Episode 28', 2009: http://jesusmarie.free.fr/islam_zakaria_boutros_28.html (accessed 23 March 2023).
21. Robert Hoyland, *Seeing Islam as Others Saw It: A Survey and Evaluation of Christian, Jewish and Zoroastrian Writings on Early Islam* (Princeton: Darwin Press, 1997), 476.
22. See Adel T. Khoury, *Polémiques byzantines contre l'Islam (VIII.-XIII.e siècles)* (Leiden: Brill, 1972), 74.
23. Ibid, 88.
24. J. R. Zaborowski, *The Coptic Martyrdom of John Phanijōit: Assimilation and Conversion to Islam in Thirteenth Century Egypt* (Leiden, Boston: Brill, 2005), 13.
25. Zakariyā Butrus, 'Les épouses du Messager: Episode 39', 2009: http://jesusmarie.free.fr/islam_zakaria_boutros_39_femmes_du_messager.html (accessed 23 March 2023).

26. Zakaryā Butrus, 'Mohammed confronté aux grands principes de la morale, et l'assassinat de ses adversaires: Episode 37', [n. d.]: http://jesusmarie.free.fr/islam_zakaria_boutros_37_Mohamed_et_ses_adversaires.html (accessed 3 May 2016).
27. Butrus, 'Mohammed confronté aux grands principes de la morale'.
28. In her study on Armenian women in Aleppo sharī'a courts, Elyse Semerdjian notes the 'paradox of harsh formulaic condemnations ['according to despicable customs (*'ala al-'ada al-qabiha*)'] coupled with the court's willingness to register Christian identities and honor requests to be buried according to the customs of their distinctive religious communities'. See her 'Armenian Women, Legal Bargaining, and Gendered Politics of Conversion in Seventeenth- and Eighteenth-Century Aleppo', *Journal of Middle East Women's Studies* 12:1 (2016), 18.
29. Sharkey, *A History of Muslims, Christians, and Jews in the Middle East*, 116. The *Hatt-i Hümayun* also granted Christians and Jews the right to vote on the municipal and provincial levels, the freedom to practice their religion, to build new churches and restore churches, as well as equality in matters of justice, military recruitment and taxes. Mayeur-Jaouen, 'Le christianisme oriental', 803.
30. Ibrahim, *The Copts of Egypt*, 17.
31. Alexander Schölch, 'Der arabische Osten im neunzehnten Jahrhundert, 1800–1914', in Ulrich Haarmann (ed.), *Geschichte der arabischen Welt* (Munich: Verlag C. H. Beck, 2004), 370–72.
32. Ibrahim, *The Copts of Egypt*, 18.
33. Mayeur-Jaouen, 'Le christianisme oriental', 807.
34. Mayeur-Jaouen, *Voyage en Haute-Égypte*, 46.
35. Ibrahim, *The Copts of Egypt*, 15.
36. Sharkey, *A History of Muslims, Christians, and Jews in the Middle East*, 141, 185.
37. Ibid, 185.
38. Jillian Schwedler, 'Conclusion: New Directions in the Study of Islamist Politics', in Hendrik Kraetzschmar and Paola Rivetti (eds), *Islamists and the Politics of the Arab Uprisings: Governance, Pluralisation and Contention* (Edinburgh: Edinburgh University Press, 2018), 359.
39. Schwedler, 'Islamists in Power?' 4.
40. Scott, *The Challenge of Political Islam*, 2.
41. See Krämer, 'Dhimmi ou citoyen'; Scott, *The Challenge of Political Islam*.
42. See Gauvain, *Salafi Ritual Purity*; Tadros, *The Muslim Brotherhood in Contemporary Egypt*.
43. Mervin (ed.), *Le Hezbollah: État des lieux*; Grafton, *The Christians of Lebanon*; Rougier, *Le jihad au quotidien*; Bernard Rougier, *L'Oumma en fragments: Contrôler le sunnisme au Liban* (Paris: Presses universitaires de France, 2011); Joas

Wagemakers, *Salafism in Jordan: Political Islam in a Quietist Community* (Cambridge: Cambridge University Press, 2016).
44. Schwedler, 'Islamists in Power?' 6.
45. Beltram Dumontier, 'L'entente du Hezbollah avec le CPL', in Mervin (ed.), *Le Hezbollah: État des lieux*, 109, 113. Michael Aoun, leader of the FPM, is originally from Haret Hreik.
46. Anna Hager, '"Lebanon is More than a Nation, More than a Country. It is a Message": Lebanon as a Model of Christian–Muslim Relations', *Journal of Beliefs and Values* 38: 3 (2017), 288.
47. Boulby, *The Muslim Brotherhood and the Kings of Jordan, 1945–1993*, 131; in Schwedler, *Faith in Moderation*, 159.
48. Ibid.
49. Wagemakers, *The Muslim Brotherhood in Jordan*, 207.
50. Joas Wagemakers, e-mail dated 25 July 2022.
51. See Hager, 'From "Polytheists" to "Partners in the Nation"', 295.
52. Ibid.
53. Ibid.
54. Tadros, *Copts at the Crossroads*, 211.
55. Gauvain, *Salafi Ritual Purity*, 240.
56. Scott, *The Challenge of Political Islam*, 106.
57. See Scott, *The Challenge of Political Islam*, 113.
58. Al-Shurūq, "أبو إسلام" المتهم بتمزيق الإنجيل, أمن الدولة تستدعى, 25 September 2012.
59. Al-Ahrām, غضب شعبي من الإساءة للرسول, 12 September 2012.
60. Al-Ahrām, البناء والتنمية يحذر من مخطط لإثارة فتنة طائفية, 19 September 2012 (number 45943, year 137), 4.
61. Ibid.
62. Watanī, حزب البناء والتنمية, 23 September 2012 (number 2648, year 54/number 614, year 12), 9.
63. Ahmad al-Asīr was born in Sidon to a Sunni father and a Shiʿi mother. Named the capital of the South, Sidon is a very important centre of Islamism and Islamist movements. It is there that *al-Jamāʿa al-Islāmiyya* was initially founded. Ahmad al-Asīr initially joined *al-Jamāʿa al-Islāmiyya* but soon criticised the movement for having a political outlook instead of focusing on religious matters. Therefore, he turned to a preaching movement that originated from southern Asia, Tablighi Jamaat (*Tablīgh-i jamāʿat*) (Al-Hayāt, أحمد الأسير بين التنصّل والتفهّم: إنّه سحر الساحر الملتبس, 15 March 2014: http://www.alhayat.com/Articles/1139661/%D8%A3%D8%AD%D9%85%D8%AF-%D8%A7%D9%84%D8%A3%D8%B3%D9%8A%D8%B1-%D8%A8%D9%8A%D9%86-%D8%A7%D9%84%D8%AA%D9%86%D8

%B5%D9%91%D9%84-%D9%88%D8%A7%D9%84%D8%AA%D9%81%D9%87%D9%91%D9%85--%D8%A5%D9%86%D9%91%D9%87-%D8%B3%D8%AD%D8%B1-%D8%A7%D9%84%D8%B3%D8%A7%D8%AD%D8%B1-%D8%A7%D9%84%D9%85%D9%84%D8%AA%D8%A8%D8%B3 (accessed 17 May 2016)

64. Al-Akhbar English, 'Ahmad al-Assir: A Salafi with a Difference', 6 March 2012: http://english.al-akhbar.com/content/ahmad-al-assir-salafi-difference (accessed 15 July 2017).
65. Al-Akhbar English, 'Ahmad al-Assir: A Salafi with a Difference'.
66. Al-Akhbar English, 'Al-Assir: A New Guardian of 'Sunni Interests' in Lebanon', 2 March 2012: http://english.al-akhbar.com/content/al-assir-new-guardian-sunni-interest-lebanon (accessed 15 July 2017). In September 2012, he was supposed to have 200 to 300 armed men and wanted to organise a resistance movement against Hezbollah and Israel (POC 63:1–2 [2013], 195).
67. Naharnet, الأسير ينتقد دعوة نصر الله الى التظاهر: 'براءة المسلمين' اساء الى الاسلام بكامله, 18 September 2012: http://www.naharnet.com/stories/ar/53922 (accessed 22 February 2023).
68. Al-Nahār, إعتصام إمام مسجد بلال بن رباح قطع أوصال بيروت, 22 September 2012 (number 24855, year 80), 5.
69. Al-Nahar Shabab, مشاركون نصرة للأسير أم للرسول؟, 27 September 2012 (number 24861, year 80), 22.
70. However, when the call for prayer at the nearby Muhammad al-Amīn Mosque built by Rafīq al-Harīrī was made, many people had already left the sit-in, with many leaving while al-Asīr was still delivering his speech. YouTube, 2012 09 21 I اعتصام انتصاراً لنبي الإسلام, 22 September 2012: https://www.youtube.com/watch?v=EPetsalWSgQ (accessed 17 March 2023).
71. Al-Nahār, إعتصام إمام مسجد بلال بن رباح قطع أوصال بيروت.
72. YouTube, 2012 09 21 الأستاذ فريد الدكان, 23 September 2012: https://www.youtube.com/watch?v=TqcBCpE7oVw (accessed 17 March 2023).
73. YouTube, 2012 09 21 اعتصام انتصاراً لنبي الإسلام, 22 September 2012.
74. Al-Safīr, اعتصام صيداوي ضد زيارة "القوات" للأسير, 5 September 2012 (number 12275, year 39), 4.
75. Ibid.
76. Al-Akhbar English, 'Salafi Cleric's Militia Ambitions Curtailed', 25 November 2012: http://english.al-akhbar.com/content/salafi-cleric%E2%80&99s-militia-ambitions-curtailed (accessed 17 May 2016).
77. The Guardian, 'Fugitive Lebanese Cleric Ahmad al-Assir Fails to Avoid Arrest with "70s Makeover"', 17 August 2015: http://www.theguardian.com/world/

2015/aug/17/fugitive-lebanese-cleric-ahmad-al-assir-arrest-70s-makeover-beirut (accessed 17 May 2016).

78. Ibid.
79. In Hager, 'From "Polytheists" to "Partners in the Nation"', 295.
80. Ibid.
81. See Scott, *The Challenge of Political Islam*, 171.
82. YouTube, (ص) كلمة نصر الله عن الفيلم المسيء للرسول, 17 September 2012.
83. Al-Ahrām, شيخ الأزهر يطالب القوى السياسية بالتوافق والبحث عن حلول حقيقية للأزمات, 27 September 2012 (number 45951, year 137), 24.
84. Albrecht Noth, 'Früher Islam', in Ulrich Haarmann (ed.), *Geschichte der Arabischen Welt* (Munich: C. H. Beck, 2004), 53.
85. Sharkey, *A History of Muslims, Christians, and Jews in the Middle East*, 152.
86. Ibid.
87. Ibid, 267.
88. Krämer, 'Dhimmi ou citoyen'.
89. Boulby, *The Muslim Brotherhood*, 55–56; in Wagemakers, *The Muslim Brotherhood in Jordan*, 89.
90. Wagemakers, *The Muslim Brotherhood in Jordan*, 222.
91. Pall, *Salafism in Lebanon*, 114.
92. Gauvain, *Salafi Ritual Purity*, 241–42.
93. Ibid, 242.
94. Al-Shurūq, الداعية السلفي محمد حسان: مصر ليست ملكا للمسلمين وحدهم, 20 October 2011 (number 992), 16.
95. Hager, 'From "Polytheists" to "Partners in the Nation"', 296.
96. Gauvain, *Salafi Ritual Purity*, 238.
97. Masress, البناء والتنمية يطلق تحالف إسلامي مسيحي لمواجهة الطائفية, 20 January 2013: https://www.masress.com/almesryoon/193075 (accessed 22 February 2023).
98. Al-Da'wa al-Salafiyya, هل نتوقف عن تنبيه المسلمين إلى كفر النصارى وكيدهم منعًا للفتنة, 21 October 2010: http://www.salafvoice.com/article.aspx?a=4837 (accessed 22 February 2023).
99. 'Abd al-Mun'im al-Shahhāt, "المسلمون والنصارى "والخيار الثالث, 30 December 2011: http://www.salafvoice.com/article.aspx?a=5910 (accessed 23 March 2023).
100. Schwedler, 'Conclusion: New Directions in the Study of Islamist Politics', 361.
101. Abouna, بيان شجب واستنكار من مجلس رؤساء الكنائس في الأردن, 14 September 2012.
102. Sabra, 'Two Ways of Being a Christian', 44.
103. Al-Anwar, حردان: الإساءة الى الإسلام جزء من مخطط أميركي - صهيوني للفتنة, 15 September 2012.

104. George Khodr, الحملة على الإسلام, *Al-Nahār*, 29 September 2012 (number 24863, year 80), 1 and 12.
105. Sabra, 'Two Ways of Being a Christian', 46.
106. Antonie Wessels, *Arab and Christian: Christians in the Middle East* (Kok Pharos: Kampen, 1995), 2.
107. Bernard Heyberger, *Les Chrétiens d'Orient* (Paris: PUF, que sais-je?, 2017), 50.
108. Stephen J. Davis, *Coptic Christology in Practice: Incarnation and Divine Participation in Late Antique and Medieval Egypt* (Oxford: Oxford University Press, 2008), 238, 251.
109. See Heleen Murre-van den Berg, 'The Language of the Nation: The Rise of Arabic among Jews and Christians (1900–1950)', *British Journal of Middle Eastern Studies* 43:2 (2016), 183.
110. Arman Akopian, 'The Syriacs of Kharberd (Kharput) on the Eve of the 1915 Genocide', *Hugoye: Journal of Syriac Studies* 23:2 (2020), 284.
111. See Anna Hager, 'The Syriac Orphanage and School in Beirut: Building an Elite for a Transnational Syriac Identity', *Studies in World Christianity* 28:3 (2022), 323–25.
112. See Sharkey, *A History of Muslims, Christians, and Jews in the Middle East*, 83, 98–99.
113. Ibid, 135–36.
114. Salameh, *Language, Memory, and Identity in the Middle East*, 8.
115. John Myhill, *Language, Religion and National identity in Europe and the Middle East: A Historical Study* (Amsterdam; Philadelphia: J. Benjamins, 2006), 249.
116. Wessels, *Arab and Christian*, 71.
117. George Sabra, 'A Response to "Christianity in a Culture Marked by Islam: Facts and Visions"', *NEST Theological Review* 35:1–2 (2014), 146.
118. Khodr, الحملة على الإسلام, *Al-Nahār*, 29 September 2012.
119. Al-Tawhīd, لقاء تضامني في عكار ندد بالفيلم المسيء الى الرسول: للتمسك بالوحدة والعروبة الجامعة ورفض المخططات الصهيونية, 22 September 2012: http://www.altawhid.org/2012/09/22/%D8%AA%D9%88%D8%A7%D8%B5%D9%84-%D8%A7%D9%84%D9%85%D9%88%D8%A7%D9%82%D9%81-%D8%A7%D9%84%D9%85%D8%B3%D8%AA%D9%86%D9%83%D8%B1%D8%A9-%D9%84%D9%84%D8%A7%D8%B3%D8%A7%D8%A1%D8%A9-%D8%A7%D9%84%D8%BA%D8%B1/ (accessed 17 May 2016).
120. Ignatius IV Hazim, *Orthodoxy and the Issues of our Time* (Balamand: University of Balamand, Dar an-Nahar, 2006), 25.

121. Maroun Lahham, 'Called by Destiny, Not by Chance', *OASIS* December 2012 (number 16, year 8), 92–96.
122. Hager, 'The Orthodox Issue in Jordan', 225.
123. Anh Nga Longva, 'From the *Dhimma* to the Capitulations: Memory and Experience of Protection in Lebanon', in Anh Nga Longva and Anne Sofie Roald (eds), *Religious Minorities in the Middle East* (Leiden: Brill, 2011), 63.
124. Al-Rai, مجلس ومجمع الكنائس يستنكران الفيلم المسيء, 15 September 2012.
125. Abouna, بيان شجب واستنكار من مجلس رؤساء الكنائس في الأردن, 14 September 2012.
126. Andrew Sharp, *Orthodox Christians and Islam in the Postmodern Age* (Leiden, Boston: Brill, 2012), 64.
127. Ibid, 68.
128. Ibid, 69.
129. Ibid, 52.
130. Al-Tawhīd, تواصل المواقف المستنكرة للإساءة الغربية للاسلام في لبنان: أئمة المساجد وقوى واحزاب ومرجعيات دينية, 22 September 2012.
131. Sharp, *Orthodox Christians and Islam*, 73.
132. Al-Tawhīd, لقاء تضامني في عكار ندد بالفيلم المسيء الى الرسول: للتمسك بالوحدة والعروبة الجامعة ورفض المخططات الصهيونية., 22 September 2012. Nāyif Istifān is also a poet and a historian who has published a number of books about Akkar and the Greek Orthodox diocese of Akkar (Al-Nahār, كتاب للأب المؤرخ نايف اسطفان وثائق تتناول أبرشية عكار الأرثوذكسية, 23 July 2014: http://newspaper.annahar.com/article/153796-%D9%83%D8%AA%D8%A7%D8%A8-%D9%84%D9%84%D8%A3%D8%A8-%D8%A7%D9%84%D9%85%D8%A4%D8%B1%D8%AE-%D9%86%D8%A7%D9%8A%D9%81-%D8%A7%D8%B3%D8%B7%D9%81%D8%A7%D9%86-%D9%88%D8%AB%D8%A7%D8%A6%D9%82-%D8%AA%D8%AA%D9%86%D8%A7%D9%88%D9%84-%D8%A3%D8%A8%D8%B1%D8%B4%D9%8A%D8%A9-%D8%B9%D9%83%D8%A7%D8%B1-%D8%A7%D9%84%D8%A3%D8%B1%D8%AB%D9%88%D8%B0%D9%83%D8%B3%D9%8A%D8%A9 (accessed 22 February 2023).
133. The Maronite village Bayt Millat was attacked, with kidnapping and harassment taking place. See Samir Kassir, *La guerre du Liban: De la dissension nationale au conflit régional* (Paris: Karthala, 2014), 151.
134. A. Mouchref, *Forgotten Akkar: Socio-Economic Reality of the Akkar Region* (Beirut: Mada Association, 2008), 1.
135. Éric Verdeil, Ghaleb Faour and Sébastien Velut (eds), *Atlas du Liban: Territoires et société* (Beirut: Ifpo, CNRS, 2007), 85–86.
136. Sabra, 'Two Ways of Being a Christian', 44.

137. See Heo, *The Political Lives of Saints*, 123–29.
138. Aubin-Boltanski, 'La Vierge, les chrétiens, les musulmans et la nation'.
139. Ibid.
140. Hager, 'Die Kopten und der Arabische Frühling', 812.
141. Adnane Mokrani, *Lebanese Christians' Point of View on Muslim-Christian Relations* (Beirut: Université Saint-Joseph, CEDRAC, Librairie Saint-Antoine, 2009), 509–10.
142. Hareth Chehab, Personal Interview, 9 December 2014, Beirut.
143. Le Comité National Islamo-Chrétien pour le Dialogue, 'Emir Hares Chakib Chehab', [n. d.]: http://chrislam.org/members.html (accessed 22 October 2015). The other general secretary of the committee, Muhammad Sammak, is a key actor in the inter-religious dialogue. He was one of the signatories of the document 'A Common Word Between Us and You' (see Chapter Five) and is an advisor to the mufti of Lebanon. Hareth Chehab, besides being from the Maronite community, also cooperates with the smaller Christian Communities: the Armenian Catholic, the Protestant, the Chaldean, the Syriac Catholic, the Syriac Orthodox, the Latin, the Assyrian and the Coptic Orthodox Churches. In addition, there is one representative for the Greek Orthodox Patriarchate, one for the Greek Catholic Melkite Patriarchate and one for the Armenian Apostolic Catholics. The Muslims are represented by one representative from the Sunni *Dār al-fatwā*, Muhammad Sammak; one representative from the Higher Islamic Shi'i Council; and one representative from the Druze *shaykh al-'aql*. See Le Comité National Islamo-Chrétien pour le Dialogue, 'Formation et Action du Comité du Dialogue', http://chrislam.org/bckground.html (accessed 22 October 2015). The Alawi sect does not have a separate representative.
144. Chehab, Interview, 2014.
145. Al-Nahār, عناوين في القمة الروحية اليوم والحضور مكتمل إسلامياً , 24 September 2012 (number 24857, year 80), 2.
146. Al-Safīr, قمة بكركي الروحية تناشد الدولية اتخاذ اجراءات لمنع الانهيار الاقتصادي, 25 September 2012 (number 12292, year 39), 2.
147. Aztabarabic, "الكاثوليكوس آرام الأول يحضر القمة الروحية المسيحية -الاسلامية في بكركي ويقول: المسيحية والاسلام تعايشتا في الشرق الأوسط لقرون طويلة", 25 September 2012: http://www.aztagarabic.com/archives/6419 (accessed 3 February 2023).
148. Bkerki, الثني - بكرك بيان القمة الروحية 24 ايلول 2012, 24 September 2012: http://www.bkerkelb.org/arabic/index.php?option=com_content&view=article&id=1714:------24--2012-&catid=263:2011-09-07-08-04-38&Itemid=66 (accessed 9 December 2013).

149. Al-Safīr, الأب ضو ... والمشاركة المميزة, 18 September 2012 (number 12286, year 39), 4.
150. See al-Safīr, السلفيون للمرة الأولى في دير ماروني: حوار حول الاختلاف . . . تأسيساً للتعايش, 20 February 2013 (number 12411), 4.
151. POC 62:1–2 (2012), 152.
152. Copts United, بالفيديو والصور الانبا كيرلس اسقف نجع حمادى: لا لازدراء الاديان ... واحترسوا من الثعالب الصغيرة, 14 September 2012.

Chapter 5

1. Haddad and Fischbach, 'Interfaith Dialogue in Lebanon', 424.
2. Picard, 'La violence milicienne', 323–24.
3. Mahmood, *Politics of Piety*, 8.
4. Ibid, 157.
5. Abouna, بيان شجب واستنكار من مجلس رؤساء الكنائس في الأردن, 14 September 2012.
6. Makari, *Conflict and Cooperation*, 109.
7. Hager, 'Die Kopten und der Arabische Frühling', 801.
8. Delhaye, 'Contemporary Muslim-Christian Relations in Egypt', 82.
9. Guirguis, *Les Coptes d'Égypte*, 153.
10. Al-Ahram Hebdo, 'Encourager l'esprit de citoyenneté'.
11. Ahram Online, 'Church-State Relations Yet to Change in Morsi's Egypt'.
12. Middle East Council of Churches, بيان من رؤساء الكنائس المسيحية بمصر حول فيلم شيفرده دافمسي, Muntada, July-September 2006, 26.
13. Arab West Report, أسقف بني مزار يعتذر للمسلمين عن الإساءة مؤكدا مخالفتها لسماحة المسيحية, 17 September 2012.
14. At a conference in Fayyum in 2010, Bishop Bishoy provoked a controversy with his claim that the Copts were the original inhabitants of Egypt, whereas Muslims were just guests. See POC 61: 1–2 (2012), 164.
15. Metropolit Bishoy, (عزازيل) كتاب: الرد على البهتان في رواية يوسف زيدان, 19 April 2009: http://metroplit-bishoy.com/ar/?p=278 (accessed 22 March 2023), 379.
16. Al-Ahrām, باخوميوس: التعدي على الأديان يحتاج لموفق حازم, 22 September 2012.
17. Al-Yawm al-Sābiʻ, بكار: التعرض للأنبياء والصحابة لا يمت لحرية الرأى بأية صلة, 10 September 2012: http://www.youm7.com/story/2012/9/10/%D8%A8%D9%83%D8%A7%D8%B1--%D8%A7%D9%84%D8%AA%D8%B9%D8%B1%D8%B6-%D9%84%D9%84%D8%A3%D9%86%D8%A8%D9%8A%D8%A7%D8%A1-%D9%88%D8%A7%D9%84%D8%B5%D8%AD%D8%A7%D8%A8%D8%A9-%D9%84%D8%A7-%D9%8A%D9%85%D8%AA-%D9%84%D8%AD%D8%B1%D9%8A%D8%

18. Sabra, 'The "Common Word" Letter in the Context of Christian–Muslim Dialogue', 90.
19. Kassir, *La guerre du Liban*, 262, 316.
20. Al-Nahār, الموسوي ويزي في مسيرة بنت جبيل: الائتلاف الإسلامي المسيحي رد مباشر, 23 September 2012 (number 24856, year 80), 5.
21. See Henley, 'Politics of a Church at War', 357.
22. Al-Nahār, الموسوي ويزي في مسيرة بنت جبيل: الائتلاف الإسلامي المسيحي رد مباشر, 23 September 2012.
23. Al-Shurūq, مسلمون وأقباط 'إيد واحدة' في مظاهرات محدودة أمام مساجد القاهرة, 15 September 2012 (number 1323, year 4), 5.
24. Al-Maṣrī al-Yawm, وفود كنسية تشارك "الإخوان" وتقفتهم رفضًا لـ "الفيلم المسيء" أمام "مصطفى محمود", 14 September 2012: http://www.almasryalyoum.com/news/details/163696 (accessed 12 July 2017).
25. Al-Shurūq, رجال 'الجماعة' داخل الكنيسة, 12 September 2012 (number 1320, year 4), 8.
26. Gate al-Ahram, الأنبا بولا: الفيلم المسيء فكرة شيطانية صهيونية لضرب الأديان.. ويطله عميلا للموساد, 15 September 2012.
27. Watanī, استقبل اللواء مهندس سمير عجلان محافظ السويس وفد الكنيسة الكاثوليكية بالسويس, 4 October, October 2012: http://www.wataninet.com/%D8%A3%D8%AE%D8%A8%D8%A7%D8%B1-%D8%A7%D9%84%D9%85%D8%AD%D8%A7%D9%81%D8%B8%D8%A7%D8%AA/%D9%85%D8%AD%D8%A7%D9%81%D8%B8-%D8%A7%D9%84%D8%B3%D9%88%D9%8A%D8%B3-%D8%A7%D9%84%D9%85%D8%B3%D9%84%D9%85%D9%88%D9%86-%D9%88%D8%A7%D9%84%D9%85%D8%B3%D9%8A%D8%AD%D9%8A%D9%88%D9%86-%D9%86%D8%B3%D9%8A/141208/ (accessed 23 May 2016). Unlike Patriarch Shinūda III, the Coptic Catholic Church had a more moderate position towards the Muslim Brotherhood: in an article published in the Coptic Catholic magazine *al-Salāh*, the 'production of fear' was criticised, and it claimed that Copts had historically been members of the early Brotherhood. See al-Salāh, الأقباط ومخاوف الانتخابات بين التهوين والتهويل 2012 (number 1, year 82), 34.
28. Haddad and Fischbach, 'Interfaith Dialogue in Lebanon', 424.
29. Mayeur-Jaouen, 'What do Egypt's Copts and Muslims share?' 149.
30. Makari, *Conflict and Cooperation*, 109.
31. Sharkey, *A History of Muslims, Christians, and Jews in the Middle East*, 124.
32. Al-Daʿwa al-Salafiyya, هل تهنئة النصارى بأعيادهم تدخل في البرّ والإقساط إليهم؟, 19 May 2007: http://www.salafvoice.com/article.aspx?a=1056 (accessed 4 April 2022).

33. Mayeur-Jaouen, 'What do Egypt's Copts and Muslims share?' 151.
34. Mervin, 'Charisme et distinction', 336.
35. Al-Ahram Hebdo, 'Prêtres, généraux et barbus', 11–17 January 2012 (number 904, year 18), 7.
36. Al-Sharq al-Awsat, تهنئة الأقباط بـ "عيد الفصح" تثير جدلا في مصر, 1 May 2013: https://archive.aawsat.com/details.asp?section=4&issueno=12573&article=726843#.Ykr1ACNCSUl (accessed 22 February 2023).
37. Masress, "الكفار" برهامي: لا يجوز للمفتي وشيخ الأزهر أن يهنيا الأقباط, 1 January 2013: https://www.masress.com/elsaba7/65273 (accessed 22 February 2023).
38. Al-Watan, مفتي الإخوان يحرم تهنئة المسيحيين بعيد القيامة.. وأقباط: فتواه تحريض على الكراهية, 30 April 2013: https://www.elwatannews.com/news/details/173429 (accessed 22 March 2023).
39. Al-Kirāza, عيد القيامة المجيد, May 2012 (number 1 and 2, year 40), 5.
40. Masress, "الكفار" برهامي: لا يجوز للمفتي وشيخ الأزهر أن يهنيا الأقباط, 1 January 2013.
41. ʿAbd al-Majīd Hāmid Subh, قالوا وقلنا, *Majallat al-Azhar*, December 2011, 148.
42. See Elsässer, *The Coptic Question in the Mubarak Era*; Iskander, 'The "Mediation" of Christian–Muslim Relations in Egypt'; Guirguis, *Les Coptes d'Égypte*.
43. Mayeur-Jaouen, *Voyage en Haute-Égypte*, 359.
44. Elsässer, *The Coptic Question*, 102.
45. Vivian Ibrahim, 'Beyond the Cross and the Crescent: Plural Identities and the Copts in Contemporary Egypt', *Ethnic and Racial Studies* 38:14 (2015), 2590.
46. Elsässer, *The Coptic Question*, 134.
47. Moheet, الأنبا بسنتي: المُنتجون للفيلم المُسيء للرسول لا يمثلون أقباط المهجر, 20 September 2012: http://moheet.com/2012/09/20/1668478/%D8%A7%D9%84%D8%A3%D9%86%D8%A8%D8%A7-%D8%A8%D8%B3%D9%86%D8%AA%D9%8A-%D8%A7%D9%84%D9%85-%D9%86%D8%AA%D8%AC%D9%88%D9%86-%D9%84%D9%84%D9%81%D9%8A%D9%84%D9%85-%D8%A7%D9%84%D9%85-%D8%B3%D9%8A.html#.VjeIWm5OfIV (accessed 21 May 2016).
48. Copts Today, بيان من نيافة الأنبا موسى ردا على الفيلم المسيء للرسول, 11 September 2012: http://www.coptstoday.com/Copts-News/Detail.php?Id=32480 (accessed 3 March 2014).
49. Al-Yawm al-Sābiʿ, "الإخوان": الحركات القبطية تنقسم بشأن المشاركة فى تظاهرات الفيلم المسيء للرسول.. المسيحيين": لسنا مطالبين بالتظاهر لتبرئة ساحتنا.. و"أقباط مصر وماسبيرو": نرفض شق الصف ونطالب بمحاكمة دولية للمسيئين, 11 September 2012.
50. Al-Ahrām, مفتي الجمهورية للأهرام: نصرة النبي تتحقق باتباع منهجه ... والإسلام يرفض العنف وإرهاب الآمنين, 21 September 2012.

51. Al-Ahrām, الغضب يجتاح مصر احتجاجا على الفيلم المسيء للرسول, 13 September 2012.
52. Al-Masrī al-Yawm, "الحرية والعدالة : الفيلم المسيء للرسول "محاولة دنيئة لإثارة الطائفية, 11 September 2012: http://www.almasryalyoum.com/news/details/163110 (accessed 23 May 2016).
53. Al-Masrī al-Yawm, تواصل الاحتجاجات ضد "الفيلم المسيء " بأنحاء مصر... ومحافظ المنيا أبرز المتظاهرين, 15 September 2012: http://www.almasryalyoum.com/news/details/163947 (accessed 23 May 2016).
54. Al-Masrī al-Yawm, الكنيسة تتبرأ من صانعى الفيلم المسيء للرسول وتؤكد: نرفض المساس بمشاعر شركاء الوطن, 11 September 2012: http://today.almasryalyoum.com/article2.aspx?ArticleID=352975 (accessed 21 May 2016).
55. Al-Shurūq, الكنيسة المصرية تنتقد الفيلم المسيء الأمريكي للرسول ... وبولس يقاضي أقباط المهجر, 11 September 2012 (number 1319, year 4), 3.
56. Al-Ahrām, غضب شعبي من الإساءة للرسول, 12 September 2012.
57. Al-Shurūq, الكنيسة: ليس مقبولًا استدعاء القائم مقام البطريك للتحقيق في القضية حرب البيانات بين الكنيسة والجبهة السلفية, 23 September 2012.
58. Al-Ahrām, باخوميوس: التعدى على الأديان يحتاج لموقف حازم, 22 September 2012.
59. Ibid.
60. Ibid.
61. Copts Today, حركة "أقباط بلا قيود" نرفض الإساءة للمقدسات الإسلامية ونطالب بوضع حد للإساءات لرموزنا المسيحية, 10 September 2012.
62. Hager, 'From "Polytheists" to "Partners in the Nation"', 297.

Chapter 6

1. 'Abd al-Majīd Hāmid Subh, قالوا وقلنا, 148.
2. See Scott, *The Challenge of Political Islam*; Tadros, *The Muslim Brotherhood in Contemporary Egypt*.
3. See Scott, *The Challenge of Political Islam*; Rachel Scott, 'Citizenship, Public Order, and State Sovereignty: Article 3 of the Egyptian Constitution and the "Divinely Revealed Religions", in Roel Meijer and Nils Butenschøn (eds), *The Crisis of Citizenship in the Arab World* (Boston: Brill, 2017), 383; Roel Meijer and Nils Butenschøn (eds), *The Crisis of Citizenship in the Arab World* (Boston: Brill, 2017); Ellis C. Kail, *Secular Nationalism and Citizenship in Muslim Countries: Arab Christians in the Levant* (London: Palgrave Macmillan, 2018).
4. Scott, 'Citizenship, Public Order, and State Sovereignty', 383.
5. POC 61:3–4 (2011), 399.
6. Al-Kirāza, الكنيسة وسط التغييرات والأحداث, 1 April 2011 (number 1–2, year 39), 1, 6.
7. See al-Kirāza, مصر بلادنا المحبوبة ... إلى أين؟, 30 December 2011 (number 15–26, year 39), 1.

8. Al-Salāh, الأقباط ومخاوف الانتخابات بين التهوين والتهويل 2012, 31.
9. OASIS, 'On the Crest of the Tahrir Square: Interview with Antonios Naguib', December 2011 (number 14, year 7), 27.
10. Al-Ahrām, المرشد: الإساءة للرسول صدرت من قلوب يملؤها الحقد, 29 September 2012 (number 45953, year 137), 4.
11. Majallat al-Azhar, بيان الأزهر ومخبة المثقفين حول مستقبل مصر, June 2011 (number 8, year 84), pages jim-waw.
12. Avon, 'Le nom chrétien sous la plume d'hommes de religion musulmans égyptiens'.
13. Al-Nahār, الراعي في القمة يتخوف من حرب سنية علوية, 28 September 2011 (number 24520, year 79), 20.
14. Al-Nahār, الراعي: زيارته دعوة للسلام في شرق الحديد والنار. الحضور المسيحي في هذه المنطقة يعطيها هوية ومعنى, 14 September 2012 (number 24848, year 80), 7.
15. Antoine Daw, مسيحيون ومسلمون معاً ضد الإساءة إلى الأديان, *Al-Safīr*, 22 September 2012 (number 12290, year 39), 4.
16. Ibrahim, *The Copts of Egypt*, 15.
17. Mahmood, *Religious Difference in a Secular Age*, 12.
18. Al-Salāh, الأقباط ومخاوف الانتخابات بين التهوين والتهويل, 33.
19. Elsässer, *The Coptic Question*, 105.
20. Al-Salāh, الأقباط ومخاوف الانتخابات بين التهوين والتهويل, 32.
21. Mayeur-Jaouen, *Voyage en Haute-Égypte*, 43.
22. Ibid.
23. Paul Sedra, 'Class Cleavages and Ethnic Conflict: Coptic Christian Communities in Modern Egyptian Politics', *Islam and Christian–Muslim Relations* 10:2 (1999), 219.
24. Al-Nahār, الكاردينال توران مخاطباً مسيحي الشرق: ابقوا أقلية فاعلة وانقذوا التعددية, 14 September 2012 (number 24848, year 80), 6.
25. Sedra, 'Class Cleavages and Ethnic Conflict', 219.
26. Mgr. Chucrallah Nabil El-Hage, 'Un combat solidaire avec les autres: L'exemple de la fondation *Adyan*', POC 61:3–4 (2011), 334–35. In Lebanon, however, the term 'minority' designates the parliamentary seat for the 'minority rites' which are the Syriac Orthodox, Syriac Catholic, Coptic Orthodox, Latin, Chaldean and Assyrian communities. The extent to which the term 'minority' is controversial was evident for instance in the 1970s, when one Syriac Orthodox leader in Zahlé bitterly wondered how long the Syriac Orthodox would remain a 'minority' in Lebanon (Majallat al-Batriyarkiyya, احتفال سرياني رائع في زحلة بعيد مار جرجس, May 1974 (number 115, year 12), 305.
27. Benjamin T. White, *The Emergence of Minorities in the Middle East: Politics and Community in French Mandate Syria* (Edinburgh: Edinburgh University Press, 2011), 21.

28. Elizabeth Monier, 'Minorities or Citizens in the Middle East? Locating the "Minority Question" in the Intersecting Histories of Collective National Belonging and State-Building', *Nations and Nationalism* 29:1 (2023), 298.
29. Chatelard, *Briser la mosaïque*, 21–22.
30. Al-Ahram Hebdo, 'Une démarche symbolique', 18–24 July 2012.
31. Al-Yawm al-Sābi', انتفاضة المؤسسات الدينية ضد الفيلم المسيء للرسول... "الأزهر": الداعون لإنتاجه هدفهم إشعال الفتنة.. "الإفتاء": ليس من الحرية ويمس أقدس رمز للمسلمين.. و"أقباط المهجر": نتبرأ من موريس صادق وزقلمة, 11 September 2012.
32. Al-Yawm al-Sābi', مطالب بشطب موريس صادق من نقابة المحامين.. مؤتمر "لا لإثارة الفتنة" يطرح وثيقة للتصدى لازدراء الأديان, 13 September 2012: http://www.youm7.com/story/2012/9/13/%D9%85%D8%A4%D8%AA%D9%85%D8%B1_%D9%84%D8%A7_%D9%84%D8%A5%D8%AB%D8%A7%D8%B1%D8%A9_%D8%A7%D9%84%D9%81%D8%AA%D9%86%D8%A9_%D9%8A%D8%B7%D8%B1%D8%AD_%D9%88%D8%AB%D9%8A%D9%82%D8%A9_%D9%84%D9%84%D8%AA%D8%B5%D8%AF%D9%89_%D9%84%D8%A7%D8%B2%D8%AF%D8%B1%D8%A7%D8%A1_%D8%A7%D9%84%D8%A3%D8%AF%D9%8A%D8%A7%D7%D9%86/784864#.VjszJF5OfVJ (accessed 23 May 2016).
33. Candace Lukasik, 'Conquest of Paradise: Secular Binds and Coptic Political Mobilization', *Middle East Critique* 25:2 (2016), 108.
34. Al-Ahram Hebdo, 'Une démarche symbolique'.
35. Hager, 'Die Kopten und der Arabische Frühling', 799.
36. Mīnā Magdī, Personal Interview.
37. McCallum, *Christian Religious Leadership in the Middle East*, 72–73.
38. Ibid, 76.
39. Arab Orthodoxy, 'Georges Khodr on the Orthodox in Lebanese Politics', 21 March 2010: http://araborthodoxy.blogspot.co.at/2010/03/georges-khodr-on-orthodox-in-lebanese.html (accessed 23 February 2023).
40. Arab Orthodoxy, 'Al-Safir Gives Some Background on the "Civil Commission" Plan', 4 October 2012, *Al-Safir*: http://araborthodoxy.blogspot.co.at/2012/10/al-safir-gives-some-background-on-civil.html (accessed 23 February 2023).
41. Arab Orthodoxy, 'The Youth Movement Rejects the Plan for a "Civil Commission"', 3 October 2012, *Al-Akhbar*: http://araborthodoxy.blogspot.co.at/2012/10/the-youth-movement-rejects-plan-for.html (accessed 23 February 2023).
42. Maximilian Felsch, 'Christian Political Activism in Lebanon: A Revival of Religious Nationalism in Times of Arab Upheavals', *Studies in Ethnicity and Nationalism* 18:1 (2018), 26.
43. Lise Paulsen Galal, 'Coptic Christian Practices: Formations of Sameness and Difference', *Islam and Christian–Muslim Relations* 23:1 (2012), 46, 47.

44. Lukasik, 'Conquest of Paradise', 115.
45. Paulsen Galal, 'Coptic Christian Practices', 47.
46. Copts Today, بيان من نيافة الأنبا موسى ردا على الفيلم المسيء للرسول, 11 September 2012.
47. Al-Yawm al-Sābi', بكار: التعرض للأنبياء والصحابة لا يمت لحرية الرأي بأية صلة, 10 September 2012.
48. Al-Shurūq, الشروق تحاور الدكتور يسرى حماد المتحدث باسم حزب النور: أتينا لنعمر لا لنخرب . . . ولا يمكننا إلغاء الاتفاقيات الدولية . . . والأقباط شركاؤنا في الوطن, 18 December 2011 (number 1051), 15.
49. Al-Daʿwa al-Salafiyya, تهنئة النصارى بأعيادهم, 31 December 2012: http://www.salafvoice.com/article.aspx?a=6567 (accessed 22 February 2023).
50. See Aubin-Boltanski, 'La Vierge, les chrétiens, les musulmans et la nation'.
51. Dima De Clerck, 'La Montagne: Un espace de partage et de ruptures', in Franck Mermier (ed.), *Liban: Espaces partages et pratiques de rencontre* (Paris, Beirut: Ifpo, 2008), 49.
52. Al-Tawḥīd, لبنان: سلسلة واسعة من المواقف المنددة من الأحزاب والجمعيات والشخصيات الإسلامية والمسيحية والوطنية بالاساءة للنبي محمد صلى الله عليه وسلم, 13 September 2012.
53. Al-Safīr, مسيرات في بعلبك وصور وصيدا وبرالياس ضد الإساءة, 22 September 2012 (number 12290, year 39), 4.
54. Al-Nahār, الحاج حسن: الدوائر الامريكية تثير الفتن معنيون بمكافحة الأقصاء والتكفير, 16 September 2012 (number 24850, year 80), 5.
55. Picard, 'La violence milicienne', 323.
56. Al-Hayāt, جنبلاط يدين الفيلم المسيء والرد عليه: لا يمكن تنزيه اسرائيل عن التحطيط له, 15 September 2012 (number 18061), 9.
57. Al-Nahār, جنبلاط: الفيلم المسيء إلى الإسلام هدفه التشويش على الثورات العربية, 15 September 2012 (number 24849, year 80), 7.
58. Massad, *Colonial Effects*, 222.
59. Luisa Gandolfo, *Palestinians in Jordan: The Politics of Identity* (London: I. B. Tauris, 2012), 108.
60. Massad, *Colonial Effects*, 265.
61. Al-Rai, مجلس ومجمع الكنائس يستنكران الفيلم المسيء, 15 September 2012.
62. A number of Transjordanian Christians actually fought on the side of the PLO (Massad, *Colonial Effects*, 265).
63. Bāssim Farrāj, Personal Interview.
64. Hager, 'The Orthodox Issue in Jordan', 226.
65. Ruhayl al-Gharāyiba, المسيحيون والمواطنة, *al-Dustūr*, 26 October 2013: https://www.ademocracynet.com/index.php?page=articles&id=4835&action=Detail (accessed 5 March 2023).
66. ʿAbd al-Amīr Qabalān, دور المسحيين في لبنان الوطن (Beirut: Université Saint-Joseph, 2003), 15.

67. Muhammad Abdallah Dirrāz, موقف الإسلام من الأديان الأخرى وعلاقته بها, Majallat al-Azhar, June 2012, 1470.
68. Fawzī Fāḍil al-Zafzāf, علاقة الإسلام بالديانات السماوية السابقة, *Majallat al-Azhar* December 2011 (number 85), 158–61.
69. Qur'an 2:136: 'Say, [O believers], "We have believed in Allāh and what has been revealed to us and what has been revealed to Abraham and Ishmael and Isaac and Jacob and the Descendants [al-Asbāṭ] and what was given to Moses and Jesus and what was given to the prophets from their Lord. We make no distinction between any of them, and we are Muslims [in submission] to Him'. https://quran.com/2/136?translations=20,49,84,17,85,101,18,95,38,19,22,31,27 (accessed 21 July 2022).
70. Qabalān, دور المسيحيين في لبنان الوطن, 19.
71. Abouna, بيان شجب واستنكار من مجلس رؤساء الكنائس في الأردن, 14 September 2012.
72. Johnny Awwad, 'Who is My God and Who is My Neighbour? A Response to "A Common Word Between Us and You"', *NEST Theological Review* 30:1 (2009), 80.
73. Wagemakers, *The Muslim Brotherhood in Jordan*, 203.
74. Grafton, *The Christians of Lebanon*, 201.
75. Qabalān, دور المسيحيين في لبنان الوطن, 16, 20.
76. Al-Yawm al-Sābiʿ, انتفاضة المؤسسات الدينية ضد الفيلم المسيء للرسول... "الأزهر": الداعون لإنتاجه هدفهم إشعال الفتنة.. "الإفتاء": ليس من الحرية ويمس أقدس رمز للمسلمين.. و"أقباط المهجر": نتبرأ من موريس صادق وزقلمة, 11 September 2012.
77. Al-Ahrām, مفتي الجمهورية للأهرام: نصرة النبي تتحقق باتباع منهجه . . . والإسلام يرفض العنف وإرهاب الآمنين, 21 September 2012.
78. Al-Ahrām, بديع: الإساءة للرسول وحدت المصريين. ولا نحمل المسيحيين وزر سفهاء الخارج, 21 September, year 137), 7.
79. Al-Ahrām, الغضب يجتاح مصر احتجاجا على الفيلم المسيء للرسول, 13 September 2012, 5.
80. Arab West Report, عبد الغفور في خطبة الجمعة بالاسكندرية, 15 September 2012.
81. Al-Yawm al-Sābiʿ, عبد الوارث: الفيلم المسيء للرسول تحرش نصراني بتيار الإسلام السياسي, 7 September 2012.
82. Al-Tawhīd, الشيخ الشعار دان الفيلم المسيء للاسلام وطالب بسحبه/ الشيخ حمود: ردات الفعل الطبيعية التي طالت السفارات الاميركية في العالم العربي كانت هبة ربانية, 14 September 2012: http://www.altawhid.org/2012/09/14/%D8%A7%D9%84%D8%B4%D9%8A%D8%AE-%D8%A7%D9%84%D8%B4%D8%B9%D8%A7%D8%B1-%D8%AF%D8%A7%D9%86-%D8%A7%D9%84%D9%81%D9%8A%D9%84%D9%85-%D8%A7%D9%84%D9%85%D8%B3%D9%8A%D8%A6-%D9%84%D9%84%D8%A7%D8%B3%D9%84%D8%A7/ (accessed 17 May 2016).

83. Al-Dustūr, تواصل الإدانة والاستنكار للفيلم المسيء لرسول الله, 17 September 2012.
84. Al-Dustūr, تواصل الادانة والاستنكار للفيلم المسيء لرسول الله, 16 September 2012, 9.
85. See Griffith, 'Christians and Christianity', 310–11.
86. Ignatius Ephrem Barsoum, المحاضرات التي القاها غبطة الحبر العلامة سيدنا مار اغناطيوس افرام برصوم بطريرك السريان الانطاكي في الجامعة الاميركية في بيروت بدعوة منها في ١-٢-٣ ايار سنة ١٩٣٣, 1933, Collection Beth Mardutho: https://archive.org/details/unset0000unse_y6a0 (accessed 23 March 2023).
87. There needs to be more study on why the use of this term ceased.
88. Rafiq Khoury, Personal Interview, 25 March 2015, Jerusalem.
89. ʿĀmir al-Hāfī, Personal Interview.
90. Al-Dustūr, فعاليات الوسطية و"عشائر الطفيلة" تستنكر الإساءة إلى النبي الكريم, 19 September 2012.
91. 'The Messenger has believed in what was revealed to him from his Lord, and [so have] the believers. All of them have believed in Allah and His angels and His books and His messengers, [saying], "We make no distinction between any of His messengers". And they say, "We hear and we obey. [We seek] Your forgiveness, our Lord, and to You is the [final] destination"'. Qur'an: http://quran.com/2 (accessed 21 May 2016).
92. See Wagemakers, *The Muslim Brotherhood in Jordan*, 203.
93. Al-Daʿwa al-Salafiyya, استعمال لفظة 'المسيحيين' بدلاً من النصارى, 25 July 2011: http://www.salafvoice.com/article.aspx?a=5537 (accessed 22 February 2023).
94. Hager, 'From "Polytheists" to "Partners in the Nation"', 301.
95. See Martin Whittingham, 'Muslims and the Bible', in David Thomas (ed.), *Routledge Handbook on Christian–Muslim Relations* (London: Routledge, 2017), 269–87.
96. Ahmad Yahya, أين إنجيل المسيح!؟, Sawt al-Salaf, 14 May 2009: http://www.salafvoice.com/article.aspx?a=3268 (accessed 23 March 2023).
97. Al-Yawm al-Sābiʿ, برهامي: لا يجوز حرق "الإنجيل".. وتمزيقه إهانة لشيء فيه ذكر الله, 14 September 2012.
98. Al-Shurūq, "ثورة غضب" إسلامية مسيحية ضد الإساءة للرسول, 12 September 2012.
99. Al-Daʿwa al-Salafiyya, حول العلاقة الاجتماعية بين المسلمين والمسيحيين, 30 December 2012: http://www.salafvoice.com/article.aspx?a=6565 (accessed 22 February 2023).
100. Al-Shurūq, "حل" لا تقدموا الإسلام ك, 16 March 2013 (number 1504), 9.
101. Wagemakers, *The Muslim Brotherhood in Jordan*, 199.
102. Ibid, 201.
103. Al-Ahrām, مفتي الجمهورية للأهرام: نصرة النبي تتحقق باتباع منهجه ... والإسلام يرفض العنف وإرهاب الآمنين, 21 September 2012.
104. Hager, 'From "Polytheists" to "Partners in the Nation"', 293.

105. Ibid.
106. Al-Shurūq, اتفقنا مع الإخوان على خذف كلمة 'مبادئ' من نص الشريعة فى الدستور, 30 June 2012 (number 1246), 6.
107. Al-Daʿwa al-Salafiyya, بيان من الدعوة السلفية بشأن أحداث ماسبيرو 9-10-2011, 11 October 2011: http://montada.khaledbelal.com/showthread.php?t=9997 (accessed 22 February 2023).
108. Al-Daʿwa al-Salafiyya, الدعوة السلفية م نَ نحن ؟ وماذا نريد؟, 28 August 2012: http://www.salafvoice.com/article.aspx?a=5615 (accessed 22 February 2023).
109. Al-Kirāza, اجتماعات المجمع المقدس وقراراته, 13 July 2012 (number 3–4, Year 40), 7.
110 Paul Sedra, 'Copts and the Power over Personal Status', *Jadaliyya*, 3 December 2012: https://www.jadaliyya.com/Details/27530/Copts-and-the-Power-over-Personal-Status (accessed 23 February 2023).
111. Scott, 'Citizenship, Public Order, and State Sovereignty', 388, 378.
112. Pizzo, 'The "Coptic Question" in Post-Revolutionary Egypt', 2599.
113. Al-Salāh, حوار العرو مع الأنبا كيرلس وليم مطران اسيوط, 2012 (number 1, year 82), 12–16 and 43–45, 45.
114. Scott, 'Citizenship, Public Order, and State Sovereignty', 383.
115. Wagemakers, *The Muslim Brotherhood in Jordan*, 208.
116. Krämer, 'Dhimmi ou citoyen'.
117. Tadros, *The Muslim Brotherhood in Contemporary* Egypt, 99, 101.
118. Krämer, 'Dhimmi ou citoyen'.
119. Al-Gharāyiba, المسيحيون والمواطنة, 26 October 2013.
120. Wagemakers, *The Muslim Brotherhood in Jordan*, 210. In the 'Zamzam Initiative', Ruhayl al-Gharāyiba as a leading figure promoted the emergence of 'a modern civil state' and ran in the 2016 elections in the same electoral list as the 'National Coalition Reform' with tribal, nationalist and Christian figures (Kirdiş, *The Rise of Islamic Political Movements and Parties*, 178–79).

BIBLIOGRAPHY

Primary Sources in Arabic: Newspapers and Websites

Abouna, بيان شجب واستنكار من مجلس رؤساء الكنائس في الأردن. 14 September 2012: http://www.abouna.org/node/1164 (accessed 21 May 2016).

———. مطرانية اللاتين تشجب العنف غير المبرر الذي راح ضحيته الكاتب ناهض حتر. 26 September 2016: http://abouna.org/content/مطرانية-اللاتين-تشجب-العنف-غير-المبرر-الذي-راح-ضحيته-الكاتب-ناهض-حتر (accessed 18 October 2020).

Al-Ahrām, غضب شعبي من الإساءة للرسول. 12 September 2012 (number 45936, year 137), 1 and 5.

———. عماد عبد الغفور مساعد رئيس الجمهورية. 12 September 2012 (number 45936, year 137), 4.

———. الغضب يجتاح مصر احتجاجا على الفيلم المسيء للرسول. 13 September 2012 (number 45937, year 137), 5.

———. النواب يطالبون أمريكا لاعتذار احتراما لمشاعر مليار ونصف مسلم. 13 September 2012 (number 45937, year 137), 4.

———. استمرار ردود الفعل الغاضبة على الفيلم المسيء: الأزهر يطالب بالتزام بضوابط الاحتجاج والبعد عن العنف. 14 September 2012 (number 45938, year 137), 6.

———. ومسيرات عارمة لنصرة الرسول في المحافظات. 15 September 2012 (number 45939, year 137), 4.

———. هدوء حذر يسود محيط السفارة بعد اشتباكات عنيفة. 16 September 2012 (number 45940, year 137), 5.

———. قوات الأمن تحكم سيطرتها على ميدان التحرير. 16 September 2012 (number 45940, year 137), 5.

———. رموز إسلامية ومسيحية تطالب بتجريم ازدراء الأديان. 17 September 2012 (number 45941, year 137), 5.

―――. 19 September 2012: http://www.ahram.org.eg/archive/The-First/News/171900.aspx (accessed 23 May 2016). 200. متظاهرون يحاصرون منزل أحد منتجي الفيلم المسيء للرسول الكريم

―――. 19 September 2012 (number 45943, year 137), 4. البناء والتنمية يحذر من مخطط لإثارة فتنة طائفية.

―――. 21 September 2012 (number 45945, year 137), 5. وزير الأوقاف يطالب بتغليب صوت العقل في التعامل مع إزدراء الأديان.

―――. 21 September 2012 (number 45945, year 137), 7. بديع: الإساءة للرسول وحدت المصريين. ولا نحمل المسيحيين وزر سفهاء الخارج.

―――. 21 September 2012 (number 45945, year 137), 40. مفتي الجمهورية للأهرام: نصرة النبي تتحقق باتباع منهجه . . . والإسلام يرفض العنف وإرهاب الآمنين.

―――. 22 September 2012 (number 45946, year 137), 3. باخوميوس: التعدى على الأديان يحتاج لموقف حازم.

―――. 27 September 2012 (number 45951, year 137), 24. شيخ الأزهر يطالب القوى السياسية بالتوافق والبحث عن حلول حقيقية للأزمات.

―――. 28 September 2012 (number 45952, year 137), 4. شيخ الأزهر: الغرب لا يزال يفكر بمنطق عصور الظلام.

―――. 29 September 2012 (number 45953, year 137), 4. المرشد: الإساءة للرسول صدرت من قلوب يملؤها الحقد.

―――. 30 September 2012 (number 45954, year 137), 22. اليوم أولى جلسات محاكمة "أبو إسلام" المتهم بحرق الإنجيل أمام السفارة الأمريكية.

Ajloun News, 6 January 2012: حراك كفرنجة للإصلاح يعقد إجتماعا لمناقشة سبل تطوير عمل الحراك الشعبي. http://www.ajlounnews.net/index.php?module=news&id=7546&category=71 (accessed 21 May 2016).

Al-Anwar, 15 September 2012 (number 18142, year 53): حردان: الإساءة الى الإسلام جزء من مخطط أميركي - صهيوني للفتنة. http://www.archive.alanwar.com/article.php?articleID=172297&issuedate=20120915 (accessed 17 May 2016).

―――. 18 September 2012 (number 18144, year 53): الجميل استنكر في مؤتمر صحافي الاساءة للإسلام وخطب مواطن: خطاب نصرالله بتوقيته ضرب وفاقاً أوجدته زيارة البابا. http://www.archive.alanwar.com/article.php?articleID=172576&issuedate=20120918 (accessed 17 May 2016).

―――. 22 September 2012 (number 18148, year 53): الأحرار: الفيلم المسيء للمسلمين عمل طائش وللحوار شروط كي لا يصبح ملهاة وغطاء. http://www.archive.alanwar.com/article.php?articleID=173042&issuedate=20120922 (accessed 17 May 2016).

Arab West Report, عبد الغفور فى خطبة الجمعة بالاسكندرية: حرق البعض للإنجيل تصرف غير محسوب ومحرم. Al-Shuruq al-Jadid. 15 September 2012: http://arabwestreport.info/ar/lsn-2012/lsbw-37/76-bd-lgfwr-f-khtb-ljm-blskndry-hrq-lbd-llnjyl-tsrf-gyr-mhswb-wmhrm (accessed 29 January 2016).

17 September 2012: أسقف بني مزار يعتذر للمسلمين عن الإساءة مؤكدا مخالفتها لسماحة المسيحية. ———
http://www.arabwestreport.info/ar/lsn-2012/lsbw-37/73-sqf-bn-mzr-ytdhr-llmslmyn-n-ls-mwkd-mkhlfth-lsmh-lmsyhy (accessed 2 November 2015).

Aztabarabic, "المسيحية والاسلام": الكاثوليكوس آرام الأول يحضر القمة الروحية المسيحية - الاسلامية في بكركي ويقول: "تعايشتا في الشرق الأوسط لقرون طويلة". 25 September 2012: http://www.aztagarabic.com/archives/6419 (accessed 3 February 2023).

Al-Balad, "مطرانية المنوفية تستنكر الإساءة للرسول... وترفع لافتة "مسلم مسيحي إيد واحدة". 15 September 2012: http://www.el-balad.com/265222 (accessed 21 May 2016).

Bkerki, الثني - بيان القمة الروحية ببكرك 24 ايلول 2012. 24 September 2012: http://www.bkerkelb.org/arabic/index.php?option=com_content&view=article&id=1714:------24--2012-&catid=263:2011-09-07-08-04-38&Itemid=66 (accessed 9 December 2013).

Coptic Catholic Patriarchate, بيان الكنيسة الكاثوليكية بشأن ما تنشره وسائل الإعلام عن ظهور فيلم يسيء للإسلام. 11 September 2012: http://coptcatholic.net/p12776/ (accessed 3 February 2023).

Copts Today, حركة "أقباط بلا قيود" نرفض الإساءة للمقدسات الإسلامية ونطالب بوضع حد للإساءات لرموزنا المسيحية. 10 September 2012: http://www.coptstoday.com/Copts-News/Detail.php?Id=32279 (accessed 23 May 2016).

——— . بيان من نيافة الأنبا موسى ردا على الفيلم المسيء للرسول. 11 September 2012: http://www.copts-today.com/Copts-News/Detail.php?Id=32480 (accessed 3 March 2014).

——— . مؤامرة شيطانية ... الفيلم المسيء للرسول .. بقلم القس فيلوباتير جميل عزيز. 12 September 2012: http://www.coptstoday.com/Copts-News/Detail.php?Id=32517 (accessed 22 March 2023).

——— . وصول مسيرة قبطية الي السفارة الامريكية وهتافات .. مسلم مسيحى ايد واحدة. 12 September 2012: http://www.coptstoday.com/Copts-News/Detail.php?Id=32628 (accessed 3 March 2015).

——— . فيديو ... حرق منزل موريس صادق بالقاهرة في وجود الشرطة المصرية. 13 September 2012: http://www.coptstoday.com/Copts-News/Detail.php?Id=32652 (accessed 3 March 2014).

——— . السلفيون يتجمهرون أمام منزل "جوزيف نصر الله" صاحب قناه الطريق. 18 September 2012: http://www.coptstoday.com/Copts-News/Detail.php?Id=33564 (accessed 3 March 2014).

——— . أمن الدولة تحقق في واقعة تمزيق الإنجيل أثناء أحداث السفارة الأمريكية. 22 September 2012: http://www.coptstoday.com/Copts-News/Detail.php?Id=34184 (accessed 23 May 2016).

Copts United, الكنيسة الأرثوذكسية ترفض الفيلم المسيء للإسلام، وتؤكد: هذا يخالف تقاليد المسيحية. 10 September 2012: http://www.copts-united.com/Article.php?I=1288&A=69777 (accessed 3 February 2023).

——. 14 September 2012 بالفيديو والصور الانبا كيرلس اسقف نجع حمادي : لا لازدراء الاديان . . . واحترسوا من الثعالب الصغيرة: http://www.copts-united.com/article.php?I=1292&A=70190 (accessed 21 May 2016).

Al-Daʿwa al-Salafiyya, هل تهنئة النصارى بأعيادهم تدخل في البرِّ والإقساط إليهم؟, 19 May 2007: http://www.salafvoice.com/article.aspx?a=1056 (accessed 22 February 2023).

——. هل نتوقف عن تنبيه المسلمين إلى كفر النصارى وكيدهم منعًا للفتنة. 21 October 2010: http://www.salafvoice.com/article.aspx?a=4837 (accessed 22 February 2023).

——. استعمال لفظة "المسيحيين" بدلاً من النصارى. 25 July 2011: http://www.salafvoice.com/article.aspx?a=5537 (accessed 22 February 2023).

——. بيان من الدعوة السلفية بشأن أحداث ماسبيرو 9-10-2011. 11 October 2011: http://montada.khaledbelal.com/showthread.php?t=9997 (accessed 22 February 2023).

——. الدعوة السلفية مَن نحن ؟ وماذا نريد؟. 28 August 2012: http://www.salafvoice.com/article.aspx?a=5615 (accessed 22 February 2023).

——. بيان من "الدعوة السلفية" بشأن الفيلم المسيء "لرسول الله -صلى الله عليه وسلم". 11 September 2012: http://www.anasalafy.com/play.php?catsmktba=35834 (accessed 22 February 2023).

——. حول العلاقة الاجتماعية بين المسلمين والمسيحيين. 30 December 2012: http://www.salafvoice.com/article.aspx?a=6565 (accessed 22 February 2023).

——. تهنئة النصارى بأعيادهم. 31 December 2012: http://www.salafvoice.com/article.aspx?a=6567 (accessed 22 February 2023).

Al-Dustūr, الحكومة تعرب عن ادانتها الشديدة ورفضها القاطع للإساءة لرسول الله ص. 14 September 2012 (number 16227), 3.

——. مسيرات واعتصامات تندد بالإساءة للرسول الكريم. 15 September 2012 (number 16228), 29.

——. رؤساء الكنائس : "مكونات مجتمعاتنا أوعى من الخديعة وأقوى أمام الافتراء". 15 September 2012 (number 16228), 16.

——. تواصل الادانة والاستنكار للفيلم المسيء لرسول الله. 16 September 2012 (number 16229), 9.

——. تواصل الإدانة والاستنكار للفيلم المسيء لرسول الله. 17 September 2012: http://www.addustour.com//16611/%D8%AA%D9%88%D8%A7%D8%B5%D9%84+%D8%A7%D9%84%D8%A5%D8%AF%D8%A7%D9%86%D8%A9+%D9%88%D8%A7%D9%84%D8%A7%D8%B3%D8%AA%D9%86%D9%83%D8%A7%D8%B1+%D9%84%D9%84%D9%81%D9%8A%D9%84%D9%85+%D8%A7%D9%84%D9%85%D8%B3%D9%8A%D8%A1+%D9%84%D8%B1%D8%B3%D9%88%D9%84+%D8%A7%D9%84%D9%84%D9%87.html (accessed 21 May 2016).

——. الأردنيون يواصلون التنديد بالفيلم المسيء للرسول. 18 September 2012: http://www.addustour.com/16612/%D8%A7%D9%84%D8%A3%D8%B1%D8%AF%D9%86%D9%8A%D9%88%D9%86+%D9%8A%D9%88%D8%A7%D8%B5%D9%84%D9%88%D9%86+%D8%A7%D9%84%D8%AA%D9%86%D8%AF%D9%8A%D8%AF+%D8%A8%D8%A7%D9%84%D9%81%D9%8A%D9%84%D9%85+%D8%A7%D9%84D

9%84%D9%85%D8%B3%D9%8A%D8%A1+%D9%84%D9%84%D8%B1%D8%B3%D9%88%D9%84.html (accessed 21 May 2016).

———. 19 September 2012 (number 16231), 29. فعاليات الوسطية و"عشائر الطفيلة" تستنكر الإساءة إلى النبي الكريم.

———. 22 September 2012: مختصون مسلمون ومسيحيون: الفيلم المشبوه مؤامرة على التعايش السلمي بين الأديان. http://www.addustour.com/16616/%D9%85%D8%AE%D8%AA%D8%B5%D9%88%D9%86+%D9%85%D8%B3%D9%84%D9%85%D9%88%D9%86+%D9%88%D9%85%D8%B3%D9%8A%D8%AD%D9%8A%D9%88%D9%86+%3A+%D8%A7%D9%84%D9%81%D9%8A%D9%84%D9%85+%D8%A7%D9%84%D9%85%D8%B4%D8%A8%D9%88%D9%87+%D9%85%D8%A4%D8%A7%D9%85%D8%B1%D8%A9+%D8%B9%D9%84%D9%89+%D8%A7%D9%84%D8%AA%D8%B9%D8%A7%D9%8A%D8%B4+%D8%A7%D9%84%D8%B3%D9%84%D9%85%D9%8A+%D8%A8%D9%8A%D9%86+%D8%A7%D9%84%D8%A3%D8%AF%D9%8A%D8%A7%D9%86.html (accessed 21 May 2016).

Enjaz News, الدكتور احمد عناب ... قائد يتمتع بحنكة استثنائية: http://www.enjaznews.com/details.aspx?id=26852 (accessed 21 May 2016).

Al-Ghad, الجرشيون يندون بالفيلم المسيء للرسول. 15 September 2012: http://www.alghad.com/articles/607348-%D8%A7%D9%84%D8%AC%D8%B1%D8%B4%D9%8A%D9%88%D9%86-%D9%8A%D9%86%D8%AF%D8%AF%D9%88%D9%86-%D8%A8%D8%A7%D9%84%D9%81%D9%8A%D9%84%D9%85-%D8%A7%D9%84%D9%85%D8%B3%D9%8A%D8%A1-%D9%84%D9%84%D8%B1%D8%B3%D9%88%D9%84 (accessed 21 May 2016).

———. عجلون: فعاليات شعبية تنتصر للرسول وتطالب بالاصلاح. 15 September 2012: http://www.alghad.com/articles/607357-%D8%B9%D8%AC%D9%84%D9%88%D9%86-%D9%81%D8%B9%D8%A7%D9%84%D9%8A%D8%A7%D8%AA-%D8%B4%D8%B9%D8%A8%D9%8A%D8%A9-%D8%AA%D9%86%D8%AA%D8%B5%D8%B1-%D9%84%D9%84%D8%B1%D8%B3%D9%88%D9%84-%D9%88%D8%AA%D8%B7%D8%A7%D9%84%D8%A8-%D8%A8%D8%A7%D9%84%D8%A7%D8%B5%D9%84%D8%A7%D8%AD?s=e3ac7a8af367d7f51c818fe724336e38&search=%D8%A7%D9%84%D9%81%D9%8A%D9%84%D9%85%20%D8%A7%D9%84%D9%85%D8%B3%D9%8A%D8%A1 (accessed 21 May 2016).

———. معان: دعوة لحملة لمقاطعة البضائع والمنتجات الأميركية. 15 September 2012: http://www.alghad.com/articles/607351-%D9%85%D8%B9%D8%A7%D9%86-%D8%AF%D8%B9%D9%88%D8%A9-%D9%84%D8%AD%D9%85%D9%84%D8%A9-%D9%84%D9%85%D9%82%D8%A7%D8%B7%D8%B9%D8%A9-%D8%A7%D9%84%D8%A8%D8%B6%D8%A7%D8%A6%D8%B9-%D9%88%D8%A7%D9%84%D9%85%D9%86%D8%AA%D8%AC%D

8%A7%D8%AA-%D8%A7%D9%84%D8%A3%D9%85%D9%8A%D8%B1%D 9%83%D9%8A%D8%A9?s=e3ac7a8af367d7f51c818fe724336e38&search=% D8%A7%D9%84%D9%81%D9%8A%D9%84%D9%85%20%D8%A7%D9%84 %D9%85%D8%B3%D9%8A%D8%A1 (accessed 21 May 2016).

—— . لجنة بلدية الطفيلة تستنكر الفيلم المسيء للرسول الكريم. 17 September 2012: http://www.alghad. com/articles/607214-%D9%84%D8%AC%D9%86%D8%A9- %D8%A8%D9%84%D8%AF%D9%8A%D8%A9-%D8%A7%D9%84%D8%B7% D9%81%D9%8A%D9%84%D8%A9-%D8%AA%D8%B3%D8%AA%D9%86%D 9%83%D8%B1-%D8%A7%D9%84%D9%81%D9%8A%D9%84%D9%85- %D8%A7%D9%84%D9%85%D8%B3%D9%8A%D8%A1- %D9%84%D9%84%D8%B1%D8%B3%D9%88%D9%84-%D8%A7%D9%84%D 9%83%D8%B1%D9%8A%D9%85?s=e3ac7a8af367d7f51c818fe724336e38&sea rch=%D8%A7%D9%84%D9%81%D9%8A%D9%84%D9%85%20%D8%A7%D9 %84%D9%85%D8%B3%D9%8A%D8%A1 (accessed 21 May 2016).

—— . سلفيو معان ينتصرون للرسول في "اسبوع الغضب". 20 September 2012: http://www.alghad. com/articles/606985-%D8%B3%D9%84%D9%81%D9%8A%D9%88- %D9%85%D8%B9%D8%A7%D9%86-%D9%8A%D9%86%D8%AA%D8%B5 %D8%B1%D9%88%D9%86-%D9%84%D9%84%D8%B1%D8%B3%D9%8 8%D9%84-%D9%81%D9%8A-%D8%A7%D8%B3%D8%A8%D9%88%D8% B9-%D8%A7%D9%84%D8%BA%D8%B6%D8%A8?s=e3ac7a8af367d7f51c818 fe724336e38&search=%D8%A7%D9%84%D9%81%D9%8A%D9%8 4%D9%85%20%D8%A7%D9%84%D9%85%D8%B3%D9%8A%D8%A1 (accessed 12 July 2017).

—— . الأنبا بولا: الفيلم المسيء فكرة شيطانية صهيونية لضرب الأديان ... وبطله عميلا للموساد, Gate al-Ahram, 15 September 2012: http://gate.ahram.org.eg/News/251298.aspx (accessed 21 May 2016).

جنبلاط يدين الفيلم المسيء والرد عليه: لا يمكن تنزيه اسرائيل عن التحطيط له. 15 September 2012, Al-Hayāt (number 18061), 9.

—— . اشتباكات بين إسلاميين وأقباط في محاكمة سلفي أحرق الإنجيل. 1 October 2012 (number 18077), 6.

—— . أحمد الأسير بين التنصّل والتفهّم: إنّه سحر الساحر الملتبس. 15 March 2014: http://www.alhayat. com/Articles/1139661/%D8%A3%D8%AD%D9%85%D8%AF-%D8%A7%D9%8 4%D8%A3%D8%B3%D9%8A%D8%B1-%D8%A8%D9%8A%D9%86-%D8 %A7%D9%84%D8%AA%D9%86%D8%B5%D9%91%D9%84-%D9%88%D8 %A7%D9%84%D8%AA%D9%81%D9%87%D9%91%D9%85-- %D8%A5%D9%86%D9%91%D9%87-%D8%B3%D8%AD%D8%B1-%D8%A7%D 9%84%D8%B3%D8%A7%D8%AD%D8%B1-%D8%A7%D9%84%D9%85%D9%8 4%D8%AA%D8%A8%D8%B3 (accessed 17 May 2016).

Al-Hurra, الفيلم المسيء للإسلام ... الأقباط في دائرة الاتهام. 19 September 2012: http://www.alhurra.com/content/video-islam-copts-situation-egypt/212035.html (accessed 23 May 2016).

Al-Jazeera, انتخاب أول مسيحي في قيادة الحزب الإسلامي الأبرز بالأردن. 20 February 2007: http://www.aljazeera.net/news/reportsandinterviews/2007/2/20/%D8%A7%D9%86%D8%AA%D8%AE%D8%A7%D8%A8-%D8%A3%D9%88%D9%84-%D9%85%D8%B3%D9%8A%D8%AD%D9%8A-%D9%81%D9%8A-%D9%82%D9%8A%D8%A7%D8%AF%D8%A9-%D8%A7%D9%84%D8%AD%D8%B2%D8%A8-%D8%A7%D9%84%D8%A5%D8%B3%D9%84%D8%A7%D9%85%D9%8A-%D8%A7%D9%84%D8%A3%D8%A8%D8%B1%D8%B2-%D8%A8%D8%A7%D9%84%D8%A3%D8%B1%D8%AF%D9%86 (accessed 21 May 2016).

———. دور النقابات المهنية في الحياة السياسية بالأردن. 12 May 2015: https://www.youtube.com/watch?v=5mcmtPXtXp8 (accessed 22 February 2023).

Al-Kirāza, الكنيسة وسط التغييرات والأحداث. 1 April 2011 (number 1–2, year 39), 1, 6.

———. بيان المجمع المقدس الصادر من الكنيسة القبطية الأرثوذكسية. 4 November 2011 (numbers 13–14, year 39), 2.

———. مصر بلادنا المحبوبة . . . إلى أين؟. 30 December 2011 (number 15–26, year 39), 1.

———. عيد القيامة المجيد. May 2012 (number 1 and 2, year 40), 5.

———. اجتماعات المجمع المقدس وقراراته. 13 July 2012 (number 3–4, year 40), 7.

Linga, مجلس رؤساء الكنائس في الأردن هو المرجعية الوحيدة لكل الشؤون المسيحية!!!. 27 January 2009: https://www.linga.org/local-news/MjMx (accessed 16 March 2023).

Majallat al-Azhar, بيان الأزهر ومخبة المثقفين حول مستقبل مصر. June 2011 (number 8, year 84), pages jim–waw.

Majallat al-Batriyarkiyya, احتفال سرياني رائع في زحلة بعيد مار جرجس. May 1974 (number 115, year 12), 304–6.

Masress, الحقوق المدنية للمسيحيين : نرفض الإساءة للأديان ونطالب بعمل فيلم للرد على المُسيء. 2 September 2012: http://www.masress.com/akhbartoday/36211 (accessed 22 February 2023).

———. برهامي: لا يجوز للمفتي وشيخ الأزهر أن يهنيا الأقباط "الكفار". 1 January 2013: https://www.masress.com/elsaba7/65273 (accessed 22 February 2023).

———. البناء والتنمية يطلق تحالف إسلامي مسيحي لمواجهة الطائفية. 20 January 2013: https://www.masress.com/almesryoon/193075 (accessed 22 February 2023).

Al-Masrī al-Yawm, "النور" و "الجبهة السلفية" ينضمان لوقفة أمام السفارة الأمريكية ضد الفيلم المسيء. 10 September 2012: http://www.almasryalyoum.com/news/details/162864 (accessed 31 January 2023).

———. الكنيسة تتبرأ من صانعي الفيلم المسيء للرسول وتؤكد: نرفض المساس بمشاعر شركاء الوطن. 11 September 2012: http://today.almasryalyoum.com/article2.aspx?ArticleID=352975 (accessed 31 January 2023).

——. "الحرية والعدالة" : الفيلم المسيء للرسول "محاولة دنيئة لإثارة الطائفية". 11 September 2012: http://www.almasryalyoum.com/news/details/163110 (accessed 31 January 2023).

——. عمرو موسى: من أعد "الفيلم المسيء" فئة حاقدة وباغية ومريضة. 12 September 2012: http://www.almasryalyoum.com/news/details/163163 (accessed 31 January 2023).

——. وفود كنسية تشارك "الإخوان" وقفتهم رفضًا لـ "الفيلم المسيء" أمام "مصطفى محمود". 14 September 2012: http://www.almasryalyoum.com/news/details/163696 (accessed 31 January 2023).

——. جورج إسحاق يُدين "الفيلم المسيء" ويؤكد: مصر سالمة بنسيجها القوي. 14 September 2012: http://www.almasryalyoum.com/news/details/163642 (accessed 31 January 2023).

——. تواصل الاحتجاجات ضد "الفيلم المسيء" بأنحاء مصر . . . ومحافظ المنيا أبرز المتظاهرين. 15 September 2012: http://www.almasryalyoum.com/news/details/163947 (accessed 31 January 2023).

Middle East Council of Churches, بيان من رؤساء الكنائس المسيحية بمصر حول فيلم شيفرده دافمسي. Muntada, July-September 2006, 26.

Moheet, الأنبا بسنتي: المُنتجون للفيلم المُسيء للرسول لا يمثلون أقباط المهجر. 20 September 2012: http://moheet.com/2012/09/20/1668478/%D8%A7%D9%84%D8%A3%D9%86%D8%A8%D8%A7-%D8%A8%D8%B3%D9%86%D8%AA%D9%8A-%D8%A7%D9%84%D9%85-%D9%86%D8%AA%D8%AC%D9%88%D9%86-%D9%84%D9%84%D9%81%D9%8A%D9%84%D9%85-%D8%A7%D9%84%D9%85-%D8%B3%D9%8A.html#.VjeIWm5OfIV (accessed 21 May 2016).

Al-Nahār, الراعي في القمة يتخوف من حرب سنية علوية. 28 September 2011 (number 24520, year 79), 20.

——. الراعي: زيارته دعوة للسلام في شرق الحديد والنار. الحضور المسيحي في هذه المنطقة يعطيها هوية ومعنى. 14 September 2012 (number 24848, year 80), 7.

——. الكاردينال توران مخاطباً مسيحي الشرق: ابقوا أقلية فاعلة وانقذوا التعددية. 14 September 2012 (number 24848, year 80), 6.

——. جنبلاط: الفيلم المسيء إلى الإسلام هدفه التشويش على الثورات العربية. 15 September 2012 (number 24849, year 80), 7.

——. الحاج حسن: الدوائر الاميركية تثير الفتن معنيون بمكافحة الأقصاء والتكفير. 16 September 2012 (number 24850, year 80), 5.

——. من زيارة البابا إلى تصاعد الاتجاجات تظاهرة الضاحية تتردّد في السفارة الأميركية. 18 September 2012 (number 24852, year 80), 1 and 12.

——. مفتي الجمهورية: زيارة البابا شهادة للبنان. 19 September 2012 (number 24853, year 80), 2.

——. اجتماع بدعوة من قباني دان "براءة المسلمين": لن يفيد أميركا التنصّل من مسؤولياتها. 21 September 2012 (number 24856, year 80), 6.

——. إعتصام إمام مسجد بلال بن رباح قطع أوصال بيروت. 22 September 2012 (number 24855, year 80), 5.

———. 23 September 2012 (number 24856, Year 80), 5. الموسوي ويزي في مسيرة بنت جبيل: الائتلاف الإسلامي - المسيحي رد مباشر.

———. 24 September 2012 (number 24857, year 80), 2. عناوين في القمة الروحية اليوم و الحضور مكتمل إسلامياً.

———. 23 July 2014: http://newspaper.annahar.com/article/153796-%D9%83%D8%AA%D8%A7%D8%A8-%D9%84%D9%84%D8%A3%D8%A8-%D8%A7%D9%84%D9%85%D8%A4%D8%B1%D8%AE-%D9%86%D8%A7%D9%8A%D9%81-%D8%A7%D8%B3%D8%B7%D9%81%D8%A7%D9%86-%D9%88%D8%AB%D8%A7%D8%A6%D9%82-%D8%AA%D8%AA%D9%86%D8%A7%D9%88%D9%84-%D8%A3%D8%A8%D8%B1%D8%B4%D9%8A%D8%A9-%D8%B9%D9%83%D8%A7%D8%B1-%D8%A7%D9%84%D8%A3%D8%B1%D8%AB%D9%88%D8%B0%D9%83%D8%B3%D9%8A%D8%A9 (accessed 22 February 2023). كتاب للأب المؤرخ نايف اسطفان وثائق تتناول أبرشية عكار الأرثوذكسية.

———. 25 September 2016: https://www.annahar.com/article/474242-حتر-ناهض-هو- (accessed 22 February 2023). مَن هو ناهض حتر؟.

Al-Nahar Shabab, مشاركون نصرة للأسير أم للرسول؟ 27 September 2012 (number 24861, year 80), 22.

Naharnet, الأسير ينتقد دعوة نصر الله الى التظاهر: "براءة المسلمين" اساء الى الاسلام بكامله. 18 September 2012: http://www.naharnet.com/stories/ar/53922 (accessed 22 February 2023).

The Orthodox Society, بيان شجب إدانة. [n. d.] Statement given to the author in May 2015.

Al-Rai, مجلس ومجمع الكنائس يستنكران الفيلم المسيء. 15 September 2012: http://www.alrai.com/article_m/539017.html (accessed 21 May 2016).

Al-Safīr, لقاء علمائي يدعو قباني إلى الاستقالة والسنيورة الى إعادة المال المسروق. 17 February 2011 (number 11816, year 37), 2.

———. اعتصام صيداوي ضد زيارة "القوات" للأسير. 5 September 2012 (number 12275, year 39), 4.

———. القاهرة فيلم يفجّر غضباً اقتحام السفارة الأمريكية. 12 September 2012 (number 12281, year 39), 1 and 17.

———. طرابلس: إحراق "كنتاكي" و "هارديز" يوقع قتيلاً و25 جريحا. 15 September 2012 (number 12284, year 39), 6.

———. الأب ضو . . . والمشاركة المميزة. 18 September 2012 (number 12286, year 39), 4.

———. مسيرات في بعلبك وصور وصيدا وبرالياس ضد الإساءة. 22 September 2012 (number 12290, year 39), 4.

———. قمة بكركي الروحية تناشد الدولية اتخاذ اجراءات لمنع الانهيار الاقتصادي. 25 September 2012 (number 12292, year 39), 2.

———. السلفيون للمرة الأولى في دير ماروني: حوار حول الاختلاف . . . تأسيساً للتعايش. 20 February 2013 (number 12411), 4.

Al-Salāh, حوار العروة مع الأنبا كيرلس مطران اسيوط, 2012 (number 1, year 82), 12–16 and 43–45.

——. الأقباط ومخاوف الانتخابات بين التهوين والتهويل, 2012 (number 1, year 82), 31–38.

Al-Sharq al-Awsat, تهنئة الأقباط بـ"عيد الفصح" تثير جدلا في مصر, 1 May 2013: https://archive.aawsat.com/details.asp?section=4&issueno=12573&article=726843#.Ykr1ACNCSUl (accessed 22 February 2023).

Al-Shurūq, : مصر ليست ملكا للمسلمين وحدهم الداعية السلفي محمد حسان. 20 October 2011 (number 992), 16.

——. الشروق تحاور الدكتور يسري حماد المتحدث باسم حزب النور: أتينا لنعمر لا لنخرب...ولا يمكننا إلغاء الاتفاقيات الدولية 18 December 2011 (number 1051), 15.

——. والأقباط شركائنا في الوطن ... . 30 June 2012 (number 1246), 6. اتفقنا مع الإخوان على خذف كلمة "مبادئ" من نص الشريعة في الدستور.

——. الكنيسة المصرية تنتقد الفيلم المسيء الأمريكي للرسول . . . وبولس يقاضي أقباط المهجر. 11 September 2012 (number 1319, year 4), 3.

——. السفارة الأمريكية تحت الحصار. 12 September 2012 (number 1320, year 4), 1.

——. "ثورة غضب" إسلامية مسيحية ضد الإساءة للرسول. 12 September 2012 (number 1320, year 4), 5.

——. رجال "الجماعة" داخل الكنيسة. 12 September 2012 (number 1320, year 4), 8.

——. مسلمون وأقباط "إيد واحدة" في مظاهرات محدودة أمام مساجد القاهرة. 15 September 2012 (number 1323, year 4), 5.

——. حرب البيانات بين الكنيسة والجبهة السلفية الكنيسة: ليس مقبولًا استدعاء القائم مقام البطريرك للتحقيق في القضية. 23 September 2012 (number 1331, year 4), 3.

——. حرب البيانات بين الكنيسة والجبهة السلفية. 23 September 2012 (number 1331, year 4), 3.

——. أمن الدولة تستدعى "أبو إسلام" المتهم بتمزيق الإنجيل. 25 September 2012 (number 1333, year 4), 6.

——. لا تقدموا الإسلام كـ"حل". 16 March 2013 (number 1504), 9.

Al-Tawhīd, لبنان: سلسلة واسعة من المواقف المنددة من الأحزاب والجمعيات والشخصيات الإسلامية والمسيحية والوطنية بالإساءة للنبي محمد صلى الله عليه وسلم. 13 September 2012: http://www.altawhid.org/2012/09/13/%D9%84%D8%A8%D9%86%D8%A7%D9%86-%D8%B3%D9%84%D8%B3%D9%84%D8%A9-%D9%88%D8%A7%D8%B3%D8%B9%D8%A9-%D9%85%D9%86-%D8%A7%D9%84%D9%85%D9%88%D8%A7%D9%82%D9%81-%D8%A7%D9%84%D9%85%D9%86%D8%AF%D8%AF%D8%A9-%D9%85/ (accessed 17 May 2016).

——. الشيخ الشعار دان الفيلم المسيء للاسلام وطالب بسحبه/ الشيخ حمود: ردات الفعل الطبيعية التي طالت السفارات الاميركية في العالم العربي كانت هبة ربانية. 14 September 2012: http://www.altawhid.org/2012/09/14/%D8%A7%D9%84%D8%B4%D9%8A%D8%AE-%D8%A7%D9%84%D8%B4%D8%B9%D8%A7%D8%B1-

%D8%AF%D8%A7%D9%86-%D8%A7%D9%84%D9%81%D9%8A%D9%84%D9%85-%D8%A7%D9%84%D9%85%D8%B3%D9%8A%D8%A6-%D9%84%D9%84%D8%A7%D8%B3%D9%84%D8%A7/ (accessed 17 May 2016).

——. تواصل المواقف المستنكرة للإساءة الغربية للإسلام في لبنان: أئمة المساجد وقوى واحزاب ومرجعيات دينية. 22 September 2012: http://www.altawhid.org/2012/09/22/%D8%AA%D9%88%D8%A7%D8%B5%D9%84-%D8%A7%D9%84%D9%85%D9%88%D8%A7%D9%82%D9%81-%D8%A7%D9%84%D9%85%D8%AA%D9%86%D9%83%D8%B1%D8%A9-%D9%84%D9%84%D8%A7%D8%B3%D8%A7%D8%A1%D8%A9-%D8%A7%D9%84%D8%BA%D8%B1/ (accessed 17 May 2016).

——. لقاء تضامني في عكار ندد بالفيلم المسيء الى الرسول: للتمسك بالوحدة والعروبة الجامعة ورفض المخططات الصهيونية. 22 September 2012: http://www.altawhid.org/2012/09/22/%D9%84%D9%82%D8%A7%D8%A1-%D8%AA%D8%B6%D8%A7%D9%85%D9%86%D9%8A-%D9%81%D9%8A-%D8%B9%D9%83%D8%A7%D8%B1-%D9%86%D8%AF%D8%AF-%D8%A8%D8%A7%D9%84%D9%81%D9%8A%D9%84%D9%85-%D8%A7%D9%84%D9%85%D8%B3%D9%8A%D8%A1/ (accessed 17 May 2016).

——. مفتي الإخوان يحرم تهنئة المسيحيين بعيد القيامة . . . وأقباط: فتواه تحريض على الكراهية. Al-Watan, 30 April 2013: https://www.elwatannews.com/news/details/173429 (accessed 22 March 2022).

——. تظاهرات أمام السفارة الامريكية لإدانة الفيلم المسىء للرسول. Waṭanī, 11 September 2012: http://www.wataninet.com/%D8%A3%D8%AE%D8%A8%D8%A7%D8%B1-%D9%85%D8%AA%D9%86%D9%88%D8%B9%D8%A9/%D8%AA%D8%B8%D8%A7%D9%87%D8%B1%D8%A7%D8%AA-%D8%A3%D9%85%D8%A7%D9%85-%D8%A7%D9%84%D8%B3%D9%81%D8%A7%D8%B1%D8%A9-%D8%A7%D9%84%D8%A7%D9%85%D8%B1%D9%8A%D9%83%D9%8A%D8%A9-%D9%84%D8%A5%D8%AF%D8%A7%D9%86/142794/ (accessed 12 July 2017).

——. المصريون "يدينون" الفيلم المسيء للرسول. 16 September 2012 (number 2647, year 54/number 613, year 12), 9.

——. حزب البناء والتنمية. 23 September 2012 (number 2648, year 54/number 614, year 12), 9.

——. استقبل اللواء مهندس سمير عجلان محافظ السويس وفد الكنيسة الكاثوليكية بالويس. 4 October 2012: http://www.wataninet.com/%D8%A3%D8%AE%D8%A8%D8%A7%D8%B1-%D8%A7%D9%84%D9%85%D8%AD%D8%A7%D9%81%D8%B8%D8%A7%D8%AA/%D9%85%D8%AD%D8%A7%D9%81%D8%B8-%D8%A7%D9%84%D8%B3%D9%88%D9%8A%D8%B3-%D8%A7%D9%84%D9%85%D8%B3%D9%84%D9%85%D9%88%D9%86-%D9%88%D8%A7%D9%84%D9%85%D8%B3

%D9%8A%D8%AD%D9%8A%D9%88%D9%86-
%D9%86%D8%B3%D9%8A/141208/ (accessed 23 May 2016).

——. الحكم بالسجن لأبو إسلام 11 سنة ولابنه ثمان سنوات. 12 June 2013: http://www.wataninet.com
/%D8%A3%D8%AE%D8%A8%D8%A7%D8%B1-%D9%85%D8%AA%D9
%86%D9%88%D8%B9%D8%A9/%D8%A7%D9%84%D8%AD%D9
%83%D9%85-%D8%A8%D8%A7%D9%84%D8%B3%D8%AC%D9
%86-%D9%84%D8%A7%D8%A8%D9%88-%D8%A5%
D8%B3%D9%84%D8%A7%D9%85-11-%D8%B3%D9%86%D8%A9-
%D9%88%D9%84%D8%A7%D8%A8%D9%86%D9%87-
%D8%AB%D9%85/121024/ (accessed 12 July 2017).

——. عبد الوارث: الفيلم المسيء للرسول تحرش نصراني بتيار الإسلام السياسي, Al-Yawm Al-Sābi, 7 September
2012: http://www.youm7.com/story/2012/9/7/%D8%B9%D8%A8%D8%AF-%
D8%A7%D9%84%D9%88%D8%A7%D8%B1%D8%AB--%D8%A7%
D9%84%D9%81%D9%8A%D9%84%D9%85-%D8%
A7%D9%84%D9%85%D8%B3%D9%89%D8%A1-%D9%84%D9%84%D8%B1
%D8%B3%D9%88%D9%84-%D8%AA%D8%AD%D8%B1%D8%B4-%D9%
86%D8%B5%D8%B1%D8%A7%D9%86%D9%89-%D
8%A8%D8%AA%D9%8A%D8%A7%D8%B1-%D8%A7%D9%84%D8%A5%
D8%B3%D9%84%D8%A7%D9%85-%D8%A7/778969#.VjI_Nm5OfVJ
(accessed 31 January 2023).

——. سياسيون ينتقدون صناع الفيلم المسيء للرسول ويهاجمون القس المتطرف تيري جونز وزقلمة وموريس صادق..
رضوان: لن نسمح لهم بإهانة الدين.. باسل عادل: الأديان السماوية خط أحمر.. السادات: هؤلاء دعاة فتنة وتقسيم. 8
September 2012: http://www.youm7.com/story/2012/9/8/%D8%B3%D9%8A
%D8%A7%D8%B3%D9%8A%D9%88%D9%86_%D9%8A%D9%86%D8%AA%
D9%82%D8%AF%D9%88%D9%86_%D8%B5%D9%86%D8%A7%D8%B9_%D
8%A7%D9%84%D9%81%D9%8A%D9%84%D9%85_%D8%A7%D9%84%D9
%85%D8%B3%D9%89%D8%A1_%D9%84%D9%84%D8%B1%D8%B3%D9%88
%D9%84_%D9%88%D9%8A%D9%87%D8%A7%D8%AC%D9%85%D9%88
%D9%86_%D8%A7%D9%84%D9%82%D8%B3_%D8%A7%D9%84%D9%85%D
8%AA/779069#.VjHXf25OfVJ (accessed 31 January 2023).

——. أقباط المهجر يشعلون الفتنة بإنتاج فيلم مسيء للرسول.. سياسيون يهاجمون القس الأمريكى تيرى جونز و"صادق"
و"زقلمة".. رضوان: المسيحيون المصريون قبل المسلمين ضد الفيلم.. ويطالبون بالملاحقة القانونية للفيلم. 9 September 2012: http://www.youm7.com/story/0000/0/0/-/780136#.Vjhs7m5OfVI
(accessed 16 March 2023).

——. بكار: التعرض للأنبياء والصحابة لا يمت لحرية الرأي بأية صلة. 10 September 2012: http://www.
youm7.com/story/2012/9/10/%D8%A8%D9%83%D8%A7%D8%B1--%D8%A7
%D9%84%D8%AA%D8%B9%D8%B1%D8%B6-%D9%84%D9%84%D8%A3%

D9%86%D8%A8%D9%8A%D8%A7%D8%A1-%D9%88%D8%A7%D9%84%D8%B5%D8%AD%D8%A7%D8%A8%D8%A9-%D9%84%D8%A7-%D9%8A%D9%85%D8%AA-%D9%84%D8%AD%D8%B1%D9%8A%D8%A9-%D8%A7%D9%84%D8%B1%D8%A3%D9%89-%D8%A8%D8%A3%D9%8A%D8%A9-%D8%B5%D9%84%D8%A9/781106#.VkGvM-F5OfVJ (accessed 31 January 2023).

———. "الحركات القبطية تنقسم بشأن المشاركة فى تظاهرات الفيلم المسيء للرسول.. 'الإخوان المسيحيين': لسنا مطالبين بالتظاهر لتبرئة ساحتنا.. و'أقباط مصر وماسبيرو': نرفض شق الصف ونطالب بمحاكمة دولية للمسيئين". 11 September 2012: http://www.youm7.com/story/2012/9/11/%D8%A7%D9%84%D8%AD%D8%B1%D9%83%D8%A7%D8%AA_%D8%A7%D9%84%D9%82%D8%A8%D8%B7%D9%8A%D8%A9_%D8%AA%D9%86%D9%82%D8%B3%D9%85_%D8%A8%D8%B4%D8%A3%D9%86_%D8%A7%D9%84%D9%85%D8%B4%D8%A7%D8%B1%D9%83%D8%A9_%D9%81%D9%89_%D8%AA%D8%B8%D8%A7%D9%87%D8%B1%D8%A7%D8%AA_%D8%A7%D9%84%D9%81%D9%8A%D9%84%D9%85_%D8%A7%D9%84%D9%85%D8%B3%D9%89%D8%A1/782863#.Vjx7ZV5OfVJ (accessed 31 January 2023).

———. "انتفاضة المؤسسات الدينية ضد الفيلم المسيء للرسول... 'الأزهر': الداعون لإنتاجه هدفهم إشعال الفتنة.. 'الإفتاء': ليس من الحرية ويمس أقدس رمز للمسلمين.. و'أقباط المهجر': نتبرأ من موريس صادق وزقلمة". 11 September 2012: https://www.youm7.com/story/2012/9/11/%D8%A7%D9%86%D8%AA%D9%81%D8%A7%D8%B6%D8%A9-%D8%A7%D9%84%D9%85%D8%B4%D8%B3%D8%B3%D8%A7%D8%AA-%D8%A7%D9%84%D8%AF%D9%8A%D9%86%D9%8A%D8%A9-%D8%B6%D8%AF-%D8%A7%D9%84%D9%81%D9%8A%D9%84%D9%85-%D8%A7%D9%84%D9%85%D8%B3%D9%89%D8%A1-%D9%84%D9%84%D8%B1%D8%B3%D9%88%D9%84-%D8%A7%D9%84%D8%A3%D8%B2%D9%87%D8%B1-%D8%A7%D9%84%D8%AF%D8%A7%D8%B9%D9%88%D9%86-%D9%84%D8%A5%D9%86%D8%AA%D8%A7%D8%AC%D9%87/782099 (accessed 31 January 2023).

———. "مؤتمر 'لا لإثارة الفتنة' يطرح وثيقة للتصدى لازدراء الأديان". 13 September 2012: http://www.youm7.com/story/2012/9/13/%D9%85%D8%A4%D8%AA%D9%85%D8%B1_%D9%84%D8%A7_%D9%84%D8%A5%D8%AB%D8%A7%D8%B1%D8%A9_%D8%A7%D9%84%D9%81%D8%AA%D9%86%D8%A9_%D9%8A%D8%B7%D8%B1%D8%AD_%D9%88%D8%AB%D9%8A%D9%82%D8%A9_%D9%84%D9%84%D8%AA%D8%B5%D8%AF%D9%89_%D9%84%D8%A7%D8%B2%D8%AF%D8%B1%D8%A7%D8%A1_%D8%A7%D9%84%D8%A3%D8%AF%D9%8A%D8%A7%D9%86/784864#.VjszJF5OfVJ (accessed 23 May 2016).

—— . القصص "ساويرس" يتصل بنادر بكار لحذف ما نشرته مواقع سلفية ضده. 13 September 2012: http://www.youm7.com/story/2012/9/13/%D8%A7%D9%84%D9%82%D9%85%D8%B5-%D8%B3%D8%A7%D9%88%D9%8A%D8%B1%D8%B3-%D9%8A%D8%AA%D8%B5%D9%84-%D8%A8%D9%86%D8%A7%D8%AF%D8%B1-%D8%A8%D9%83%D8%A7%D8%B1-%D9%84%D8%AD%D8%B0%D9%81-%D9%85%D8%A7-%D9%86%D8%B4%D8%B1%D8%AA%D9%87-%D9%85%D9%88%D8%A7%D9%82%D8%B9-%D8%B3%D9%84%D9%81%D9%8A%D8%A9-%D8%B6%D8%AF%D9%87/784996#.VjDYa25OfVJ (accessed 31 January 2023).

—— . برهامي: لا يجوز حرق "الإنجيل".. وتمزيقه إهانة لشىء فيه ذكر الله. 14 September 2012: https://www.youm7.com/story/2012/9/14/%D8%A8%D8%B1%D9%87%D8%A7%D9%85%D9%89-%D9%84%D8%A7-%D9%8A%D8%AC%D9%88%D8%B2-%D8%AD%D8%B1%D9%82-%D8%A7%D9%84%D8%A5%D9%86%D8%AC%D9%8A%D9%84-%D9%88%D8%AA%D9%85%D8%B2%D9%8A%D9%82%D9%87-%D8%A5%D9%87%D8%A7%D9%86%D8%A9-%D9%84%D8%B4%D9%89%D8%A1-%D9%81%D9%8A%D9%87-%D8%B0%D9%83%D8%B1/786012 (accessed 2 February 2023).

—— . مناظرة وسام عبد الوارث وجمال أسعد الفيلم المسيء للرسول. 9 September 2012: https://www.youtube.com/watch?v=sqhRj3ArQRQ (accessed 23 May 2016).

—— . كلمة نصر الله عن الفيلم المسيء للرسول (ص). 17 September 2012: https://www.youtube.com/watch?v=EjGlC1LbZHE (accessed 17 May 2016).

—— . السيد حسن نصرالله: مسيرة الولاء للنبي محمد (ص). 17 September 2012: https://www.youtube.com/watch?v=7Tv8YGVZycY (accessed 17 May 2016).

—— . اعتصام انتصاراً لنبي الإسلام I 21 09 2012. 22 September 2012: https://www.youtube.com/watch?v=EPetsalWSgQ (accessed 17 March 2023).

—— . الأستاذ فريد الدكان 21 09 2012. 23 September 2012: https://www.youtube.com/watch?v=TqcBCpE7oVw (accessed 17 March 2023).

Sources in Arabic with an Author

Barsoum, Ignatius Ephrem, المحاضرات التي القاها غبطة الحبر العلامة سيدنا مار اغناطيوس افرام برصوم بطريرك السريان الانطاكي في الجامعة الاميركية في بيروت بدعوة منها في ١-٢-٣ ايار سنة ١٩٣٣. Collection 1933, Beth Mardutho: https://archive.org/details/unset0000unse_y6a0 (accessed 23 March 2023).

Metropolit Bishoy, كتاب: الرد على البهتان في رواية يوسف زيدان (عزازيل). 19. April 2009: http://metroplit-bishoy.com/ar/?p=278 (accessed 22 March 2023).

Daw, Antoine, مسيحيون ومسلمون معاً ضد الإساءة إلى الأديان. *Al-Safīr*. 22 September 2012 (number 12290, year 39), 4.

Dirrāz, Muhammad 'Abdallah, موقف الإسلام من الأديان الأخرى وعلاقته بها. Majallat al-Azhar, June 2012, 1470.

Ferzli, Elie, 'Elie Ferzli Blog', 26 September 2012: http://elieferzli.blogspot.co.at/2012_09_01_archive.html (accessed 15 July 2017).

al-Gharāyiba, Ruhayl, المسيحيون والمواطنة. *al-Dustūr*, 26 October 2013: https://www.ademocracynet.com/index.php?page=articles&id=4835&action=Detail (accessed 5 March 2023).

Khodr, George, الحملة على الإسلام. *Al-Nahār*, 29 September 2012 (number 24863, year 80), 1 and 12.

Mokrani, Adnane, *Lebanese Christians' Point of View on Muslim-Christian Relations* (Beirut: Université Saint-Joseph, CEDRAC, Librairie Saint-Antoine, 2009).

Qabalān, 'Abd al-Amīr, دور المسيحيين في لبنان الوطن (Beirut: Université Saint-Joseph, 2003).

al-Shahhāt, 'Abd al-Mun'im, "المسلمون والنصارى "والخيار الثالث". *Sawt al-Salaf*, 30 December 2011: http://www.salafvoice.com/article.aspx?a=5910 (accessed 23 March 2023).

Subh, 'Abd al-Majid Hāmid, قالوا وقلنا, *Majallat al-Azhar*, December 2011 (number 1, year 85), 148–49.

Yahya, Ahmad, أين إنجيل المسيح!؟, *Sawt al-Salaf*, 14 May 2009: http://www.salafvoice.com/article.aspx?a=3268 (accessed 23 March 2023).

al-Zafzāf, Fawzī Fādil, علاقة الإسلام بالديانات السماوية السابق, *Majallat al-Azhar*, December 2011 (number 1, year 85), 158–61.

Sources in English

Ahram Online, 'Church-State Relations Yet to Change in Morsi's Egypt', 18 November 2011: http://english.ahram.org.eg/NewsContent/1/64/58089/Egypt/Politics-/-Churchstate-relations-yet-to-change-in-Morsis-Egy.aspx (accessed 23 February 2023).

Al-Akhbar English, 'Tripoli Clashes: Keeping Conflict Alive', 14 February 2012: http://english.al-akhbar.com/content/tripoli-clashes-keeping-conflict-alive (accessed 15 July 2017).

——. 'Al-Assir: A New Guardian of "Sunni Interests" in Lebanon', 2 March 2012: http://english.al-akhbar.com/content/al-assir-new-guardian-sunni-interest-lebanon (accessed 15 July 2017).

——. 'Ahmad al-Assir: A Salafi with a Difference', 6 March 2012: http://english.al-akhbar.com/content/ahmad-al-assir-salafi-difference (accessed 15 July 2017).

——. 'Geagea and the Maronite Church: A Battle for Patriarchy', 18 March 2012: http://english.al-akhbar.com/content/geagea-and-maronite-church-battle-patriarchy (accessed 17 May 2016).

——. 'Lebanon-Syria Border: A Weapons Market Boom', 5 May 2012: http://english.al-akhbar.com/content/lebanon-syria-border-weapons-market-boom (accessed 15 July 2017).

——. 'Lebanon's Mufti: The Future Movement Wants My Turban', 16 August 2012: http://english.al-akhbar.com/content/lebanons-mufti-future-movement-wants-my-turban (accessed 17 May 2016).

——. 'A Shadow State in Lebanon for the Syrian Opposition', 9 October 2012: http://english.al-akhbar.com/content/shadow-state-lebanon-syrian-opposition (accessed 15 July 2017).

——. 'Salafi Cleric's Militia Ambitions Curtailed', 25 November 2012: http://english.al-akhbar.com/content/salafi-cleric%E2%80%99s-militia-ambitions-curtailed (accessed 17 May 2016).

The Amman Message, 'The Amman Message', 2004: https://ammanmessage.com/the-amman-message-full/ (accessed 22 March 2023).

ANERA, 'Palestinian Refugees in Lebanon', Volume 3 (June 2012): http://bit.ly/1Ty1RcJ (accessed 23 February 2023).

Arab Orthodoxy, 'Georges Khodr on the Orthodox in Lebanese Politics', 21 March 2010: http://araborthodoxy.blogspot.co.at/2010/03/georges-khodr-on-orthodox-in-lebanese.html (accessed 23 February 2023).

——. 'The Youth Movement Rejects the Plan for a "Civil Commission"', 3 October 2012: http://araborthodoxy.blogspot.co.at/2012/10/the-youth-movement-rejects-plan-for.html (accessed 23 February 2023).

——. 'Al-Safir Gives Some Background on the "Civil Commission" Plan', 4 October 2012: http://araborthodoxy.blogspot.co.at/2012/10/al-safir-gives-some-background-on-civil.html (accessed 23 February 2023).

BBC, 'Obama: Egypt is Not US ally, Nor an Enemy', 13 September 2012: http://www.bbc.com/news/world-middle-east-19584265 (accessed 20 February 2023).

Byzantine Catholic Church in America, 'Prelate: Muslim Refugees Place Future of Lebanon's Christians in Jeopardy', 22 August 2015: http://byzcath.org/index.php/news-mainmenu-49/4841-prelate-muslim-refugees-place-future-of-lebanon-s-christians-in-jeopardy (accessed 23 February 2023).

Daily News Egypt, 'Families of Maspero Victims Attack Maspero Youth Union', 6 October 2012: http://www.dailynewsegypt.com/2012/10/06/families-of-maspero-victims-attack-maspero-youth-union/ (accessed 23 February 2023).

The Guardian, 'Protests in Cairo and Benghazi over American Film', 11 September 2012: http://www.theguardian.com/world/2012/sep/11/egypt-protest (accessed 23 February 2023).

———. 'Muhammad Film: Director Goes into Hiding after Protests', 12 September 2012: http://www.theguardian.com/world/2012/sep/12/ant-islam-israeli-film-protests?INTCMP=SRCH (accessed 23 February 2023).

———. 'Anti-Islamic Film Search Leads to Coptic Christian in California', 12 September 2012: http://www.theguardian.com/world/2012/sep/13/anti-islamic-film-us-nakoula?INTCMP=SRCH (accessed 23 February 2023).

———. 'Fugitive Lebanese Cleric Ahmad al-Assir Fails to Avoid Arrest with "70s Makeover"', 17 August 2015: http://www.theguardian.com/world/2015/aug/17/fugitive-lebanese-cleric-ahmad-al-assir-arrest-70s-makeover-beirut (accessed 23 February 2023).

Haaretz, 'Monastery near Jerusalem Torched: Catholics Blame Israeli "Hatred"', 5 September 2012 (number 28380, volume 92), 1 and 2.

Los Angeles Times, 'Christian Charity, Ex-Con Linked to Film on Islam', 13 September 2012: http://articles.latimes.com/2012/sep/13/local/la-me-filmmaker-20120914 (accessed 22 March 2023).

The New York Times, 'Protesters in Beirut Set Danish Consulate on Fire', 5 February 2006: http://www.nytimes.com/2006/02/05/international/middleeast/05cnd-beirut.html?_r=0 (accessed 22 March 2023).

———. 'Updates on Rage Over Anti-Islam Film', 12 September 2012: http://thelede.blogs.nytimes.com/2012/09/12/latest-updates-on-rage-over-anti-islam-film/ (accessed 12 July 2017).

———. 'Man of Many Names is Tied to a Video', 13 September 2012: http://www.nytimes.com/2012/09/14/us/origins-of-provocative-video-are-shrouded.html?_r=0 (accessed 12 July 2017).

———. 'Cultural Clash Fuels Muslims Angry at Online Video', 16 September 2012: http://www.nytimes.com/2012/09/17/world/middleeast/muslims-rage-over-film-fueled-by-culture-divide.html?_r=0 (accessed 23 May 2016).

———. 'Hezbollah Aids Syrian Military in a Key Battle', 19 May 2013: http://www.nytimes.com/2013/05/20/world/middleeast/syrian-army-moves-to-rebel-held-qusayr.html?pagewanted=all&_r=0 (accessed 15 July 2017).

OASIS, 'On the Crest of the Tahrir Square: Interview with Antonios Naguib', December 2011 (number 14, year 7), 24–27.

RT, 'Law Enforcement Confirms Convicted Fraudster behind Anti-Muslim Movie', 13 September 2012/2 October 2012: https://www.rt.com/usa/nakoula-confirmed-anti-muslim-movie-063/ (accessed 12 July 2017).

UNHCR, 'Syrian Refugees in Lebanon Surpass One Million', 3 April 2014: https://www.unhcr.org/news/press/2014/4/533c15179/syrian-refugees-lebanon-surpass-million.html (accessed 23 February 2023).
Watani, 'Copts Pushed Back into the Church?' 2 September 2012 (number 2645, year 54/number 611, year 12).
The World Bank, 'Population, Total: Egypt, Arab Rep.', [n. d.]: https://data.worldbank.org/indicator/SP.POP.TOTL?locations=EG (accessed 31 May 2022).
Who's Who in Lebanon 2007-2008, Munich: Publitec Publications in co-edition with K. G. Saur (Munich, 2007), 'Ferzli, Elie Najib'; 'Fares, Marwan'.

Sources in English with an Author

Bishoy, Metropolitan, 'Revival of the Egyptian Church since the Middle of the Nineteenth Century', in Habib Badr (ed.), *Christianity: A History in the Middle East* (Beirut: MECC, 2005), 775–96.
Butrus, Zakaryā, 'Fr Zakaria Statement concerning his relationship to the making of Mohamed movie', September 2012: http://www.fatherzakaria.net/main/fr-zakaria-mohamed-movie.htm (accessed 23 March 2023).
Casper, Jayson, 'Salafis, Muslim Youth Protest Anti-Muhammad Film at US Embassy', *A Sense of Belonging*, 11 September 2012: http://asenseofbelonging.org/2012/09/11/salafis-muslim-youth-protest-anti-muhammad-film-at-us-embassy/ (accessed 22 March 2023).
——. 'The Coptic Movements: Coptic Activism in a Revolutionary Setting', *Arab West Report*, 15 May 2013: http://www.arabwestreport.info/sites/default/files/pdfs/AWRpapers/paper44.pdf (accessed 22 March 2023).
Fisk, Robert, 'A Year on From the Murder of Christian Writer Nahed Hattar in Jordan, Many Questions Remain Unanswered', *Independent*, 21 September 2017: https://www.independent.co.uk/voices/middle-east-jordan-christians-nahed-hattar-murder-king-abdullah-government-a7959026.html (accessed 23 March 2023).
Gomaa, Ali, 'Egypt's Mufti: To Muslims, Prophet Muhammad is "the Mercy to all Worlds"', *Washington Post*, 18 September 2012: http://www.faithstreet.com/onfaith/2012/09/18/prophet-muhammad-is-the-mercy-to-all-worlds-to-muslims-egypts-mufti/10018 (accessed 12 July 2017).
Hazim, Ignatius IV, *Orthodoxy and the Issues of our Time* (Balamand: University of Balamand, Dar an-Nahar, 2006).
Lahham, Maroun, 'Called by Destiny, Not by Chance', *OASIS*, December 2012 (number 16, year 8), 92–96.

El-Shater, Khayrat, '"Our Condolences", the Muslim Brotherhood Says', *The New York Times*, 13 September 2012: http://www.nytimes.com/2012/09/14/opinion/our-condolences-the-muslim-brotherhood-says.html?_r=1 (accessed 23 May 2016).

Sadek, Morris, Twitter: https://twitter.com/morrissadek/status/244998938401308672 (accessed 5 March 2023).

Sidhom, Youssef, 'Code Name: Sectarian Strife', *Watani*, 15 May 2011 (number 2577, year 53/number 543, year 11).

Sources in French

Al-Ahram Hebdo, 'Encourager l'esprit de citoyenneté', 22–28 December 2010 (number 850, year 17), 3–4.

——. 'Prêtres, généraux et barbus', 11–17 January 2012 (number 904, year 18), 7.

——. 'Un deuxième bastion islamisé', 7–13 March 2012 (number 912, year 18), 6.

——. 'Les tentacules se déploient', 28 March–3 April 2012 (number 915, year 18), 3.

——. 'Une démarche symbolique', 18–24 July 2012 (number 931, year 18), 8.

——. 'Morsi ne sait pas sur quel pied danser', 19–25 September 2012 (number 940, year 18), 6.

——. 'Al-Azhar: Le jeu de la politique et de la religion', 17–23 April 2013 (number 970, year 19), 3.

Butrus, Zakaryā, 'Les preuves de la Révélation dans l'Islam et dans le Christianisme: Episode 28', 2009: http://jesusmarie.free.fr/islam_zakaria_boutros_28.html (accessed 23 March 2023).

——. 'Mohammed confronté aux grands principes de la morale, et l'assassinat de ses adversaires. Episode 37', [n. d.]: http://jesusmarie.free.fr/islam_zakaria_boutros_37_Mohamed_et_ses_adversaires.html (accessed 23 March 2023).

——. 'Les épouses du Messager. Episode 39', 2009: http://jesusmarie.free.fr/islam_zakaria_boutros_39_femmes_du_messager.html (accessed 23 March 2023).

Le Comité National Islamo-Chrétien pour le Dialogue, 'Formation et Action du Comité du Dialogue', [n. d.]: http://chrislam.org/bckground.html (accessed 22 October 2015).

——. 'Emir Hares Chakib Chehab', [n. d.]: http://chrislam.org/members.html (accessed 22 October 2015).

El-Hage, Mgr. Chucrallah Nabil, 'Un combat solidaire avec les autres: L'exemple de la fondation *Adyan*', *Proche-Orient Chrétien* 61: 3–4 (2011), 333–39.

Le Monde, 'Dans la diaspora copte, des extrémistes minoritaires mais très actifs', 20 September 2012: https://www.lemonde.fr/afrique/article/2012/09/19/dans-la-diaspora-copte-des-extremistes-minoritaires-mais-tres-actifs_1762299_3212.html (accessed 31 May 2020).

L'Orient le Jour, 'Geagea: Le Hezbollah n'est pas prêt au dialogue et utilise le film islamophobe pour se créer la dimension politique qu'il espère', 18 September 2012 (number 13557), 3.

Interviews

Bishop Benedict. Personal Interview, 24 April 2015. Amman.
Chehab, Hareth. Personal Interview, 9 December 2014. Beirut.
Farrāj, Bāssim. Personal Interview, 27 April 2015. Amman.
Fādī, Yūsuf. Personal Interview, 20 January 2015. Cairo.
Habāsh, Jiryis. Personal Interview, 28 April 2015. Amman.
Al-Hāfī, 'Āmir. Personal Interview, 9 April 2015. Personal Interview. Amman.
Kildānī, Hannā. Personal Interview, 8 April 2015. Marj al-Hammām, Amman.
Khoury, Rafiq. Personal Interview, 25 March 2015. Jerusalem.
Lahhām, Mārūn. Personal Interview, 20 April 2015. Amman.
Magdī, Mīnā. Personal Interview, 21 January 2015. Cairo.
Sabra, George. Personal Interview, 21 November 2014. Beirut.

Secondary Sources

Akopian, Arman, 'The Syriacs of Kharberd (Kharput) on the Eve of the 1915 Genocide', *Hugoye: Journal of Syriac Studies* 23: 2 (2020): 279–321.

American Historical Review, 'AHR Conversation: Religious Identities and Violence', December 2007: 1433–81.

Armanios, Febe, *Coptic Christianity in Ottoman Egypt* (New York: Oxford University Press, 2011).

Al-Attiyat, Ibtissam, Shteiwi, Musa; and Sweiss, Suleiman, *Building Democracy in Jordan: Women's Political Participation, Political Party life and Democratic Elections* (Stockholm: International Institute for Democracy and Electoral Assistance & the Network for Development, 2005): https://www.idea.int/sites/default/files/publications/building-democracy-in-jordan.pdf (accessed 22 March 2023).

Avon, Dominique, 'Al-Azhar ou l'expression d'un désarroi des autorités sunnites', 2015: https://hal.science/halshs-03263255v1 (accessed 17 February 2023).

——. 'Le nom chrétien sous la plume d'hommes de religion musulmans égyptiens', *Les Cahiers d'EMAM* 32 (2020): http://journals.openedition.org/emam/2669 (accessed 17 February 2023).

Aubin-Boltanski, Emma, 'La Vierge, les chrétiens, les musulmans et la nation', *Terrain* 51 (2008): http://journals.openedition.org/terrain/10943 (accessed 16 February 2023).

Auge, Oliver, and Witthöft, Christiane (eds), *Ambiguität im Mittelalter: Formen zeitgenössischer Reflexion und interdisziplinärer Rezeption* (Berlin, Boston: de Gruyter, 2016).

Awwad, Johnny, 'Who is My God and Who is My Neighbour? A Response to "A Common Word Between Us and You"', *NEST Theological Review* 30:1 (2009), 78–88.

Baroudi, Sami E., and Tabar, Paul, 'Spiritual Authority versus Secular Authority: Relations between the Maronite Church and the State in Postwar Lebanon, 1990–2005', *Middle East Critique* 18:3 (2009): 195–230.

Bauer, Thomas, *Die Kultur der Ambiguität: Eine andere Geschichte des Islams* (Berlin: Verlag der Weltreligionen, 2011).

Baumann, Hannes, 'The "New Contractor Bourgeoisie" in Lebanese Politics: Hariri, Mikati and Fares', in Knudsen, Are, and Kerr, Michael (eds), *Lebanon after the Cedar Revolution* (London: Hurst, 2012), 125–44.

Bayat, Asef, *Post-Islamism: The Changing Faces of Political Islam* (Oxford: Oxford University Press, 2013).

van den Boogert, Maurits H., 'Millets: Past and Present', in Roald, Anne Sofie, and Longva, Anh Nga (eds), *Religious Minorities in the Middle East: Domination, Self-Empowerment, Accommodation* (Leiden, Boston: Brill, 2012), 27–45.

Boulby, Marion, *The Muslim Brotherhood and the Kings of Jordan, 1945–1993* (Atlanta: Scholars Press, 1999).

Chatelard, Géraldine, *Briser la mosaïque: Les tribus chrétiennes de Madaba, Jordanie, XIX-XXe siècles* (Paris: CNRS, 2004).

——. 'Les chrétiens en Jordanie, dynamiques identitaires et gestion du pluralisme', *Les Cahiers de l'Orient* 93:1 (2009), 41–56.

Davis, Stephen J., *Coptic Christology in Practice. Incarnation and Divine Participation in Late Antique and Medieval Egypt* (Oxford: Oxford University Press, 2008).

De Clerck, Dima, 'La Montagne: Un espace de partage et de ruptures', in Mermier, Franck (ed.), *Liban: espaces partages et pratiques de rencontre* (Paris, Beirut: Ifpo, 2008).

Delhaye, Grégoire, 'Contemporary Muslim-Christian Relations in Egypt: Local Dynamics and Foreign Influences', in Roald, Anne Sofie, and Longva, Anh Nga (eds), *Religious Minorities in the Middle East: Domination, Self-Empowerment, Accommodation* (Leiden, Boston: Brill, 2012), 71–96.

Dietrich, Regina, *Transformation oder Stagnation? Die jordanische Demokratisierungspolitik seit 1989* (Hamburg: Deutsches Orient Institut, 1999).
van Doorn-Harder, Nelly, *Between Desert and City: The Coptic Orthodox Church Today*, ed. with Kari Vogt (Oslo: Novus Forlag, 1997; Portland: Wipf and Stock Publishers, 2004).
——. *Copts in Context: Negotiating Identity, Tradition, and Modernity* (Columbia: University of South Carolina Press, 2017).
Droeber, Julia, '"We are different!" Similarities between Christian and Muslim Women in Jordan', *Islam and Christian-Muslim Relations* 23:1 (2012), 59–78.
Dumontier, Beltram, 'L'entente du Hezbollah avec le CPL', in Mervin, Sabrina (ed.), *Le Hezbollah: État des lieux* (Arles: Actes Sud, 2008), 109–16.
El-Husseini, Rola, *Pax Syriana: Elite Politics in Postwar Lebanon* (Syracuse: Syracuse University Press, 2012).
Elsässer, Sebastian, *The Coptic Question in the Mubarak Era* (New York: Oxford University Press, 2014).
Felsch, Maximilian, 'Christian Political Activism in Lebanon: A Revival of Religious Nationalism in Times of Arab Upheavals', *Studies in Ethnicity and Nationalism* 18:1 (2018): 19–37.
Gandolfo, Luisa, *Palestinians in Jordan: The Politics of Identity* (London, New York: I. B. Tauris, 2012).
Gauvain, Richard, *Salafi Ritual Purity: In the Presence of God* (Abingdon: Routledge, 2013).
Carlo Ginzburg, 'Microhistory: Two or Three Things That I Know about It', trans. John and Anne C. Tedeschi, *Critical Inquiry* 20:1 (Autumn 1993): 10–35.
Grafton, David D., *The Christians of Lebanon: Political Rights in Islamic Law* (London: Tauris Academic Studies, 2003).
Griffith, Sidney, 'Christians and Christianity', in Dammen McAuliffe, Jane (ed.), *Enyclopaedia of the Qur'ān* (Leiden: Brill, 2006), 307–16.
Guirguis, Laure, *Les Coptes d'Égypte: Violences communautaires et transformations politiques (2005–2012)* (Paris: Karthala, 2012).
Haddad, Yvonne Yazbeck, and Smith, Jane I., 'The Quest for "A Common Word": Initial Christian Responses to a Muslim Initiative', *Islam and Christian-Muslim Relations* 20:4 (2009): 369–88.
Haddad, Yvonne, and Donovan, Joshua, 'Good Copt, Bad Copt: Competing Narratives on Coptic Identity in Egypt and the United States', *Studies in World Christianity* 19:3 (2013): 208–32.

Haddad, Yvonne Yazbeck, and Fischbach, Rahel, 'Interfaith Dialogue in Lebanon: Between a Power Balancing Act and Theological Encounters', *Islam and Christian-Muslim Relations* 26:4 (2015), 423–42.

Hager, Anna, '"Lebanon is More Than a Nation, More Than a Country. It is a Message": Lebanon as a Model of Christian-Muslim Relations', *Journal of Beliefs and Values* 38:3 (2017): 286–95.

——. 'From "Polytheists" to "Partners in the Nation": Islamist Attitudes towards Coptic Egyptians in Post-Revolutionary Egypt (2011–2013)', *Islam and Christian-Muslim Relations* 29:3 (2018): 289–308.

——. 'Die Kopten und der Arabische Frühling: Zwischen politischer Emanzipation und Minderheitenstatus', *Études Asiatiques/Asiatische Studien* 72:3 (2018): 795–817.

——. 'The Orthodox Issue in Jordan: The Struggle for an Arab and Orthodox Identity', *Studies in World Christianity* 24:3 (2018): 212–33.

——. 'Die Christen in Jordanien nach 2011', *Ostkirchliche Studien* 69:1 (2020): 103–16.

——. 'The Syriac Orphanage and School in Beirut: Building an Elite for a Transnational Syriac Identity', *Studies in World Christianity* 28:3 (2022): 311–33.

Hasan, S. S., *Christians versus Muslims in Modern Egypt: The Century-Long Struggle for Coptic Equality* (Oxford: Oxford University Press, 2003).

Haykel, Bernard, 'On the Nature of Salafi Thought and Action', in Meijer, Roel (ed.), *Global Salafism: Islam's New Religious Movement* (Oxford: Oxford University Press, 2014), 33–57.

Henley, Alexander D. M., 'Politics of a Church at War: Maronite Catholicism in the Lebanese Civil War', *Mediterranean Politics* 13:3 (2008): 353–69.

——. 'The Maronites', in Rowe, Paul (ed.), *Routledge Handbook of Minorities in the Middle East* (Milton: Routledge, 2018), 89–99.

Heo, Angie, *The Political Lives of Saints: Christian-Muslim Mediation in Egypt* (Berkeley: University of California Press, 2018).

Hermann, Katja, *Aufbruch von Unten: Möglichkeiten und Grenzen von NGOs in Jordanien* (Hamburg: Lit, 2000).

Heyberger, Bernard, *Les chrétiens au Proche-Orient: De la compassion à la compréhension* (Paris: Manuels Payot 2013).

——. *Les Chrétiens d'Orient* (Paris: PUF, que sais-je?, 2017).

Hoyland, Robert, *Seeing Islam as Others Saw It: A Survey and Evaluation of Christian, Jewish and Zoroastrian Writings on Early Islam* (Princeton: Darwin Press, 1997).

Ibrahim, Vivian, *The Copts of Egypt: The Challenges of Modernisation and Identity* (London: I. B. Tauris, 2013).

———. 'Beyond the Cross and the Crescent: Plural Identities and the Copts in Contemporary Egypt', *Ethnic and Racial Studies* 38:14 (2015): 2584–97.

International Crisis Group, 'Jordan's 9/11: Dealing with Jihadi Islamism', 23 November 2005. Middle East Report Number 47: https://icg-prod.s3.amazonaws.com/47-jordan-s-9-11-dealing-with-jihadi-islamism.pdf (accessed 15 March 2023).

———. 'Popular Protest in North Africa and the Middle East (IX): Dallying with Reform in a Divided Jordan', 12 March 2012, Middle East/North Africa Report Number 118: https://d2071andvip0wj.cloudfront.net/118-popular-protest-in-north-africa-and-the-middle-east-ix-dallying-with-reform-in-a-divided-jordan.pdf (accessed 31 May 2022).

Iskander, Elizabeth, 'The "Mediation" of Muslim-Christian Relations in Egypt: The Strategies and Discourses of Official Egyptian Press during Mubarak's Presidency', *Islam and Christian-Muslim Relations* 23:1 (2012): 31–44.

Kail, Ellis C., *Secular Nationalism and Citizenship in Muslim Countries: Arab Christians in the Levant* (London: Palgrave Macmillan, 2018).

Kanafani-Zahar, Aïda, *Liban, la guerre et la mémoire* (Rennes: Presses Universitaires de Rennes, 2011).

Kårtveit, Bård Helge, *Dilemmas of Attachment: Identity and Belonging among Palestinian Christians* (Boston: Brill, 2014).

Kassir, Samir, *La guerre du Liban: De la dissension nationale au conflit régional* (Paris: Karthala, 2014).

Katz, Kimberley, *Jordanian Jerusalem: Holy Places and National Spaces* (Gainesville: University Press of Florida, 2005).

Kerr, Michael, 'Before the Revolution', in Knudsen, Are, and Kerr, Michael (eds), *Lebanon after the Cedar Revolution* (London: Hurst, 2012), 23–38.

El-Khawaga, Dina, 'L'affirmation d'une identité chrétienne copte: Saisir un procéssus en cours', in Décobert, Christian (ed.), *Itinéraires d'Egypte: Mélanges offerts au père Maurice Martin, s.j.* (Cairo: Institut français d'archéologie orientale du Caire, 1992), 345–65.

Khoury, Adel T., *Polémiques byzantines contre l'Islam (VIII.-XIIIe siècles)* (Leiden: Brill, 1972).

Kirdiş, Esen, *The Rise of Islamic Political Movements and Parties: Morocco, Turkey and Jordan* (Edinburgh: Edinburgh University Press, 2019).

Knudsen, Are, and Kerr, Michael (eds), 'Introduction', in *Lebanon after the Cedar Revolution*, 3–21.

Krämer, Gudrun, 'Dhimmi ou citoyen: Réflexions réformistes sur le statut des non-musulmans en société islamique', in Roussillon, Alain (ed.), *Entre réforme sociale et mouvement national: Identité et modernisation en Égypte (1882–1962)* (Cairo:

CEDEJ, 1995), 577–90: https://books.openedition.org/cedej/1446 (accessed 23 February 2023).

——. 'Anti-Semitism in the Muslim World: A Critical Review', *Die Welt des Islams* 46:3 (2006): 243–76.

——. *Hasan al-Banna* (Oxford: Oneworld Publication, 2010).

Kraetzschmar, Hendrik, and Rivetti, Paola (eds), *Islamists and the Politics of the Arab Uprisings: Governance, Pluralisation and Contention* (Edinburgh: Edinburgh University Press, 2018).

Kunelius, Risto (ed.), *Reading the Mohammed Cartoons Controversy: An International Analysis of Press Discourses on Free Speech and Political Spin* (Bochum: Projekt Verlag, 2007).

Lacroix, Stéphane, 'Sheikhs and Politicians: Inside the New Egyptian Salafism', Brookings Doha Center, 2012: http://www.brookings.edu/~/media/research/files/papers/2012/6/07-egyptian-salafism-lacroix/stephane-lacroix-policy-briefing-english.pdf (accessed 20 February 2023).

Longva, Anh Nga, 'From the *Dhimma* to the Capitulations: Memory and Experience of Protection in Lebanon', in Longva, Anh Nga, and Roald, Anne Sofie (eds), *Religious Minorities in the Middle East* (Boston: Brill, 2011), 47–69.

Longva, Anh Nga, and Roald, Anne Sofie (eds), *Religious Minorities in the Middle East: Domination, Self-Empowerment, Accommodation* (Boston: Brill, 2011).

Luizard, Pierre-Jean, 'Al-Azhar: Institution Sunnite réformée', in Roussillon, Alain (ed.), *Entre réforme sociale et mouvement national: Identité et modernisation en Égypte (1882–1962)* (Cairo: CEDEJ, 1995), 519–48: https://books.openedition.org/cedej/1442 (accessed 23 February 2023).

Lukasik, Candace, 'Conquest of Paradise: Secular Binds and Coptic Political Mobilization', *Middle East Critique* 25:2 (2016): 107–25.

——. '*The Politics of Persecution: Middle Eastern Christians in an Age of Empire.* By Mitri Raheb', *Journal of Church and State* 64:4 (2022): 744–46.

Maggiolini, Paolo, 'Christian Churches and Arab Christians in the Hashemite Kingdom of Jordan', *Archives de sciences sociales des religions* 171 (2015): 37–58: http://journals.openedition.org/assr/27010 (accessed 23 February 2023).

Mahmood, Saba, *Politics of Piety: The Islamic Revival and the Feminist Subject* (Princeton: Princeton University Press, 2011).

——. *Religious Difference in a Secular Age: A Minority Report* (Princeton: Princeton University Press, 2016).

Makari, Peter E., *Conflict and Cooperation: Christian-Muslim Relations in Contemporary Egypt* (Syracuse: Syracuse University Press, 2007).

Makdisi, Ussama, *The Culture of Sectarianism: Community, History and Violence in Nineteenth Century Ottoman Lebanon* (Berkeley, Los Angeles, London: California University Press, 2000).
Maktabi, Rania, 'The Lebanese Census of 1932 Revisited: Who are the Lebanese?' *British Journal of Middle Eastern Studies* 26:2 (1999): 219–41.
Marzouki, Nadia, 'The U.S. Coptic Diaspora and the Limit of Polarization', *Journal of Immigrant & Refugee Studies* 14:3 (2016): 261–76.
Massad, Joseph, *Colonial Effects. The Making of National Identity in Jordan* (New York: Columbia University Press, 2001).
Mayeur-Jaouen, Catherine, 'Le christianisme oriental, Les chrétiens d'Orient au XIXe siècle: Un renouveau lourd de menace', in Mayeur, Jean-Marie, Piétri, Charles, Piétri, Luce, Vauchez, André, and Vénard, Marc (eds), *Histoire du Christianisme, Tome 11, Libéralisme, industrialisation, expansion européenne (1830–1914)* (Paris: Desclée, 1995), 793–849.
——. *Pèlerinages d'Egypte: Histoire de la piété copte et musulmane, XVe –XXe siècles* (Paris: Éditions de l'École des Hautes Études en Sciences Sociales, 2005).
——. 'What Do Egypt's Copts and Muslims Share? The Issue of Shrines', in Dionigi, Albera, and Couroucli, Maria (eds), *Sharing Sacred Spaces in the Mediterranean: Christians, Muslims, and Jews at Shrines and Sanctuaries* (Bloomington: Indiana University Press, 2012), 148–73.
——. *Voyage en Haute-Égypte: Prêtres, coptes et catholiques* (Paris: CNRS, 2019).
McCallum, Fiona, 'Muslim-Christian Relations in Egypt: Challenges for the Twenty-First Century', in Loosley, Emma, and O'Mahoney, Anthony (eds), *Christian Responses to Islam and Muslim-Christian Relations in the Modern World* (Manchester: Manchester University Press, 2008), 66–84.
——. *Christian Religious Leadership in the Middle East: The Political Role of the Patriarch* (Lewiston: The Edwin Mellen Press, 2010).
Meijer, Roel, and Butenschøn, Nils (eds), *The Crisis of Citizenship in the Arab World* (Boston: Brill, 2017).
Mermier, Franck, 'À l'ombre du leader disparu: Antoun Saadé et le Parti syrien national social', in Mermier, F., and Mervin, S (eds), *Leaders et Partisans au Liban* (Paris: Karthala, IFPO, ISSMM, 2012), 187–217.
Mervin, Sabrina (ed.), *Le Hezbollah: État des lieux* (Arles: Actes Sud, 2008).
——. 'Le lien iranien', in *Le Hezbollah: État des lieux*, 75–87.
——. 'La religion du Hezbollah', in *Le Hezbollah: État des lieux*, 181–206.
——. 'Charisme et distinction: L'élite religieuse chiite', in Mermier, F., and Mervin, S. (eds), *Leaders et Partisans au Liban* (Paris: Karthala, IFPO, ISSMM, 2012), 321–51.

Mikdashi, Maya, 'Blaming Others: A History of Violence in Lebanon', *Jadaliyya*, 5 June 2012: https://www.jadaliyya.com/Details/26160/Blaming-Others-A-History-of-Violence-in-Lebanon (accessed 23 February 2023).

——. 'What is Political Sectarianism?' *Jadaliyya*, 25 March 2011: http://www.jadaliyya.com/pages/index/1008/what-is-political-sectarianism (accessed 23 February 2023).

Monier, Elizabeth, 'Minorities or Citizens in the Middle East? Locating the "Minority Question" in the Intersecting Histories of Collective National Belonging and State-Building', *Nations and Nationalism* 29:1 (2023): 295–310.

Mouchref, A., *Forgotten Akkar: Socio-Economic Reality of the Akkar Region* (Beirut: Mada Association, 2008).

Murre-van den Berg, Heleen, 'The Language of the Nation: The Rise of Arabic among Jews and Christians (1900–1950)', *British Journal of Middle Eastern Studies* 43:2 (2016): 176–90.

Myhill, John, *Language, Religion and National Identity in Europe and the Middle East: A Historical Study* (Amsterdam, Philadelphia: J. Benjamins, 2006).

Neveu, Norig, *Le Prince Hasan, Héraut du rapprochement islamo-chrétien en Jordanie* (unpubl. MA thesis, Paris IV-Sorbonne, 2004–5).

Noe, Nicolas (ed.), *Voice of Hezbollah: The Statements of Hasan Nasrallah* (London, New York: Verso, 2007).

Noth, Albrecht, 'Möglichkeiten und Grenzen islamischer Toleranz', *Saeculum* 29:2 (1978): 190–204.

——. 'Früher Islam', in Haarmann, Ulrich (ed.), *Geschichte der Arabischen Welt* (Munich: C. H. Beck, 2004), 11–100.

Pall, Zoltan, *Lebanese Salafis Between the Gulf and Europe: Development, Fractionalization and Transnational Networks of Salafism in Lebanon* (Amsterdam: Amsterdam University Press, 2013).

——. *Salafism in Lebanon: Local and Transnational Movements* (Cambridge: Cambridge University Press, 2018).

Paulsen Galal, Lise, 'Coptic Christian Practices: Formations of Sameness and Difference', *Islam and Christian-Muslim Relations* 23:1 (2012): 45–58.

Picard, Élizabeth, 'La violence milicienne et sa légitimation religieuse', in Scheffler, Thomas (ed), *Religion between Violence and Reconciliation* (Beirut: Orient-Institut Beirut; Würzburg: Ergon-Verl., 2002), 319–32.

Pizzo, Paola, 'The "Coptic Question" in Post-Revolutionary Egypt: Citizenship, Democracy, Religion', *Ethnic and Racial Studies* 38:14 (2015): 2598–2613.

Pollack, Alexander, 'Antisemitismus: Probleme der Definition und Operationalisierung eines Begriffs', in Bunzl, John, and Senfft, Alexander (eds), *Zwischen*

Antisemitismus und Islamophobie: Vorurteile und Projektionen in Europa und Nahost (Hamburg: VSA, 2008), 17–32.

Proche-Orient Chrétien (POC) 61:1–2 (2011).

———. 61:3–4 (2011).

———. 63:1–2 (2013).

———. 66: 3–4 (2016).

Reiss, Wolfram, *Erneuerung in der koptisch-orthodoxen Kirche: Die Geschichte der koptisch-orthodoxen Sonntagsschulbewegung und die Aufnahme ihrer Reformansätze in den Erneuerungsbewegungen der koptisch-orthodoxen Kirche der Gegenwart* (Hamburg: LIT, 1998).

———. 'Die Situation der Kopten in der Gegenwart', in Hölscher, A., Middelbeck-Varwick, A., and Thurau, M. (eds), *Kirche in Welt: Christentum im Zeichen kultureller Vielfalt* (Frankfurt: Peter Lang Verlag, 2013), 45–90.

Reiss, W., Kriener, J., and Hock, K., *Die Darstellung des Christentums in Schulbüchern islamisch geprägter Länder, 3: Libanon und Jordanien* (Berlin: EB-Verlag, 2012).

Robson, Laura, 'Recent Perspectives on Christianity in the Modern Arab World: Christianity in the Modern Arab World', *History Compass* 9:4 (2011): 312–25.

Rogan, Eugene L., *Frontiers of the State in the Late Ottoman Empire: Transjordan, 1850–1921* (Cambridge, New York: Cambridge University Press, 1999).

Rowe, Paul S., 'The Middle Eastern Christian as Agent', *IJMES* 42:3 (2010): 472–74.

Rougier, Bernard, *Le jihad au quotidien* (Paris: PUF, 2004).

———. *Everyday Jihad: The Rise of Militant Islam among Palestinians in Lebanon* (Cambridge, MA, London: Harvard University Press, 2007).

———. *L'Oumma en fragments: Contrôler le sunnisme au Liban* (Paris: Presses universitaires de France, 2011).

Sabra, George, 'Two Ways of Being a Christian in the Muslim Context of the Middle-East', *Islam and Christian-Muslim Relations* 17:1 (2006): 43–53.

———. 'The "Common Word" Letter in the Context of Christian-Muslim Dialogue', *NEST Theological Review* 30:1 (2009): 89–98.

———. 'A Response to "Christianity in a Culture Marked by Islam: Facts and Visions"', *NEST Theological Review* 35:1–2 (2014): 145–48.

Salameh, Franck, *Language, Memory, and Identity in the Middle East: The Case for Lebanon* (Lanham: Lexington Books, 2010).

Schölch, Alexander, 'Der arabische Osten im neunzehnten Jahrhundert 1800–1914', in Haarmann, Ulrich (ed.), *Geschichte der arabischen Welt* (Munich: Verlag C. H. Beck, 2004), 365–431.

Scott, Rachel, *The Challenge of Political Islam: Non-Muslims and the Egyptian State* (Palo Alto: Stanford University Press, 2010).

———. 'Citizenship, Public Order, and State Sovereignty: Article 3 of the Egyptian Constitution and the "Divinely Revealed Religions"', in Meijer, Roel, and Butenschøn, Nils (eds), *The Crisis of Citizenship in the Arab World* (Boston: Brill, 2017), 375–406.

Schulze, Kirsten E., *The Jews of Lebanon: Between Coexistence and Conflict* (Brighton: Sussex Academic Press, 2001).

Schwedler, Jillian, *Faith in Moderation: Islamist Parties in Jordan and Yemen* (Cambridge: Cambridge University Press, 2006).

———. 'Islamists in Power? Inclusion, Moderation, and the Arab Uprisings', *Middle East Development Journal* 5:1 (2013): 1–18.

———. 'Conclusion: New Directions in the Study of Islamist Politics', in Kraetzschmar, Hendrik, and Rivetti, Paola (eds), *Islamists and the Politics of the Arab Uprisings: Governance, Pluralisation and Contention* (Edinburgh: Edinburgh University Press, 2018), 359–74.

Sedra, Paul, 'Class Cleavages and Ethnic Conflict: Coptic Christian Communities in Modern Egyptian Politics', *Islam and Christian-Muslim Relations* 10:2 (1999): 219–35.

———. 'The Church, Maspero, and the Future of the Coptic Community', *Jadaliyya*, 19 May 2012: http://www.jadaliyya.com/pages/index/4735/the-church-maspero-and-the-future-of-the-coptic-co (accessed 23 February 2023).

———. 'Copts and the Power over Personal Status', *Jadaliyya*, 3 December 2012: https://www.jadaliyya.com/Details/27530/Copts-and-the-Power-over-Personal-Status (accessed 23 February 2023).

———. 'Religious Difference in a Secular Age: Book Review', 8 May 2016: https://www.madamasr.com/en/2016/05/08/opinion/u/religious-difference-in-a-secular-age-book-review/ (accessed 23 February 2023).

Semerdjian, Elyse, 'Armenian Women, Legal Bargaining, and Gendered Politics of Conversion in Seventeenth- and Eighteenth-Century Aleppo', *Journal of Middle East Women's Studies* 12:1 (2016): 2–30.

Sharkey, Heather, *A History of Muslims, Christians, and Jews in the Middle East* (Cambridge: Cambridge University Press, 2017).

Sharp, Andrew, *Orthodox Christians and Islam in the Postmodern Age* (Leiden, Boston: Brill, 2012).

Shenoda, Anthony, 'Reflections on the (In)visibility of Copts in Egypt', *Jadaliyya*, 18 May 2011: http://www.jadaliyya.com/pages/index/1624/reflections-on-the-%28in%29visibility-of-copts-in-egyp (accessed 8 February 2023).

Tadros, Mariz, *Copts at the Crossroads: The Challenges of Building Inclusive Democracy in Contemporary Egypt* (Cairo: American University in Cairo Press, 2013).

——. *The Muslim Brotherhood in Contemporary Egypt: Democracy Redefined or Confined?* (London: Routledge, 2012).

——. 'Participation not Domination: Morsi on an Impossible Mission?' in Kraetzschmar, Hendrik, and Rivetti, Paola (eds), *Islamists and the Politics of the Arab Uprisings: Governance, Pluralisation and Contention* (Edinburgh: Edinburgh University Press, 2018), 17–35.

Verdeil, Éric, Faour, Ghaleb, and Velut, Sébastien (eds), *Atlas du Liban: Territoires et société* (Beirut: Ifpo, CNRS, 2007).

Voile, Brigitte, *Les coptes d'Égypte sous Nasser: Sainteté, miracles, apparitions* (Paris: CNRS Éditions, 2004).

Wagemakers, Joas, *Salafism in Jordan: Political Islam in a Quietist Community* (Cambridge: Cambridge University Press, 2016).

——. *The Muslim Brotherhood in Jordan* (Cambridge: Cambridge University Press, 2020).

Wessels, Antonie, *Arab and Christian: Christians in the Middle East* (Kok Pharos: Kampen, 1995).

White, Benjamin T., *The Emergence of Minorities in the Middle East: Politics and Community in French Mandate Syria* (Edinburgh: Edinburgh University Press, 2011).

Whittingham, Martin, 'Muslims and the Bible', in Thomas, David (ed.), *Routledge Handbook on Christian-Muslim Relations* (London: Routledge, 2017), 269–87.

Zaborowski, J. R., *The Coptic Martyrdom of John Phanijōit: Assimilation and Conversion to Islam in Thirteenth Century Egypt* (Leiden, Boston: Brill, 2005).

Other

Brown, Dan, *Da Vinci Code* (Paris: JC Lattès, 2004).

Yousef, M. H., with R. Brackin, *Son of Hamas* (Carol Stream, Israel: Tyndale Momentum, 2001).

Zaydān, Yusif, عزازيل (Cairo: Dār al-Shurūq, 2008).

INDEX

al-ʿAbādī, ʿAbd al-Salām, 29, 58
Abbasid Caliphate, 74
ʿAbd al-Ghanī, Safwat, 81
ʿAbd Allāh, Emir of Jordan, 54
Abdullah II, King of Jordan, 28, 29, 41, 56, 92, 126
Abdulmajid, Sultan, 107
Abū Fāris, 80
Abū Ghanīma, Ziyād, 80
Abū Islām, 18, 20, 42–3, 81, 102, 111, 131
Abū Jābir family, 61
Abū Yahyā, 18, 37
Abū Yusūf, 74
ʿAfīfī, Talʿat, 47, 48
Aflaq, Michel, 91
agency, 3, 5–7, 18, 31, 33, 44, 50, 52, 99, 103, 137–9
ahl al-kitāb, 77, 80, 128, 129, 133
al-Ahrām, 36, 59, 84, 102, 110–11
ʿĀʾisha, 76
ʿAjlūn, 28
Akkar, 27, 83, 91, 93–4, 97, 128, 137
Alawis, 23, 26, 53, 94, 178n
Aleppo, 90, 172n

Alexandria, 15, 20, 37, 38, 43, 66, 97
ʿAlī, Muhammad, 77, 117
Allāh, Fr Maryūs Khayr, 104
Amal Movement, 22, 23, 26, 27, 33, 68, 72, 83, 96, 104, 105, 116, 125, 136
ambiguity, 6–7, 9, 39, 50, 52, 72–3, 88, 90, 92–4, 97, 99, 113, 115, 137, 138
American Historical Review (AHR), 4–5
Amman, 29, 30, 40, 53, 62, 65
'Amman Message', 29, 41, 56, 92
Andalusia, 59, 75
antagonism, 8, 13, 18–21, 25, 50, 78, 81, 82, 99, 101, 107, 113, 126, 138
anti-colonialism, 49, 69, 79–80, 88–9
anti-Semitism, 45–50
anti-Western sentiment, 14, 41–2, 58–9, 88–9
Aoun, Michel, 23, 79, 173n
Arab identity, 62, 89–94, 98, 121
Arab Islamic Democratic Movement (*Hizb al-duʿāʾ*), 30, 129
Arab League, 18
Arab nationalism, 49, 90–1, 121
Arab Spring, 2, 11, 12–13, 27, 28, 54, 55, 57, 66, 80, 84, 86, 115–16

Arab West Foundation, 42
Arabic language, 24–5, 42, 82, 89–90
Arkoub, 104
Armenian Apostolic Church, 4, 30, 65, 165n, 178n
Armenian Catholic Church, 90
Armenians, 53, 77, 85, 118, 172n
al-ʿAryān, ʿIsām, 107
Asʿad, Gamāl, 80, 120–1
al-Asīr, Ahmad, 24, 26, 78, 82–3, 98, 105, 113, 129, 132, 136, 138, 174n
al-Assad, Bashar, 22
assassinations, 15, 23, 24
Aswan, 36, 111
Asyut, 36, 37
ʿAtāʾ Allāh, Samʿān, 25, 27, 53, 83, 125
Atfih, 67, 70, 86, 169n
Athanāsyūs, Bishop of Beni Mazar, 43, 101
Aubin-Boltanski, Emma, 94
authority, 10, 52, 56, 57, 60, 71, 111, 116, 134, 139
avoidance, 5, 7, 11, 85–6, 88, 95, 98–103, 127, 139
Avon, Dominique, 116
Awwad, Johnny, 128
Ayn Ibl, 104
ʿAzab, Mahmūd, 97
Azazeel (Ziedan), 12, 43–4, 101–2, 103
al-Azhar, 2, 41, 51, 55–6, 57, 58–9, 97, 105, 107, 108, 116, 128, 132–3, 139
ʿAzīz, Fīlūbātir Gamīl, 32, 42, 154n

Baalbek, 22, 53, 69, 83, 125
backlash, 1–2, 7, 21, 32–3, 39–41, 99, 136, 138
Badīʿ, Muhammad, 20, 32, 116, 129
Badrān, ʿAbd Allāh, 17–18
Bahīrā, 76
Bākhūmyūs, Bishop, 21, 64, 65, 101, 102, 103, 111

Bakkār, Nādir, 20, 81, 102, 103, 124
Balfour Declaration, 47
al-Bannā, Hasan, 14
Baroudi, Sami, 63–4
Baʿth party, 91
Bauer, Thomas, 6–7, 39
Bayt al-ʿāʾila, 37, 95, 97
Al Bayt Institute for Islamic Thought, 56, 92
Bazzī, ʿAlī, 104
Bebnine, 93
Beirut, 2, 22, 24–6, 32, 49, 79, 82
Benedict XVI, 2, 22, 26, 32, 42, 43, 50, 56–7, 79, 96, 116, 119, 124–5, 129
Benedict, Bishop of Amman, 40
Benedict, Philip, 5–6, 41, 43, 44
Beni Mazar, 43
Beni Suef, 36, 86
Beqaa Valley, 26, 94
Bible, 1, 18, 20, 43, 44, 81, 93, 102, 111, 131
Bint Jbeil, 22, 104, 105
al-Birr, ʿAbd al-Rahman, 107, 108
Bishoy, Bishop, 101–2, 103, 179n
al-Biyādī, Safwat, 39
Bkerké, 64, 95–6
Boogert, Maurits H. van den, 61
Boulby, Marion, 80
Brown, Dan, 43–4, 101
Building and Development Party, 15–16, 81
Būlā, Bishop of Tanta, 46, 105, 111, 123
Burhāmī, Yāsir, 20, 107–8, 131, 132–3
al-Bustānī, Butrus, 90
Butrus, Fr Zakaryā, 46, 75–7
Byzantine Empire, 74, 123

Cairo, 1, 2, 13, 17, 32–3, 35, 36–7, 41–3, 46, 66, 70, 101, 104, 110
Camp David Accords, 49
canon law, 54, 133

Casper, Jayson, 42
Catholic Church *see* Coptic Catholic Church; Greek Catholic Church; Roman Catholic Church
Cedar Revolution, 23
censorship, 43–4
Chalcedonians, 74, 89
Chameini, Ali, 23
charisma, 10, 24, 56, 57, 75
Chartier, Roger, 9
Chatelard, Géraldine, 7, 53, 69, 120
Chehab, Hareth, 96, 178n
Christian Brothers, 67, 70, 120, 121, 134
Christian identity, 52, 68–71, 94, 118–24
Christian laity, 11, 21, 39–40, 52, 60–8
Christian symbols, 42–4, 101–2, 121
Christmas, 36, 37, 62, 66, 100, 105–9, 128
Church of the East, 74, 76, 166n
citizenship, 53–4, 79, 115, 117, 120, 121, 133–4
Coalition of Egypt's Copts, 67, 70, 95, 98, 110, 168n
Coalition of Jirash for Reform, 28
colonialism, 49, 69, 79–80, 88–9
'Common Word, A', 56–7, 92, 127, 128
conferences, 2, 3, 21, 37–8, 46, 69, 81, 86–7, 91, 93, 105, 120–1, 128, 137
conspiracies, 45–50, 138
conversion, 37, 44, 46, 60, 74
cooperation, 5, 28, 31, 79, 80, 117, 137, 138, 139
Coptic Catholic Church, 21, 39, 60, 105, 115–16, 118–19, 134, 138, 154n, 180n
Coptic diaspora, 1, 2, 19–20, 45–6, 59
Coptic Lay Council, 61–2, 65
Coptic–Muslim violence, 1–2, 11, 12, 32–8
Coptic Orthodox Church, 1, 2, 12, 18, 19, 21, 32, 35–9, 43, 46, 53, 55, 60–8, 70, 86–7, 97, 100–3, 105, 107–11, 113–15, 119, 121–4, 133, 138

Coptic Reform Association, 62
Copts 38, 84
Copts Without Restrictions, 40, 67–8, 70, 111, 168n
corruption, 27, 58, 61, 62
Council for Islamic Research, 128
Council of Chalcedon, 123
Council of Churches, 30, 40, 44, 48, 65, 72, 88, 92, 100, 117, 128
Council of Evangelical Churches, 92, 126
Covenant of 'Umar, 75

Da Vinci Code, The (Brown), 43–4, 101
Dahshur, 37
Dā'irat al-iftā', 60, 130
Damascus, 63, 85, 90
Damietta, 17, 102
Danish cartoons controversy, 2, 32, 44
Dār al-fatwā, 56, 57–8, 59, 178n
Darbāla, 'Isām, 16, 132
Daw, Fr Antoine, 27, 83, 96, 116–17
al-Da'wa al-Salafiyya, 7, 15–18, 20, 41–2, 48, 51, 84, 87, 98, 107–8, 112, 124, 127, 129, 131–3, 136
democracy, 8, 16, 17, 52, 58, 83, 115, 116, 133
denial, 7, 35–6, 98, 100, 138, 139
dhimma, 6, 8, 11, 72–3, 74–5, 77, 81, 88–94, 120, 134, 139
differentiation, 54–5, 110, 114, 117–23, 135
Dirāz, Muhammad 'Abd Allāh, 127
displacement, 24, 90; *see also* refugees
divorce, 84, 133
Donovan, Joshua, 2
Druze, 23, 53, 69, 118, 125, 178n
al-Dustūr, 28, 30

East Bank Jordanians, 4, 49, 53, 54
Easter, 62, 106–8

ecclesiastical courts, 54, 64
Egypt
  appearances of Virgin Mary, 94
  and the Arab Spring, 2, 11, 12–13, 57, 66, 80, 84, 115–16
  army, 38
  attack on US embassy in Cairo, 1, 2, 17, 32–3, 41–2, 44, 46, 70, 104, 110
  al-Azhar, 2, 41, 51, 55–6, 57, 58–9, 97, 105, 107, 108, 116, 128, 132–3, 139
  Bayt al-ʿāʾila, 37, 95, 97
  British occupation, 55, 109
  Building and Development Party, 15–16, 81
  Christian laity, 21, 39–40, 60–8
  constituent assembly, 13, 105, 107
  constitution, 57, 102, 115, 120, 133
  Coptic Catholic Church, 21, 39, 60, 105, 115–16, 118–19, 134, 138, 154n
  Coptic Orthodox Church, 1, 2, 12, 18, 19, 21, 32, 35–9, 43, 46, 53, 55, 60–8, 70, 86–7, 97, 100–3, 105, 107–11, 113–15, 119, 121–4, 133, 138
  al-Daʿwa al-Salafiyya, 7, 15–18, 20, 41–2, 48, 51, 84, 87, 98, 107–8, 112, 124, 127, 129, 131–3, 136
  demographics, 3–4, 34, 52–4
  elections, 2, 13–14, 15, 124, 128
  Freedom and Justice Party, 13, 15–17, 80, 105, 107, 110
  al-Gamāʿa al-Islāmiyya, 7, 8, 10, 15–17, 20, 43, 51, 78, 80–1, 83–4, 87, 98, 104–8, 112–13, 127, 132, 138
  Jewish community, 49, 53
  Latin Church, 105
  legal system, 54, 57, 84, 87, 132–3
  media, 1, 18–19, 21, 36, 38, 39–40, 46, 50, 68, 81, 87, 110–11, 132
  monarchy, 109
  Mubarak regime, 4, 14–15, 35–6, 101, 115
  Mursī regime, 2, 13, 17, 57, 65, 67, 87, 107, 110, 129
  Muslim Brotherhood, 2, 7, 13–17, 20, 21, 51, 57, 80, 99, 103–7, 122, 134, 138
  Nasser regime, 14, 15, 55, 62, 64–5
  national unity, 36, 38, 48, 59, 68, 86, 87, 102, 109–11, 123–4
  nationalism, 39, 42, 49, 109, 121, 123
  1919 Revolution, 86, 117
  numbers of Christians, 3, 34–5, 52–3
  Nur Party, 7, 8, 10, 13–21, 31–2, 41–2, 51, 73, 80–1, 84, 86–7, 102, 108, 113, 124, 129, 132, 138
  official Islam, 2, 14, 18, 55–9, 107, 108, 110, 116
  People's Party, 84
  political quota system, 4, 54, 64, 68
  Protestant Churches, 21, 39, 60
  protests, 1, 2, 13, 17, 32–3, 37–8, 41–2, 66–7, 70, 72, 104–5
  Sadat regime, 14, 15, 49, 101
  Salafi Front, 20, 21, 84, 111, 123
  sectarian violence, 1–2, 11, 12, 32–8, 86–7, 100–1, 111
  socio-economic status of Christians, 4, 53, 61–2
  Supreme Constitutional Court, 14, 57
  Supreme Council of Armed Forces, 13–14, 37, 70, 86
  25 January revolution, 2, 13, 36, 57, 105, 127
  wars with Israel, 15, 49
elections, 2, 8, 13–14, 15, 28, 124, 128
electoral law, 27–8, 54
Elsässer, Sebastian, 34, 48
emigration, 115, 116
equality, 10, 58, 73, 77, 92, 103, 113–15, 121–4, 127, 132, 134, 139
Evangelical Church, 39

Facebook, 20, 70, 107
Fahmī, Mīkhāʾīl, 121
family law, 54, 84
family members, targeting of, 32, 41, 42, 44, 102
Fāris, Marwān, 25, 69
Farrāj, Bāssim, 40, 62, 126
fascism, 14
Fatimid dynasty, 55
fatwas, 20, 56, 57, 87, 107, 131
al-Fayyum, 17, 36
fear, 7, 11, 21, 32, 39–41, 50, 88, 97, 111, 115–17, 135, 138, 139
Felsch, Maxilian, 122
Ferzli, Elie, 47–8, 161n
First World War, 90, 119
Fischbach, Rachel, 99, 106
fitna, 8, 35, 41, 59, 73, 84–8, 97, 100–1, 111, 139
Free Patriotic Movement (FPM), 23, 79
Freedom and Justice Party (FJP), 13, 15–17, 80, 105, 107, 110
freedom of speech, 12, 17, 28
Future Movement, 23, 56

Galal, Lise Paulsen, 122–3
al-Gamāʿa al-Islāmiyya, 7, 8, 10, 15–17, 20, 43, 51, 78, 80–1, 83–4, 87, 98, 104–8, 112–13, 127, 132, 138
Gandolfo, Luisa, 125–6
Garīsh, Fr Rafīq, 39
Gauvain, Richard, 15, 37, 81
Gaza, 2, 32
Geagea, Samīr, 23, 40, 83, 136
Gemayel, Amin, 26, 136
Gemayel, Bachir, 92
al-Ghad, 28
al-Ghaffūr, ʿImād ʿAbd, 16, 20, 32, 80, 129
al-Gharāyiba, Ruhayl, 126, 132, 134
Giza, 18, 35, 37, 42, 66, 81, 104

Grafton, David, 8
Greek Catholic Melkite Church, 25, 30, 40–1, 60, 63, 65, 69, 95, 104, 178n
Greek Orthodox Church, 4, 27, 30, 40, 47, 54, 60–3, 65, 68–9, 74, 89–91, 93–4, 114, 121–2, 126, 178n
Guardian, 42
Guirguis, Laure, 35, 43, 63
Gulf War, 53
Gumʿa, ʿAlī, 36, 55, 58, 59, 108, 110, 116, 129, 132, 156n

Habāsh, Jiryis, 65
Haddād, Fr Nabīl, 40–1
Haddād, Ridā, 71
Haddad, Yvonne Yazbeck, 2, 99, 106
al-Hāfī, ʿĀmir, 53, 130
al-Hage, Chucrallah Nabil, 119, 120
Halba, 93
Hamas, 46
Hammād, Yusrī, 19–20, 81, 87, 125, 131, 132
Hammūd, Māhir, 57–8, 129, 164n
Hardān, Asʿad, 69, 83, 88–9
al-Harīrī, Rafīq, 23, 24, 56, 58, 82
al-Harīrī, Saʿad, 24, 82
al-Hasan, Husayn al-Hajj, 125
Hasbaya, 69, 104
Hashimite monarchy, 27–9, 55, 56–7, 71, 80, 86, 92, 98, 125–6
Hassān, Muhammad, 70, 86–7
Hassan bin Talal, Prince of Jordan, 56
Hatt-i Hümayun, 77, 92, 107, 172n
Hattar, Nāhid, 70–1, 126
Haykal, Muhammad, 118
Haykel, Bernard, 15
Helwan, 37, 70, 86, 169–70n
Heo, Angie, 5, 9, 34, 35, 38, 63, 65, 66
Hermel, 22, 69
Heyberger, Bernard, 52

Hezbollah, 7, 11, 13, 22–7, 31, 33, 51, 68–9, 72, 79–83, 96, 98, 104–5, 113, 116, 125, 129–31, 136, 138
hierarchisation of targets, 41–5, 102–3
Higher Islamic Shi'i Council, 2, 55, 96, 127, 178n
al-Hikma, 18, 66, 129
Hizb al-dustūr, 69
Hizb ut-Tahrir, 42
hospitality, 5, 96, 99
human rights, 58, 117

Ibrahim, Vivian, 34, 109
identity, 7, 14, 25, 62, 68–71, 89–94, 98, 118–24
iftār, 10, 106–7
Ighnātiyūs Afrām I, Patriarch, 130
Ignatius IV, Patriarch, 91, 122
Imbaba, 18, 37, 44
Incarnation, 74, 131
inclusion-moderation hypothesis, 7–8, 78, 84
Iran, 23
Iraq, 4, 90, 116, 118, 135
Ishāq, George, 69–70, 86, 121, 170n
Iskander, Elizabeth, 36
Islamic courts, 54
Islamic Action Front (IAF), 7, 27, 28, 29, 31, 51, 80, 126, 130, 132
Islamic Awakening, 14, 15
Islamic Jihad, 86–7
Islamic State (IS), 70–1
Ismailiyya, 14
Israel, 4, 15, 23, 24, 45–50, 69, 89, 95, 103–4, 125, 126
Istifān, Fr Nāyif, 91, 93, 128, 177n

Jābir, Kāmil, 91
al-Jamā'a al-Islāmiyya see Muslim Brotherhood: Lebanon
al-Jazeera, 123–4

Jerusalem, 49, 62, 63, 68, 168n
Jesus, 39, 43, 58, 74, 80, 107, 108, 128, 130–1
Jesus Christ Superstar (Rice), 44, 101
Jews, 3, 6, 45–50, 53, 59, 61, 77, 80, 92, 109
jihadism, 23, 29, 42
Jirash, 28
jizya, 74, 75
John of Damascus, 76, 92
John Paul II, 124
Jones, Terry, 46, 47
Jordan
    annexation of West Bank, 49, 53
    Arab Islamic Democratic Movement, 30, 71
    and the Arab Spring, 11, 12–13, 27, 28, 54, 116
    Armenian Apostolic Church, 30, 65, 90, 168n
    army, 27
    Christian laity, 40, 60–4, 65, 68
    Council of Churches, 30, 40, 44, 48, 65, 72, 88, 92, 100, 117, 128
    Council of Evangelical Churches, 92, 126, 153–4n
    Dā'irat al-iftā', 60, 130
    demographics, 3–4, 52–4
    dissatisfaction with the regime, 13, 27–30, 130
    East Bank Jordanians, 4, 49, 53, 54
    elections, 28
    electoral law, 27–8, 54
    Greek Catholic Church, 30, 40–1, 60, 63, 65
    Greek Orthodox Church, 30, 40, 60–3, 65, 68, 121, 126
    Islamic Action Front, 7, 27, 28, 29, 31, 51, 80, 126, 130, 132
    Jewish community, 49

Latin Church, 30, 40, 60, 62, 63, 65
legal system, 54
media, 28, 30, 126
Ministry of Islamic Endowments, 29, 30, 51, 58, 60
monarchy, 27–9, 55, 56–7, 71, 80, 86, 92, 98, 125–6
murder of Nāhid Hattar, 70–1, 126
Muslim Brotherhood, 7, 27–8, 31, 51, 80, 86, 131, 134
national unity, 71, 92, 109, 122, 123, 125–6
nationalism, 125
numbers of Christians, 3, 52–3
official Islam, 30, 55–60, 136
Orthodox Society, 40, 49, 51, 61, 62–3, 68, 71
Palestinian Jordanians, 4, 27, 49, 53, 54, 125–6
political quota system, 4, 28, 54, 64, 68
professional associations, 2, 27, 29, 30, 51, 136–7
Protestant Churches, 30, 168n, 178n
protests, 11, 28, 29
socio-economic status of Christians, 4, 30, 61–3
tribes, 27, 29, 48, 126, 136
Tribes of the Tafileh Governorate Province Demanding Reform, 48, 130
wars with Israel, 49
Jordanian Interfaith Coexistence Research Centre, 40–1
Jumblatt, Walid, 125

Kanafani-Zahar, Aïda, 36
Kaslik University, 104
Kataeb *see* Phalange Party
Kerbala, battle of, 25, 149n
Khadīja, 75–6
Khanka, 34

Khodr, George, 89, 91, 92–3, 98, 122, 127, 136
Khomeini, Ruhollah, 23
Khoury, Amal, 10, 106
Khoury, Fr Rafiq, 130
kidnappings, 44, 177n
Kildānī, Hannā, 30, 40, 44, 65
al-Kirāza, 108, 115
Kirdiş, Esen, 16, 28
Kīrillus I, Patriarch, 43
Krämer, Gudrun, 8, 14, 49, 74, 86, 134
Kufranja, 28, 151n
Kurds, 54, 118
Kuwait, 53
Kīrillus, Bishop, 36, 37
Kyrillos VI, Patriarch, 65

Lahhām, Bishop Mārūn, 40, 53, 62, 64, 70–1, 91, 120
Latin Church, 30, 40, 53, 60, 62, 63, 65, 70, 91, 105, 130, 165–6n
League of Nations, 119
Lebanese Forces, 23, 40, 83
Lebanon
 Alawis, 23, 26, 53, 94, 178n
 Amal Movement, 22, 23, 26, 27, 33, 68, 72, 83, 96, 104, 105, 116, 125, 136
 appearances of Virgin Mary, 94–5
 and the Arab Spring, 11, 12–13, 57, 116
 assassination of al-Harīrī, 23, 24
 Cedar Revolution, 23
 Christian laity, 40, 60, 63–4
 citizenship, 53–4
 Civil War, 5, 22–3, 24, 26, 36, 38, 54, 56, 57, 83, 75, 97, 103–4, 122, 124
 Dār al-fatwā, 56, 57–8, 59, 178n
 demographics, 3–4, 52–4
 Druze, 23, 53, 69, 118, 125, 178n
 Free Patriotic Movement, 23, 79
 French Mandate, 56

Lebanon (cont.)
  Future Movement, 23, 56
  Greek Catholic Melkite Church, 25, 40, 60, 69, 95, 104, 178n
  Greek Orthodox Church, 27, 47, 54, 60, 69, 89, 93–4, 122, 178n
  Hezbollah, 7, 11, 13, 22–7, 31, 33, 51, 68–9, 72, 79–83, 96, 98, 104–5, 113, 116, 125, 129–31, 136, 138
  Higher Islamic Shiʿi Council, 2, 55, 96, 127, 178n
  Israeli occupation, 23, 49, 103–4
  Jewish community, 49
  Lebanese Forces, 23, 40, 83
  Marada Movement, 23, 79
  March 8 Alliance, 23, 25, 79
  March 14 Alliance, 23, 25, 26, 93, 136, 149n
  Maronite Church, 2, 4, 23, 25–6, 32, 53–4, 60, 63–4, 83, 89–90, 92, 94–6, 104, 116, 119, 124–5, 141n, 178n
  media, 22, 25, 89, 96
  Muslim Brotherhood (al-Jamāʿa al-Islāmiyya), 23, 145n, 149n, 174n
  National Committee for Dialogue, 95–6
  National Liberal Party, 26
  national unity, 109, 123, 124–5
  numbers of Christians, 3, 52–3
  official Islam, 2, 8, 55–9
  Palestinian refugees, 53–4, 82
  Phalange Party, 23, 26
  political polarisation, 2, 22–3, 83
  political quota system, 4, 54, 64, 68
  protests, 1, 2, 22, 24–7, 32–3, 42, 68, 72, 103–5, 116, 125
  sectarian violence, 82
  Shiʿa Islam, 3, 4, 22–6, 31, 53, 54, 69, 79, 96, 103, 107
  socio-economic status of Christians, 4
  spiritual summits, 95–6
  Sunni Islam, 4, 22, 24, 26, 53, 54, 56, 57–8, 94, 103
  Syrian refugees, 2, 53, 82
  Syrian Social National Party, 23, 25, 68, 69, 79, 83, 88–9, 121, 136
  Syrian troops withdraw from, 23
  and the Syrian war, 22, 26, 83
  visit of Benedict XVI, 22, 26, 42, 50, 79, 96, 116, 119, 124–5
  wars with Israel, 24, 95, 103–4
Longva, Anh Nga, 6
Lukasik, Candace, 121, 123
Luxor, 36

Maʿān, 29, 161n
McCallum, Fiona, 121
Magdī, Minā, 40, 67, 121
Mahmood, Saba, 6, 35, 44, 54, 73, 99, 117–18
Majallat al-Azhar, 38, 108, 127, 132, 156n
Makari, Peter, 5, 57
al-Manār, 22, 25, 45, 47
Mansūr, Bishop Bāsīlyūs, 27, 93
Marada Movement, 23, 79
March 8 Alliance, 23, 25, 79
March 14 Alliance, 23, 25, 26, 93, 136, 149n
Maronite Church, 2, 4, 23, 25–6, 32, 53–4, 60, 63–4, 83, 89–90, 92, 94–6, 104, 116, 124–5, 141n, 178n
Mārtīrūs, Bishop, 120–1
martyrdom, 38, 76, 101
Martyrdom of John Phanijōit, 76
Mary, Virgin, 94–5
Maspero Massacre, 38, 66–7, 86, 101, 111, 131, 169n
Maspero Youth Union (MYU), 40, 67, 70, 111, 169n
al-Masrī al-Yawm, 110
Massad, Joseph, 125
Mayeur-Jaouen, Catherine, 35, 106

Mecca, 56
media, 1, 18–22, 25, 28, 30, 36, 38–40, 42, 45–7, 50, 58, 68, 81, 87, 89, 96, 110–11, 126, 132, 137
Medina, 56
Mervin, Sabrina, 24
Mikdashi, Maya, 53–4
millet, 61, 65, 74, 90
Ministry of Islamic Endowments, 29, 30, 47, 51, 58, 60
minority status, 6, 63, 73, 80, 86, 87, 91, 118–20, 134
al-Minya, 36, 110
Mīqātī, Najīb, 24
moderation, 7–8, 14, 29, 55, 56, 58, 72, 78–85, 97, 108, 116, 127
Monier, Elizabeth, 119–20
Mossad, 46
Mount Lebanon, 36, 75, 90, 93, 136
Movement for Civil Rights for Christians, 67
Mubarak, Hosni, 4, 14–15, 35–6, 101, 115
Muhammad, Prophet, 1, 2, 12, 34, 47, 56, 58, 75–7, 88–9, 93, 96, 132
Murqus, Bishop of Shubra al-Khayma, 115
Mursī, Muhammad, 2, 13, 17, 57, 65, 67, 87, 107, 110, 129
Mūsā, ʿAmr, 18
Mūsā, Bishop, 110, 124
Mūsāʿada, ʿAzīz, 71, 80
al-Mūsawī, Nawwāf, 104, 105
Muslim Brotherhood
  Egypt, 2, 7, 13–17, 20, 21, 51, 57, 80, 99, 103–7, 122, 134, 138
  Jordan, 7, 27–8, 31, 51, 80, 86, 131, 134
  Lebanon, 23, 145n, 149n, 174n

Nabatieh, 104, 125
Nablus, 2, 32
Nag Hammadi, 36, 37, 66, 97, 105

Naguīb, Antūnyūs, 116
al-Nahār, 89, 96, 120
Nāsif, Fr Bāsīl, 104
Nasr Allāh, Hasan, 22, 24–6, 31, 45, 47, 48, 79–80, 81–2, 83, 85, 104, 130–1, 136
Nasr Allāh, Jūzīf, 42, 46
Nasser, Gamal Abdel, 14, 15, 55, 62, 64–5
Nasserism, 15, 49
National American Coptic Assembly, 46
National Committee for Dialogue, 95–6
National Liberal Party, 26
national unity, 36, 38, 48, 59, 68, 71, 86, 87, 92, 102, 109–11, 122, 123–6
nationalism, 39, 42, 49, 90–1, 109, 121, 123, 125
Nestorians *see* Church of the East
New York Times, 17
1956 war, 49
1967 war, 15, 49
Niqūlā, Niqūlā Bāsilī, 42, 45–6, 49–50, 158n, 159n
non-determinism, 8–9
Nur Party, 7, 8, 10, 13–21, 31–2, 41–2, 51, 73, 80–1, 84, 86–7, 102, 108, 113, 124, 129, 132, 138

Obama, Barack, 17
objectification, 44
official Islam, 2, 8, 10, 11, 14, 18, 30, 51–2, 55–60, 98, 107, 108, 110, 116, 136, 137
Orthodox Church *see* Coptic Orthodox Church; Greek Orthodox Church
Orthodox Congress, 68
Orthodox Society, 40, 49, 51, 61, 62–3, 68, 71
Orthodox Youth Movement, 122
Ottoman Empire, 6, 54, 61, 77–8, 85, 90, 92, 109, 119–20

Palestine, 2, 4, 24, 32, 53, 89, 90, 126
Palestinian Jordanians, 4, 27, 49, 53, 54, 125–6
Pall, Zoltan, 57, 86
People's Party, 84
Persian Sasanian Empire, 74, 166n
Phalange Party (Kataeb), 23, 26
Phoenicianism, 124
Picard, Élizabeth, 5, 45, 95, 99, 125
Pizzo, Paola, 134
pluralism, 8, 79, 128–9
polarisation, 2, 22–3, 83
polemics, 10, 20, 31, 50, 59, 72, 75–8, 92, 128
police, 1, 34, 35, 37, 42, 66
political quota systems, 4, 28, 54, 64, 68
Popular Movement of Kufranja for Reform and Change, 28, 151n
population growth, 34
potential violence, 3, 33, 45–50, 72, 84, 138
poverty, 4, 26, 40, 54, 93–4
Proche-Orient Chrétien (POC), 33
professional associations, 2, 27, 29, 30, 51, 136–7
Protestant Churches, 4, 21, 30, 39, 60
protests
    in Egypt, 1, 2, 13, 17, 32–3, 37–8, 41–2, 66–7, 70, 72, 104–5
    joint Christian–Muslim protests, 2, 25–6, 33, 37–8, 68, 72, 103–5
    in Jordan, 11, 28, 29
    in Lebanon, 1, 2, 22, 24–7, 32–3, 42, 68, 72, 103–5, 116, 125
proximity, 7, 11, 22, 24–5, 73, 78–85, 88–9, 91–2, 94–7, 98, 105–7, 114, 117, 127, 137–9

Qabalān, ʿAbd al-Amīr, 55, 96, 127, 128, 129
Qabbānī, Rashīd, 50, 55, 56, 59, 85, 124–5
al-Qaraḍāwī, Yūsuf, 57, 128
Qena, 36
Qunstuntīn, Wafāʾ, 44
Qurʾan, 15, 47, 49, 58, 60, 74, 76, 77, 93, 102, 108, 127, 128–31, 133
al-Qusayr, battle of, 26

al-Rāʿī, Patriarch Bishāra Butrus, 64, 83, 96, 116
reciprocity, 7, 10, 11, 83, 96, 99–100, 103–5, 108, 113–15, 127, 134, 139
reconciliation, 35–6
refugees, 2, 53–4, 78, 82
religious feasts, 62, 100, 105–9, 139
resistance, 6, 99, 115
revelation, 75–6, 93, 102, 108, 128, 131
Riḍā, Muhammad Rashīd, 14
ritual, 10, 11, 96, 98–112, 113, 115, 127, 137, 139
ritualised language, 7, 98, 100–3, 113, 127
ritualised behaviour, 11, 98, 100, 103–5
Rmeich, 103–4
Robson, Laura, 4, 9
Roman Catholic Church, 2, 4, 22, 26, 93, 119; *see also* Benedict XVI; John Paul II; Latin Church
Rowe, Paul, 6
Royal Institute of Inter-Faith Studies, 53, 91, 92, 130
rural–urban migration, 34–5
Rushdie, Salman, 47

Saadeh, Antoun, 69
Sabra, George, 10, 68–9, 88–9, 94, 102
al-Sadat, Anwar, 14, 15, 49, 101
Sadek, Morris, 19, 42, 46
Sadr, Musa, 107, 149n
al-Safīr, 116–17
Salafi Front, 20, 21, 84, 111, 123
al-Salāh, 115, 180n

Sammak, Muhammad, 96, 170n
Al-Saʿūd, ʿAbd al-ʿAzīz, 56
Sawiris, Naguib, 4
Sāwirīs, Salīb Matā, 20
Schwedler, Jillian, 79, 88
Scott, Rachel, 115, 133
sectarian violence, 1–2, 8, 11, 12, 32–8, 86–7, 90, 100–1, 111
secularism, 13, 15, 19, 41, 56, 76, 80, 122, 135, 145n, 164n, 166n
Sedra, Paul, 119
sensationalism, 9, 11, 36
sexuality, 75–6
al-Shahhāt, ʿAbd al-Munʿim, 87
shariʿa law, 14, 57, 58, 84, 87, 108, 114, 132
Sharkey, Heather, 61, 85, 107
al-Shātir, Khayrat, 17
Shenoda, Antony, 37
Shiʿa Islam, 3, 4, 22–6, 31, 53, 54, 56, 69, 79, 96, 103, 107
Shin Bet, 46
Shinūda III, Patriarch, 21, 63, 64, 66, 75, 84, 100–1, 105–8, 115, 119, 123–4
Shubra al-Khayma, 35, 115
Shūfānī, Fr Shukr Allāh, 104
al-Shurūq, 110, 132
Sidhom, Youssef, 35, 37
Sidon, 24, 82, 83, 174n
Sinai, 34
Siniora, Fouad, 56, 58
Sleiman, Michel, 83
soccer clubs, 42
social media, 20, 46, 70, 107
Sohag, 36
solidarity, 10, 11, 19, 21, 39, 40, 45, 83, 100–3, 104, 106, 110
Son of Hamas (Yusuf), 46
Soviet Union, 47
spiritual summits, 95–6

statesmanship, 8, 17, 18, 20, 21, 80
Subh, ʿAbd al-Majīd Hāmid, 108, 114, 127
Suez, 17, 35, 105, 138
Sufism, 14
Sunday School Movement, 63
Sunni Islam, 2, 4, 22, 24, 26, 53, 54, 56, 57–8, 82, 94, 103
Supreme Constitutional Court, 14, 57
Supreme Council of Armed Forces (SCAF), 13–14, 37, 70, 86, 170n
suspicion, 1, 5, 19, 21, 32, 45, 81, 116, 137
Syria, 2, 4, 22, 23, 26, 53, 75, 83, 90
Syriac Christians, 53, 90, 130, 165n, 178n, 183n
Syriac language, 76, 166n
Syrian Social National Party (SSNP), 23, 25, 68, 69, 79, 83, 88–9, 121, 136

Tabar, Paul, 63–4
Tadros, Mariz, 80, 134
Taef Agreement, 23
tahrīf, 108, 127, 130–2, 138
Tahrir Square, Cairo, 13, 17, 67, 101
Tauran, Jean-Louis, 119
Tawādrūs II, Patriarch, 21
taxation, 61, 74–5, 126, 172n
al-Tayyib, Ahmad, Shaykh al-Azhar, 37, 38, 55, 58–9, 85, 97, 129, 156n
terrorism, 2, 29, 32, 34, 38, 42, 47, 58
Theodosius, Bishop of Giza, 104
Theophilos, Patriarch, 91
tolerance, 5, 6, 29, 48, 58, 60, 73, 79, 87, 115, 130
tribes, 27, 29, 48, 61, 71, 74, 126, 130, 136
Tribes of the Tafileh Governorate Demanding Reform, 48, 130
Trinity, 74, 92–3, 131
Tripoli, 1, 26, 41, 42, 43, 96
Tulkarem, 2, 32

Tunisia, 13
al-Turtūshī, Abū Bakr Muhammad, 75
25 January revolution, 2, 13, 36, 57, 105, 127
Twitter, 46
2006 war, 24, 104
Tyre, 22, 104

al-Umraniyya, 66, 101
United Nations, 23
United States, 1, 17–18, 24, 41–2, 45–6, 59, 70, 97
unity, 11, 36, 38, 48, 59, 68, 71, 86, 87, 92, 102, 104, 109–11, 113–35, 138–9
Upper Egypt, 4, 34, 35, 36–8, 81
US embassy, Cairo, 1, 2, 17, 32–3, 41–2, 44, 46, 70, 104, 110

Wagemakers, Joas, 80, 134
al-Wārith, Wisām ʿAbd, 18, 19, 66, 129

Washington Post, 58
Waṭanī, 35
West Bank, 2, 49, 53, 161–2n
Western symbols, 41–2
White, Benjamin, 119
women, 34, 37, 44, 58, 67, 76, 77, 132

Yāsīn, Hānī, 43
al-Yawm al-Sābiʿ, 18, 19, 39, 47
al-Yāzijī, Nāsīf, 90
Yūsuf, Fādī, 98, 110
Yusuf, Musʿab Hasan, 46

al-Zafzāf, Fawzī Fāḍil, 128
Zaynab, 76
Ziedan, Yusuf, 12, 43–4, 101–2, 103, 147n
Zionism, 43, 45–50, 69, 70–1, 80, 85, 89, 101, 125, 126
al-Zumur, ʿAbbūd, 15, 80, 81
al-Zumur, Tāriq, 15